*In laudem Caroli*

*Habent sua fata libelli*

*Volume XLIX*
*of*
*Sixteenth Century Essays & Studies*

*Raymond A. Mentzer, General Editor*

*Composed by Thomas Jefferson University Press*
*at Truman State University*
*Cover art and title page by Timothy Rolands*
*Manufactured in the United States of America*
*Text is set in Minion 11/13.*

# IN LAUDEM CAROLI

### Renaissance *and* Reformation Studies

### *for*

## Charles G. Nauert

Edited by
James V. Mehl

VOLUME XLIX
Sixteenth Century Essays & Studies

This book has been brought to publication with the generous
support of Truman State University, Kirksville, Missouri

*Library of Congress Cataloging-in-Publication Data*

In laudem Caroli : Renaissance and Reformation studies for Charles G.
Nauert / edited by James V. Mehl
    p.   cm. – (Sixteenth century essays & studies : v. 49)
    Includes bibliographical references and index
    ISBN 0–940474–53–0 (hb : alk. paper). ISBN 0–940474–54–9 (pb :
alk. paper)
    1. Renaissance. 2. Humanism–Europe–16th century. 3. Human-
ists–Europe. I. Nauert, Charles Garfield. 1928–. II. Mehl, James V. III.
Series. Sixteenth century essays & studies : v. 49.
    CB369.15   1998                 98–3775
    940.2'1–dc21                       CIP

# Contents

# Foreword

THOROUGH, ORGANIZED, PREPARED, and with enthusiasm for his subject that seemed to burst out from such a normally reserved demeanor, Charles Nauert could leave students who attended his lectures in awe. As one of his first graduate students during the 1960s, I remember how Charles always entered the classroom early for his upper-level Renaissance and Reformation classes, filling the board (these were the days before Powerpoint) with all the names and special terms to which he would refer in the course of the lecture. At the top of the hour, he would launch off on a perfectly structured presentation, offering all the latest research and so packed with ideas that students struggled to keep pace. His graduate seminars, held most fittingly in the library, demanded detailed research, critical thinking, and good writing. Naturally, they provoked lively discussion. As a dissertation advisor, Charles promptly returned drafts with carefully written suggestions for revision and encouraging words. Charles came to embody for me what a university professor should be.

This volume is dedicated, then, to Charles G. Nauert on the occasion of his retirement from the University of Missouri–Columbia. The contributors of essays to this Festschrift represent the many current/former students and colleagues who wish to honor Charles and to show their appreciation for his many years of service as a teacher and scholar. His promotion of Renaissance and Reformation studies over the years has been significant.

Charles has had a distinguished academic career. He received his B.A. in history from Quincy College in 1950, followed by the M.A. and Ph.D. in history (1951 and 1955) from the University of Illinois. His dissertation on Agrippa von Nettesheim was directed by William Bouwsma. After teaching for a year at Bowdoin College, Charles was an instructor and assistant professor at Williams College (1956–61). He then went to the University of Missouri–Columbia where he has continued to teach in the Department of History. He was appointed professor in 1966 and served as chairman from 1965 to 1968. Between 1982 and 1985 he was honored as Middlebush Professor of History. In 1964 he was visiting associate professor of history at the University of California, Berkeley.

Charles has received fellowships and research awards from the American Philosophical Society, the American Council of Learned Societies, and the University of Missouri Research Council. In 1991 his many contributions as a teacher-scholar were recognized when he was given the prestigious Thomas Jefferson Award at the University of Missouri.

Charles has also provided important service to several professional associations. He has been very active, from the beginning, in the Sixteenth Century Studies Conference. Besides serving as president of the conference in 1978 and on the editorial board since 1972, he was the first editor of the "Sixteenth Century Essays and Studies" series from 1979 to 1996. During his tenure as editor, some volumes were published in that series. He also was elected to the Council of the Renaissance Society of America (1991–93) and was chairman of the New England Renaissance Conference (1962) and president of the Central Renaissance Conference (1974 and 1991). He was on the Council of the Society for Reformation Research between 1985 and 1988 and has provided service for several committees of the American Historical Association over the years.

His publications show broad scholarly interests. In 1965, the University of Illinois Press published his revised dissertation, "Agrippa and the Crisis of Renaissance Thought." It remains a standard reference source on Agrippa. A book-length article treating Renaissance commentaries on Pliny, "Caius Plinius Secundus," was included in the *Catalogus Translationum et Commentarium*, edited by F. Edward Cranz in 1980. Charles continues to edit several volumes of the Erasmus correspondence for the Toronto edition. He wrote the introductions and annotations for the *Collected Works of Erasmus*, vol. 11 (1994), which covers Erasmus' letters from January to December 1525. In what may be his most important work to date, *Humanism and the Culture of Renaissance Europe* (Cambridge University Press, 1995), there is a careful distillation and synthesis of his reflections on the subject of Renaissance humanism. Several earlier articles, beginning with his "The Clash of Humanists and Scholastics: An Approach to Pre-Reformation Controversies" in 1973, have led to new views on the relationship of humanism and scholasticism. These publications by Charles, along with recent studies by Erika Rummel, Hans Peterse, Laetitia Boehm, and others, have contributed to a revised consideration of the humanist-scholastic debate. His articles have appeared in such journals as *Renaissance Quarterly, Studies in the Renaissance, Sixteenth Century Journal, Journal of the History of Ideas, American Historical Review, Journal of the Warburg and Courtauld Institutes, Daphnis: Zeitschrift für mittlere deutsche Literatur, Historical Reflections/Réflections historiques*, as well as in volumes of collected essays. His textbook, *The Age of Renaissance and Reformation* (1977; rept. 1982) remains popular.

The essays by current/former students and colleagues, that have been collected for this Festschrift reflect many of Charles's scholarly and academic interests. Some of the studies are related to dissertations for which he was advisor. Although the subjects of the fifteen studies which follow are quite varied, they are all focused primarily on Renaissance and Reformation topics of the sixteenth century. A number of the essays treat humanism and humanist education, while some others include discussion of Erasmus. The Italian Renaissance humanists, Paolo Manuzio and Angelo Poliziano, are the subjects of Paul Grendler and Keith Shafer. Erika Rummel considers the intricacies of friendship among European humanists. The relationships among German humanists are the focus of essays by Eckhard Bernstein and James Mehl, while Paul Casey explores Luther's first printed hymn and Bonner Mitchell describes Emperor Charles V's triumphal entries. French Renaissance literary topics concerning Marguerite de Navarre and Rabelais are treated by Paula Sommers and Barbara Bowen. Both Gwendolyn Blotevogel and Janet Glenn Gray explain the humanist educational reform efforts in the French provinces. Dynastic and political considerations in Tudor England are the subjects of Kim Schutte and Robert Babcock. To round out the volume, Guy Wilson discusses humanist treatments of Renaissance battle accounts and Jill Raitt discusses the spiritual advice of Ignatius Loyola and Teresa of Avila for women. The hard work and cooperation of all these authors are very much appreciated.

In addition to these essays, there have been other contributions to acknowledge. Special thanks go to Bob Schnucker and others at the Sixteenth Century Journal, Publishers, for printing this volume in the "Sixteenth Century Essays and Studies" series. Besides the financial underwriting of the publisher, support has come from Paul Casey, Bonner Mitchell, Carol Heming, Stanley Burgess, Barbara Miller, Gwendolyn Blotevogel, Kim Schutte, Janet Gray, Guy Wilson, Erika Rummel, and James and Jan Mehl, to help cover the printing and mailing costs. I also want to thank Charles Timberlake, chairman of the Department of History at the University of Missouri–Columbia, for his cooperation, assistance, and encouragement in this project "in laudem Caroli."

This volume is dedicated to Charles G. Nauert in appreciation for his many years of faithful service as a teacher-scholar of the Renaissance and Reformation and in gratitude for his constant friendship as a mentor and colleague.

James V. Mehl
St. Joseph, Missouri

# THE ADAGES OF PAOLO MANUZIO

## Erasmus and the Roman Censors

*Paul F. Grendler*

IN 1985 A CATALOG FROM AN ANTIQUARIAN BOOK DEALER IN FLORENCE appeared in my mail. It offered for sale the first edition (1575) of the *Adages* of Paolo Manuzio, printed by the Florentine publishing house of the Giunti. Aware of its true authorship, I wrote to the bookseller without real hope of obtaining it. To my surprise, I got the volume for the modest price of $140 plus postage. I rejoiced in my good fortune, because the *Adages* of Paolo Manuzio are an expurgated edition of the *Adages* of Erasmus of Rotterdam, but lacking the author's name. Had the bookseller been aware of the book's true authorship, the price would have been considerably higher.

Erasmus scholars have long been aware of this edition, but know little about it. How did it come into existence? Who expurgated it? What does the process reveal about Italian ecclesiastical attitudes toward Erasmus' works in the third quarter of the sixteenth century? So far as is known, Manuzio's letters have not been read for information on this subject, nor the story of the expurgation told. The tale of Paolo Manuzio's adages boasts a cast of cardinals, censors, scholars, and publishers, and offers insight into sixteenth-century Italian Catholicism.

Rome began to lose patience with Erasmus in the mid-1520s, but moved only slowly and fitfully to ban or censor Erasmus' books.[1] While

---

[1] This account is limited to the *Adagia*; for a fuller story of the various works of Erasmus that Italian church and state authorities denounced and/or banned between the *Consilium de emendanda ecclesia* of 1537 and the Pauline Index of 1559, see Marcella and Paul Grendler, "The Survival of Erasmus in Italy," *Erasmus in English* 8 (1976): 5–6; this is reprinted in Paul F. Grendler, *Culture and Censorship in Late Renaissance Italy and France* (London: Variorum Reprints, 1981), Study 11, 1–5; idem, *The Roman Inquisition and the Venetian Press, 1540–1605* (Princeton: Princeton University Press,

1

the *Colloquia*, the *Moria*, and some religious texts were banned in some of the unofficial or stillborn indexes of the late 1540s and early 1550s, the *Adagia* escaped notice until 1559. In that year the very restrictive Index of Prohibited Books proclaimed by Pope Paul IV condemned all Erasmus' works. But scholars strongly criticized the Pauline Index and members of the book trade fought it tenaciously. Compliance was grudging until Paul IV suddenly died on 18 August 1559. His Index was quickly withdrawn, and the whole question referred to the Council of Trent.[2]

In recess since 1552, the Council of Trent resumed meeting in January 1562. It turned to the question of an Index of Prohibited Books on 26 January and discussions continued through 26 February.[3] The Council fathers expressed a variety of opinions, ranging from strong affirmations of Paul IV's severe Index to pleas for moderation. One Italian prelate condemned Erasmus directly. The Franciscan Dionisio Zannettini (d. 1566), bishop (1538–55) of Mylopotamos in Crete, then under Venetian control, saw no differences between Luther, Erasmus, and Melanchthon (in that order). He condemned Erasmus with the cliché: "aut Erasmus lutherizat aut Lutherus erasmizat" ("either Erasmus lutherizes or Luther erasmizes").[4]

After the opening speeches in February 1562, the council appointed a commission to draft a new Index, empowering it to revise, if necessary, the entries of the Pauline Index of 1559. The commission worked at its task from February 1562 to November 1563, debating controversial authors such as Erasmus. For example, Archbishop (not yet cardinal) Gabriele Paleotti of Bologna argued that certain scholarly books by suspect authors, including Erasmus' *Adagia*, should be permitted.[5] But the commission

---

1977), 79, 96, 101–2, 115, 117; *Index de Venise 1549, Venise et Milan 1554*, ed. J. M. De Bujanda et al. "Introduction historique," Index des livres interdits, 3 (Sherbrooke, Quebec: Centre d'Études de la Renaissance, 1987), ab indice; *Index de Rome 1557, 1559, 1564. Les premiers index romains et l'index du Concile de Trente*, ed. J. M. De Bujanda et al., Index des livres interdits, 8 (Sherbrooke, Quebec: Centre d'Études de la Renaissance, 1990), ab indice; and Silvana Seidel Menchi, *Erasmo in Italia 1520–1580* (Turin: Bollati Boringhieri, 1987), ch. 9.

[2]Grendler, *Roman Inquisition*, 115–27; and *Index de Rome 1557, 1559, 1564*, 37–50.

[3]Grendler, *Roman Inquisition*, 144–45; and *Index de Rome 1557, 1559, 1564*, 55–62.

[4]"Milopotamensis Dionisius verbosas ex sinu chartas protulit, quibus legendis saepe etiam oculis fallebatur. In iis invehi coepit contra Lutherum, Erasmum, Melanchthonem et quosdam alios, subdens: aut Erasmus lutherizat aut Lutherus erasmizat." *Concilium Tridentinum. Diariorum, actorum, epistularum. Nova Collectio edidit Societas Goerresiana*, vol. 3: *Diariorum pars tertia, volumen Prius*, ed. Sebastian Merkle, 2d ed. (Freiburg im Breisgau: Herder, 1964), 250–74, quote at 252. For the identification of Zannettini, see *Hierarchia Catholica medii et recentioris aevi*, ed. C. Eubel et al., 6 vols. (Munich: Regensburg, 1923; rpt. Padua, 1960), 3:244.

[5]See a letter of Camillo Paleotti for Gabriele Paleotti with the list of books to be permitted in *Concilium*

could not agree. On 3 February 1563 Anton Brus von Müglitz, archbishop of Prague, a leading commission member, reported to Emperor Ferdinand I that it was very divided on Erasmus' works. Some wanted to ban the *Moria, Colloquia*, some apologetical works, and many letters; others wanted to correct his works, but so severely that if Erasmus returned to earth he would not recognize them. Still others argued that Pope Leo X had supported Erasmus' literary scholarship and that Erasmus had died as a Catholic. They honored his works on the church fathers and wanted them preserved. But the majority had another view: It was enough for them that the Index of Paul IV had judged Erasmus to be an author of the first class, i.e., a heretic, all of whose works were banned.[6]

At some point in 1563 the commission reached a decision concerning Erasmus' works and the *Adagia* in particular. The commission authorized the universities (i.e., the faculties of theology) of Paris and Louvain to expurgate Erasmus' works, without naming any specific texts. And it charged one of its members, Egidio Foscarari, bishop of Modena, with censuring the *Adagia*.[7] Thus, the Tridentine Index commission decided that Erasmus' works could be permitted in expurgated form.

Foscarari was one of the first clergymen to undertake the new role of censor. Known as a church reformer of exemplary life, Foscarari was born in Bologna in 1512 and joined the Dominican Order in 1524 or 1526.[8] He

---

*Tridentinum*, vol. 13: *Tractatuum pars altera prius ex collectionibus Vincentii Schweitzer*, ed. Hubert Jedin, 2d ed. (Freiburg im Breisgau: Herder, 1967), 587–607, at 602–3. Also quoted in *Index de Rome 1557, 1559, 1564*, 80 n. 146. See also Paolo Prodi, *Il Cardinale Gabriele Paleotti (1522–1597)*, vol. 1 (Rome: Edizioni di Storia e Letteratura, 1959), 125–26. For the work of the commission, see *Index de Rome 1557, 1559, 1564*, 62–94.

[6]See the copy of his letter in *Index de Rome 1557, 1559, 1564*, 79–80 n. 145.

[7]"ERASMI *Opera* pene omnia fuerunt examinata. Verum quia edere in lucem expurgata et censuras longum esset et prolixum opus, ad Universitatem Parisiensem et Lovaniensem remissum est. Censurae in *Adagia* sunt apud D. Mutinensem." Document of 1563: "Nomina librorum qui in concilio Tridentino a Patribus deputatis sunt expurgati et eorum quibus ut examinarentur ab eisdem Patribus dati sunt" (n.d., but 1563), from the Archive of the Holy Office, Rome, as printed in *Index de Rome 1557, 1559, 1564*, 106–8, quote at 107. Although this document seems to be an interim statement, the Tridentine Index repeated many of its decisions.

[8]For Foscarari's career, see Jacobus Quétif and Jacobus Echard, *Scriptores Ordinis Praedicatorum*, vol. 2, part 1: *1499–1639 A.D.* (Paris, 1719–23; rpt. New York, n.d.), 184–86; Alfonso D'Amato, "Foscarari, Egidio," *Enciclopedia cattolica*, vol. 5 (Vatican City, n.d.), 1545; Pedro Rodríguez and Raúl Lanzetti, *El Catecismo Romano: Fuentes e historia del texto y de la redacción: Bases críticas para el estudio teológico del Catecismo del Consilio de Trento (1566)* (Pamplona, 1982), 96–100, et ab indice; and *Il processo inquisitoriale del cardinal Giovanni Morone: Edizione critica*, ed. Massimo Firpo and Dario Marcatto, vol. 2 in two parts: *Il processo d'accusa* (Rome, 1984), 400–2. Michelle M. Fontaine, "For the Good of the City: The Bishop and the Ruling Elite in Tridentine Modena," *Sixteenth Century Journal* 28 (1997): 29–43, focuses on his role as resident bishop of Modena.

acquired a doctorate in theology, then served as inquisitor in Bologna (1546–47). Paul III appointed him Master of the Sacred Palace, i.e., personal theologian to the pope, in April 1547, a post which he held until May 1550. At some point in those years, the Congregation of the Holy Office commissioned Foscarari and another Dominican, Pietro Bertano (1501–58), bishop (later cardinal) of Fano, to draft the first papal index. They completed their work in 1552. The Index of 1554, as it is called, was briefly promulgated in late 1554 and early 1555 in Venice and Milan, before being withdrawn when Paul IV became pope on 23 May 1555.[9]

Foscarari became bishop of Modena in 1550, succeeding Cardinal Giovanni Morone, who had never resided in Modena. Except for the absences noted below, Foscarari was an effective resident bishop, very much respected by the Modenese. He participated in the sessions of the Council of Trent in 1551 and 1552, then returned to his diocese, where he dealt mildly with local heretics. But the sweeping inquisition trial of Cardinal Giovanni Morone, his patron and friend, under the harsh Paul IV caught up Foscarari as well. Arrested under suspicion of heresy, he spent seven months (21 January to 18 August 1558) in a Roman prison. In January 1560, Pius IV exonerated him with the statement that the accusations had come from impious and lying men. Nevertheless, the imprisonment probably cost him the cardinal's hat. Returning to his diocese, Foscarari then entered the most important part of his career in service of the larger church. In addition to membership on the Index commission, he argued forcefully in the 1562–63 sessions of Trent that bishops must reside in their dioceses. In 1563 and 1564 Foscarari labored on the revisions of the Tridentine Catechism (published 1566), Breviary (1568), and Missal (1570) before suddenly dying on 23 December 1564.

Because of his other activities and his premature death, it is not likely that Foscarari did much work, if any, on the *Adages*. When the Tridentine Index appeared in 1564 (with a papal bull of 24 March 1564), it permitted the *Adagia* as expurgated by Paolo Manuzio. In other words, the task had been given to Paolo Manuzio, although who made this decision is unknown. Until Manuzio's edition appeared, readers were ordered to cancel out suspect passages following the judgment of faculties of theology of Catholic universities or the Inquisition.[10]

[9]For the story of the 1554 index, see Grendler, *Roman Inquisition*, 93–101, at 100 for Foscarari; and Grendler, "Introduction historique," in *Index de Venise 1549*, 50–65.

[10]Adagia vero ex editione, quam molitur Paulus Manutius, permittentur; interim vero, quae iam edita sunt, expunctis locis suspectis iudicio alicuius facultatis theologicae universitatis catholicae vel inquisitionis alicuius generalis, permittantur." *Index de Rome 1557, 1559, 1564*, 432, 834. The Tridentine Index also banned six titles outright (*Colloquia, Moria, Lingua, Christiani matrimonii institutio,*

Paolo Manuzio (1512–74), the third and youngest son of the famous Aldo Manuzio (ca. 1450–1515), was the only one to continue in any meaningful way the family tradition of scholarship and publishing.[11] As a youth he lived and studied in several places, but especially in Venice. After Aldo Senior's death, a consortium consisting of Andrea Torresani, Paolo's uncle, and Torresani's sons, operated the Aldine Press until Torresani died in 1529. In 1533 a new group was formed which included Paolo, his two brothers, and Torresani's sons. Paolo now played a major role in the press and may have been the intellectual leader of the group. In 1540 Paolo took full control of the Aldine Press of Venice, which now published books under the name of The Sons of Aldo. In the next twenty years the Aldine Press published many more works than in the period 1515 to 1540. Overall, the Aldine Press published or financed 575 editions between 1533 and 1570 under Paolo's leadership.[12]

Paolo was also a talented humanist. An admirer of Cicero, he earned a high scholarly reputation with his editions of Cicero's letters, speeches, and philosophical writings first published in 1540–41 and frequently reprinted.[13] But like many other humanists, Paolo was restless; he traveled

---

*De interdicto esu carnium*, and the Italian translation of the *Paraphrases on Matthew* prepared by Bernardino Tomitano), and ordered that unnamed other works dealing with religious matters should be prohibited until the faculties of theology of Paris or Louvain could expurgate them. *Index de Rome 1557, 1559, 1564*, 429–32.

[11]There is no biography of Paolo Manuzio, but much information can be found in Ant. Aug. Renouard, *Annales de l'imprimerie des Alde, ou histoire des trois Manuce et de leurs éditions* (Paris: Jules Renouard, 1834); repr. *Annali delle edizioni Aldine con notizie sulla famiglia dei Giunta e repertorio delle loro edizioni fino al 1550* (Bologna: Fiammenghi, 1953), 425–60. Also see Martin Lowry, *Facing the Responsibility of Paulus Manutius*. UCLA University Research Library, Department of Special Collections, Occasional Papers 8 (Los Angeles: University Research Library, 1995). The brief summaries of Paolo's letters found in Ester Pastorello, *L'epistolario manuziano. Inventario cronologico-analitico 1483–1597* (Florence: Leo S. Olschki, 1957), 35–125, 294–302, offer a chronology of his movements. However, this volume does not reprint any of the letters. The most important published sources are the 155 letters found in *Lettere di Paolo Manuzio copiate sugli autografi esistenti nelle Biblioteca Ambrosianaa*, ed. Antoine-Augustin Renouard (Paris: Giulio Renouard, 1834); and some 270 letters by and to Paolo printed in Ester Pastorello, *Inedita manutiana 1502–1597. Appendice all'inventario* (Florence: Leo S. Olschki, 1960), 23–378. However, none of the letters in the last volume deals with the expurgation of Erasmus' *Adagia*.

[12]See Lowry, *Paulus Manutius*, 4. Between 1558 and 1561, Manuzio was the publisher for the Accademia Venetiana, a group of scholars and Venetian patricians who planned a vast program of scholarly learning and publication. After nearly sixty works appeared, its chief sponsor, Federico Badoer, became insolvent, and the Venetian government suppressed the Accademia. Paul Lawrence Rose, "The Accademia Venetiana: Science and Culture in Renaissance Venice," *Studi veneziani* 11 (1969):191–242. See Renouard, *Annali delle edizioni aldine*, 266–81, for a list of Accademia Venetiana publications issued by Manuzio, plus additions noted by Rose.

[13]Lowry, *Paulus Manutius*, 4. His many editions of Cicero and other classical authors are listed

in search of the income that would support scholarly *otium*. And Paolo wanted a great deal of income. Hence, he sought patronage from cardinals and princes, angled for university professorships at Rome and elsewhere, and pursued knighthoods for himself and his son. He also had to cope with his brothers' personal difficulties and his own chronic ill health. He mentioned his aches and pains in practically every letter, while maintaining a very active schedule.

Over the course of two decades, Paolo made several visits to Rome where he secured the friendship of a group of prelates committed to Catholic scholarly renewal. These men concluded that simply banning the works of Protestants would not stop the spread of Protestantism, let alone win back religious defectors. Catholicism had to prove its religious and intellectual superiority through biblical, liturgical, and patristic scholarship that met the highest humanistic standards. Instructed by the Council of Trent and supported by the papacy, Catholic scholars with excellent humanistic credentials sought to match and better Protestant scholarship on the fundamental works of Christianity. Rome also needed a publisher to present the fruit of their labors to the learned public. Who better than Paolo Manuzio, son of the most famous scholarly publisher of the Renaissance and a leading scholar in his own right?

Pope Paul IV (1555–59) began the wooing by sending an emissary to Manuzio, but no agreement resulted. Paul's successor, Pius IV (1559–65), renewed the pursuit. The scholarly Cardinal Girolamo Seripando (1492/3–1563), who had known Manuzio for many years and was convinced of the need to bring him to Rome, played a major role. Manuzio demanded and obtained an extremely high price for his services: A twelve-year contract; annual payment of 500 gold scudi to be advanced every six months; 300 scudi to cover the expenses of moving his household from Venice to Rome; free housing in Rome; a knighthood with an annual value of 150 scudi (later relinquished in favor of a pension of 100 scudi) for his son, Aldo Junior; the papacy to bear printing costs against future profits; and profits to be divided equally between the papacy and Manuzio.[14] Manuzio moved to Rome in June 1561.

---

in Renouard, *Annali delle edizioni aldine*, passim. However, Manuzio's scholarship has attracted little scholarly attention. An exception is Gustavo Costa, "Paolo Manuzio e lo Pseudo-Longino," *Giornale storico della letteratura italiana* 102 (no. 161; 1984): 60–77.

[14]For a copy of the contract, see Lowry, *Paulus Manutius*, 6–9, 78–80. The terms are also mentioned in Manuzio's 17 May 1561 letter to his brother, *Lettere di Paolo Manuzio*, 25:54–55; Ludovico Beccadelli's 3 May 1561 letter, *Inedita manutiana*, 1006:155–56; and Hubert Jedin, *Papal Legate at the Council of Trent: Cardinal Seripando*, trans. Frederic C. Eckhoff (St. Louis: Herder, 1947), 557–58.

Called the Stamperia del Popolo Romano, Manuzio's Roman press set up operations near the Trevi Fountain in the second half of 1561, and issued its first book in February 1562, Reginald Pole's *De Concilio*. The press issued seven to eleven editions annually from 1562 through 1566, a total of forty-four editions, among them editions of the works of Gregory of Nyssa, Cyprian, Jerome, and Theodoret, an impressive list of church fathers.[15] It also published works summarizing the results of the Council of Trent: the *Canones et decreta* of Trent (1564), the Tridentine Index (1564), the Tridentine Catechism (both Latin and Italian in 1566), and the revised Breviary (1568). Manuzio simultaneously published editions of Latin secular classics, often reissues of earlier Aldine imprints. He also kept a close eye on the Aldine Press of Venice.[16]

Although Manuzio published an impressive list of books meeting exacting humanistic standards, not everything went smoothly. He was unable to realize the grandest projects, a new edition of the Vulgate (Latin Bible) and editions of the Greek fathers. Over time, papal support for the press eroded, as the group of cardinals who had brought Manuzio to Rome died or lost influence. Pius V, who became pope in January 1566, had less interest in the press than his predecessor. Manuzio complained that overly zealous ecclesiastical officials concerned with doctrinal orthodoxy looked over his shoulder and slowed production. Finally, the press did not realize Manuzio's probably unrealistic profit expectations. Manuzio issued only ten editions, several of them reprints, between 1567 and 1570. Disappointed and restless, Manuzio wanted to leave Rome. Even though the papacy and various cardinals begged him to continue, Manuzio broke his contract in August 1570, three years before its termination. Sold to Fabrizio Galletti, the Stamperia del Popolo Romano continued to publish but without achieving scholarly distinction. Manuzio left Rome for Venice in September or October 1570.[17]

---

[15]The fundamental works on the Stamperia del Popolo Romano are Francesco Barberi, *Paolo Manuzio e la Stamperia del Popolo Romano (1561–1570) con documenti inediti* (Rome, 1942; rpt. Rome: Gela Reprints, 1985), 101–61, for the list of editions; and Lowry, *Paulus Manutius*. See also Renouard, *Annali delle edizioni aldine*, passim. Curt F. Bühler, "Paulus Manutius and His First Roman Printings," *Papers of the Bibliographical Society of America* 46 (1952): 209–14, demonstrates that Manuzio took pains to print his first publication accurately.

[16]Manuzio's many letters of the 1560s and early 1570s to his son Aldo Manuzio Junior in Venice mostly concern press matters. Indeed, it is thanks to Manuzio's letters to his absent son that one can follow the expurgation of the *Adages*. Aldo Junior (1547–97) began to publish under his own name in Venice in 1567. Like Paolo, he combined publishing and scholarship, but was less accomplished in both than his father.

[17]See Pastorello, *L'epistolario manuziano*, 112–13, for his movements.

Financial and intellectual disappointment probably persuaded Manuzio to give up.[18] Manuzio's press was not technically equipped to take advantage of the most lucrative profit opportunities, mass production of the newly revised liturgical works, which required complex page layouts, many different typefaces, copious illustrations, and red and black ink on the same page. Lacking expertise, Manuzio sold the rights to print the liturgical works to others after issuing some first editions.

The intellectual disappointment may have been just as great. Publication of improved texts of the Bible and patristic authors according to the principles of humanistic scholarship was only the end of the process. Preparation took years.[19] Standards of humanistic scholarship had risen considerably from the time when Aldo Senior and his associates edited and published the first editions of ancient pagan Greek and Latin authors, sometimes on the basis of brief study of a manuscript or two. Now expert scholars needed years of painstaking labor with manuscripts and earlier printed versions in order to establish the correct text and to prepare commentary. They proceeded slowly, because they could not afford to make mistakes in an age of religious controversy. And Manuzio was not always fortunate in his collaborators, as ill health, death, and scandal removed some from the scene. It is likely that both Manuzio and his cardinal supporters harbored unrealistic scholarly expectations for the Stamperia del Popolo Romano. Only in 1587 did the papacy establish the Vatican Press, which did publish the revised Vulgate and other works long in preparation.

Although not his primary concern, moving to Rome also inserted Paolo Manuzio into the world of papal censorship. The Tridentine Index commission, which included Cardinal Seripando, Manuzio's strong supporter, had charged him with preparing an expurgated edition of Erasmus' *Adages*. The members of the commission obviously believed that Manuzio had the learning and probity to do the job. Possibly they felt that the scholarly world would accept an expurgated version of the *Adages* only if the scholarly son of Aldo Senior did it, because the father published the important 1508 edition, called *Adagiorum Chiliades*, which increased the adages from 818 to 3,260. But Manuzio seems to have done nothing about the *Adages* in the years in which he operated the Stamperia del Popolo Romano.

---

[18]What follows is based on Barberi, *Paolo Manuzio*, 83–97; Lowry, *Paulus Manutius*, 52–71; and my own speculation.

[19]Experience as a member of the Editorial Board of the Collected Works of Erasmus and as editor-in-chief of the forthcoming *The Encylopedia of the Renaissance* has taught me that large scholarly enterprises take longer than anticipated to realize.

By June 1572 he was back in Rome, enjoying a monthly stipend of twenty-five ducats from Gregory XIII (elected 13 May 1572), thanks to the intervention of friends among the cardinals.[20] Manuzio's letters from this period show him busily working on his own scholarship, sending directions on press matters to Aldo Junior, now in Venice, and raising money for the dowry for his daughter, about to be married. Manuzio first mentioned Erasmus' *Adages* at this time.

On 23 August 1572, Paolo wrote to Aldo Junior in Venice concerning various books in preparation (paraphrased as follows):

> Between my Latin letters, the commentary on Cicero's *Letters to Atticus*, and the "Proverbij d'Erasmo," Manuzio began, many presses of the Company [presumably the Aldine Press in Venice] will be busy.[21] In addition to everything else, the corrections alone of the "Proverbij di Erasmo" will keep a good corrector busy. There is considerable Greek in the work, as I have seen in the Paris copy, which I have in my room. You told me that the Greek had been eliminated [from the Paris edition], but that is not so. All this labor has passed to a theologian and myself. And the book has been given to me as my work [*cosa mia*], as promised by the Council of Trent, as you will see from the *motus proprius* of the pope, which has already been sent. I hope to get some use from this in several respects. I will tell you this little bit in confidence, which you should not pass on to your colleagues. I also have in hand the *Apophthegmata* of Erasmus, which has been given to me to review. And, because now they intend to expurgate books prohibited by the Council, I believe that I will be able to get part of this for myself, that is, for us, if I remain here in Rome. But God knows that I have little wish to do so.[22]

---

[20]For the stipend, see Manuzio's letter to Aldo Junior, Venice, 19 December 1573, *Lettere di Paolo Manuzio*, 105:309; *L'epistolario manuziano*, 1657; and Barberi, *Paolo Manuzio*, 96.

[21]I am not translating, but closely paraphrasing, Manuzio's words throughout his letters in an effort to render meaning and style fluently. Literal translation would involve too many awkward constructions and explanatory notes to be smooth.

[22]"Perche tra le mie Epistole latine, il Commento delle *ad Atticum*, i Proverbij d'Erasmo che sono in ordine, e bisogna subito cominciarli, si occuperanno molti torcoli della Compagnia. Oltra che il mio Commento vorrà un altro torcolo fuor della Compagnia. Si che ci sarà che far assai, e la coretione sola de' Proverbij di Erasmo occuperà un correttore buono. Dove ci è greco assai, per quanto ho veduto nella copia di Parigi, la quale ho in camera; e, parmi, che tu mi dicessi, che'l greco era levato via: che non è così. Tutta la fatica è passata per mano d'un Teologo, e mia; et a me è dato il libro, come cosa mia, promessa dal Concilio: come si vedrà nel *Motu proprio* di N. S.^re già spedito. E però intendo di haverne utile particolare per diversi rispetti. Io te ne do per hora questo poco di lume: però non ne dir altro a' compagni. Ho anco in mano gli Apoftegmi di Erasmo, che mi son dati a rivedere. E, perchè

This letter sheds considerable light about the expurgation of the *Adagia* and Manuzio's motives in doing it. Manuzio and an unnamed theologian had been expurgating the *Adagia*. They used the Paris 1570 edition as the base text for at least part of their work, just as Ferdinand van der Haeghen concluded one hundred years ago.[23] The pope had authorized Manuzio to publish Erasmus' *Adagia* as his own work, omitting Erasmus' name, because the Council had promised this. Manuzio hoped to profit from his expurgation of the *Adagia*, probably by publishing it with the Aldine Press of Venice. He had also been given Erasmus' *Apophthegmata* to expurgate.[24] Finally, the papacy intended to allow the expurgation of other prohibited books, and Manuzio and the Aldine Press hoped to publish some of them. What the letter suggests is that Manuzio, whatever his unspoken views concerning the legitimacy of expurgating one of the classics of Renaissance humanistic scholarship, hoped to profit from his work of expurgation.

---

hora si attende a purgar i libri proibiti dal Concilio, io crederei di poterne impetrar una parte per me, cioè per noi, se rimanessi qui. Ma Dio sa che n'ho poca voglia." 23 August 1572, Rome; *Lettere di Paolo Manuzio*, 66:231–32; 1573 in *L'epistolario manuziano*.

This is copied exactly from the printed text, even though it is unlikely that Manuzio italicized titles when writing. "N. S.re" is "Nostro Signore," i.e., the pope. An expanded edition of Manuzio's Latin letters was published as *Epistolarum Pauli Manutii libri xi* (Venice: Aldine Press, 1573). A new edition of the *Ad Atticum* appeared in Venice (Aldine Press, 1570) but no subsequent edition has been located. Renouard, *Annali delle edizioni aldine*, 209, 216.

[23] According to van der Haeghen, the first part of the expurgated version is based on the edition of Basel: Hieronymous Froben and Nikolaus Episcopius, 1559; and the second part on the edition of Paris: Nicolas Chesneau, printed by Jean Charron, 1570. F. van der Haeghen, *Bibliographie des oeuvres d'Érasme: Adagia* (Gand: C. Vyt, 1897), 146–55, 171. Van der Haeghen's descriptions of the various editions of the *Adagia* are copied exactly in *Bibliotheca belgica: Bibliographie Générale des Pays-Bays*, ed. Marie-Thérèse Lenger, vol. 2 (Brussels: Culture et Civilisation, 1964), passim.

[24] Unfortunately, there is no other information about the expurgation of the *Apophthegmata* in the published letters of Paolo Manuzio. The Aldine Press of Venice published the expurgated *Apophthegmata* under the name of Paolo Manuzio in 1577: *Apophthegmatum ex optimis utriusque, linguae scriptoribus libri iix Paulli Manutii studio, atque industria, doctissimor. Theologor. consilio, atque ope, ab omnib. me(n)dis vindicati, quae pium, & veritatis Catholicae studiosum lectorem poterant offendere. Gregorio XIII. Pont. Max. hanc unam editionem approbante ut in extremo libro videre est.* Venetiis. MDLXXVII. Ex aedibus Manutianis.

This description is based on the copy at the Ahmanson-Murphy Aldine Collection at the Department of Special Collections, University of California at Los Angeles. The book contains an uninformative introductory letter of Aldo Junior, dated 13 November 1576, which does not mention his father or Erasmus. The volume also reprints the same *motus proprius* of Gregory XIII found in the 1575 expurgated *Adagia*. I am grateful to James Davis of the UCLA Department of Special Collections who furnished me copies of the title page and introductory matter. This work was reprinted in 1583, 1590, 1604, and 1620. *Bibliotheca Belgica*, vol. 2, E369, E370, and E373. I own a copy of the 1620 edition, which is not listed in *Bibliotheca Belgica*.

The unnamed theologian was probably Eustachio Locatelli. When the expurgated *Adagia* appeared in 1575, it contained a first-person affirmation by Locatelli dated 27 February 1573, Rome, that he had participated in expurgating Erasmus' *Adages*.[25] Locatelli wrote that on the request of Fra Tomás Manrique, former Master of the Sacred Palace, he, Friar Eustachio Locatelli, Order of Preachers and bishop of Reggio (Emilia), read through and corrected the *Adages* of Erasmus, expurgating everything offensive to the Christian religion and pious readers, and that he showed his corrections and expurgations to the Master of the Sacred Palace. The latter approved what had been done. Locatelli also affirmed that the preparation of the work had been entrusted to Paolo Manuzio according to the order of the Council of Trent. In other words, Manrique had passed the charge of reviewing Manuzio's expurgations to a second clergyman, Eustachio Locatelli.

Locatelli specialized in expurgating famous authors. Born in Bologna in 1518, Locatelli entered the Dominican Order there and served as a theological expert at the Council of Trent from 1547 to 1548, later as inquisitor of Bologna from 1554 to 1560.[26] At that time he questioned witnesses in the long heresy trial of Cardinal Giovanni Morone. Locatelli became procurator general of the Dominican Order in 1561, was confessor to Pius V, and was named bishop of Reggio Emilia in 1569. He died in October 1575. In February 1572, Locatelli (and Tomás Manrique; see below) gave advice to a Florentine concerning the first expurgation of Boccaccio's *Decameron*, which was published by the Florentine Giunti Press at the end of 1573, but immediately withdrawn as not severe enough. He simultaneously advised in another project the expurgation of Machiavelli's works. This project never came to fruition.[27] The point is that Locatelli reviewed Manuzio's

---

[25]"Ego frater Eustachius Locatellus ordinis Predicatorum Episcopus Reggij attestor quatenus precibus Reverendi fratris Thommae Manrique, olim Magistri Sacri Palatij, Adagia Erasmi perlegi, & castigavi, & ea ab omnibus, quae religionem Christianam, & pias lectoris aures offendere poterant, expurgavi, & sic castigata, & expurgata eidem Reverendo Magistro Sacri Palatij ostendi; quae demum ipso approbante Paullo Manutio excudenda tradita fuerunt iuxta ordinem Concilij Tridentini, in quorum fidem praesentes manu propria scripsi, & solitum meum sigillum apposui hac die xxvij, Februarij. MDLXXIII. Romae. Ita est frater Eustachius Locatellus Episcopus, qui sup." *Adagia quaecumque ad hanc diem exierunt, Paullii Manutii studio, atque industria, doctissimorum Theologorum consilio, atque ope....Florentiae. Apud Iuntas MDLXXV, Sig. 3 verso. The original capitalization and punctuation have been retained in both the statement and the title.

[26]For a capsule biography, see *Il processo di Morone*, 2:348–49 n. 1. See also Quétif and Echard, *Scriptores Ordines Praedicatorum*, 231–32.

[27]Pio Paschini, *Cinquecento romano e riforma cattolica: Scritti raccolti in occasione dell'ottantesimo compleanno dell'autore* (Rome: Lateranum, 1958), 59, 245–58, esp. 247, 256–57; and John Tedeschi, *The Prosecution of Heresy: Collected Studies on the Inquisition in Early Modern Italy* (Binghamton, N.Y.: Medieval & Renaissance Texts & Studies, 1991), 310–11, and bibliography therein.

work and made the final decision as to what would be expurgated and permitted. Barring discovery of working drafts, the extent to which the final version reflected Manuzio's or Locatelli's expurgations will probably never be determined.

In his next letter to Aldo Junior on 30 August 1572, Manuzio briefly mentioned that he had received the letter of Gregory XIII, and that the *Motus proprius* did not name Erasmus.[28] On 6 September 1572, Manuzio again mentioned the *Adages* in his letter to Aldo Junior, telling him that if they would like to have Aldo Junior's "Proverbij d'Erasmo," he would be happy to satisfy him, although they would not be able to see the other one (presumably the expurgated text) that Manuzio had written. Manuzio told Aldo Junior that he would speak of it with Fra Gabriele; but that Gabriele would not give up the *Adages* without permission from the Master of the Sacred Palace. "But," Manuzio wrote, "that is like crashing against a rock, especially now that the reprinting of the new [*Adages*] is completely his project."[29] This letter suggests that (1) Manuzio continued to expect that the Aldine Press in Venice would publish the expurgated version, (2) Fra Gabriele was the corrector that the papacy provided,[30] and (3) the Master of the Sacred Palace was playing a key, if difficult, role.

Originating with St. Dominic in the thirteenth century, the Master of the Sacred Palace (always a Dominican) was the chief theological consultant to the pope.[31] But from the 1550s onward, he was also the chief censor for the city of Rome, and these activities probably occupied much of his time. He was also a permanent consultant member of the Congregations of the Index and of the Inquisition. He advised the cardinals of the congregations on heresy and censorship matters and carried out their instructions.

---

[28]"Ho ricevuto la epistola di Gregorio. Nel *Motu proprio* non è nominato Erasmo." Letter to Aldo Junior, Venice, 30 August 1572, *Lettere di Paolo Manuzio*, 67:232; letter 1574 in *L'epistolario manuziano*. It is not clear whether "the letter of Gregory" meant the *Motus proprius* itself, a letter accompanying the *Motus proprius*, or something else.

[29]"Se si potranno haver i tuoi Proverbij d'Erasmo, mi sarà caro per sodisfarti, benchè non sappia veder quello, che importi. Ne parlerò con fra Gabriel; ma lui non li darà senza licenza del Mastro Sacri Palatij: che è come urtar in uno scoglio, massime hora che il ristampar i nuovi è tutta impresa sua." Letter to Aldo Junior, Venice, 6 September 1572, *Lettere di Paolo Manuzio*, 68:234; letter 1576 in *L'epistolario manuziano*.

[30]"Il Papa ha voluto che fra Grabriele venga a star qui in casa per la correttione, e che gli dia due stanze: e cosi gli ho dato le tue." Letter to Aldo Junior, Venice, 26 June 1568, *Lettere di Paolo Manuzio*, 29:128; letter 1367 in Pastorello, *L'epistolario manuziano*. Fra Gabriele has not been further identified.

[31]For a succinct history of the office, see Gregory Cleary, "Master of the Sacred Palace," *The Catholic Encyclopedia*, vol. 10 (New York: Appleton, 1911), 39–40. For additional censorship activity by Masters of the Sacred Palace, see William McCuaig, *Carlo Sigonio: The Changing World of the Late Renaissance* (Princeton, N.J.: Princeton University Press, 1989), 261–62 n. 25, and 287–89.

Manuzio referred to Friar Tomás Manrique (or Manriquez), a Spanish Dominican priest appointed Master of the Sacred Palace in 1565.[32] Little is known about Manrique. A Spaniard, he joined a Dominican convent in Piedrahíta (in Castile, west of Madrid) at a young age. Election as procurator general of the order in 1553 brought him to Rome, if he was not there already. As a scholar, Manrique concentrated on the works of St. Thomas Aquinas; he was the principal editor of the Aquinas edition appearing in nineteen folio volumes in Rome in 1570 and 1571. As Master of the Sacred Palace, he enjoyed the confidence of Pope Pius V (1566–72), a fellow Dominican. He participated in the preparation of the Tridentine Catechism. He and Eustachio Locatelli selected the passages to be deleted or changed in the first attempt to expurgate Boccaccio's *Decameron*. Manrique was one of several clergymen who reviewed the texts that the Stamperia del Popolo Romano published; Manuzio complained about him more than once.[33] This probably fueled Manuzio's comment that Manrique left few friends when he died on 11 January 1573 (see below).

Manuzio did not mention the *Adages* in his correspondence during the next sixteen months. Then on 16 January 1574, Manuzio again wrote to Aldo Junior in Venice. "Filippo Giunti writes," Manuzio began:

> that you have some additions to the "Proverbij di Erasmo."[34] Now I want to warn you that if they are drawn from those written after Erasmus, your labor has been in vain, because all were printed with the last edition of the *Adages*, published in Paris, which has been revised here by the Master of the Sacred Palace and myself. I believe that I have removed two hundred items included as proverbs, that are not, plus many others of Adriaen de Jonge (Hadrianus Junius) and Gilbert Cousin and their comrades.[35] I have

---

[32]See the brief biography in Quétif and Echard, *Scriptores Ordinis Praedicatorum*, vol. 2, part 1, 229–30. For his death date, see Pio Paschini, *Cinquecento romano*, 59 n. 7. For other references to his activity, see ibid., 59, 60, 265–66; and Paschini, *Tre illustri prelati del Rinascimento: Ermolao Barbaro, Adriano Castellesi, Giovanni Grimani* (Rome: Lateranum, 1957), 175–76; and Ludwig von Pastor, *The History of the Popes*, ed. Ralph Francis Kerr, vol. 17: *Pius V (1566–72)* (London: Herder, 1929), 130, 203, 336 n. 1, 345, 355. For Manrique's participation in the Stamperia del Popolo Romana, see Barberi, *Paolo Manuzio, 105, 123, 141, 157*; for the Catechism, see Paschini, *Cinquecento romano*, 58–60; and Rodríguez and Lanzetti, *El catecismo Romano*, ab indice.

[33]For example, see *Lettere di Paolo Manuzio*, 100:303; 102:305; 103:306; and letters 1648, 1652, and 1653 in *L'epistolario manuziano*.

[34]Giunti was more than likely already in possession of the text of the expugated *Adagia*; see below.

[35]Gilbert Cousin or Cognatus (1506–72) served as Erasmus' amanuensis (1530–35) and friend; he often echoed Erasmus' religious views after the latter died in 1536. PGB, "Gilbert Cousin," in *Contemporaries of Erasmus: A Biographical Register of the Renaissance and Reformation*, ed. Peter G. Bietenholz

made a body without a name of these non-Erasmian proverbs, and inscribed it "Appendix Proverbiorum." Now if you have something different, I fear some difficulty. Because that which pertains to the "Proverbij di Erasmo" must be seen here and approved by the Master of the Sacred Palace, and by him presented to the Cardinals of the Congregation of the Index. They all have a bad opinion of Erasmus because of his heresies. Moreover, the Master of the Sacred Palace is dead. Although little is missing [i.e., the work is almost ready to be printed], it would not take much for the book to be prohibited anew, after the revision of the Master of the Sacred Palace, who has left few friends. And if it were not my work, the *Adages* would never be printed. But [Cardinal Guglielmo] Sirleto and [Cardinal Vincenzo] Giustiniani, who love and respect me, knowing the work that I have done, hesitate to offend me by not printing them according to the order of the Council of Trent. And by their authority they moved the other cardinals [of the Congregation of the Index].[36]

This letter introduces Filippo Giunti (1533–1600), who with his brother Jacopo (d. 1591), directed the Florentine Giunti publishing firm which would publish the expurgated *Adages* in 1575.[37] The Manuzio and

---

and Thomas B. Deutscher, vol. 1 (Toronto, Buffalo, and London: University of Toronto Press, 1985), 350–52. Adriaen de Jonge (1511–75) was a prolific Dutch humanist best known for a lexicography and a book on emblems.

[36]"Mi scrive M. Philippo Giunti, che tu hai alcune aggiunte sopra li Proverbij di Erasmo. Onde ho voluto avertirti, che, se sono cavate da quelli che hanno scritto dopo Erasmo, la fatica è soverchia, perchè tutti sono stampati con gli ultimi Proverbij di Erasmo, fatti in Parigi; li quali poi sono stati revisti qui dal M.ro S. Palazzo e da me. E credo haver levate di Erasmo 200 cose poste come Proverbij, che non sono, et altre assai di Adrian Junio, di Cogneto, e suoi compagni. E di tutti poi ho fatto un corpo senza nome, et inscrittolo *Appendix Proverbiorum*. Hor vedi tu, se hai cosa diversa; dove dubito di qualche difficultà. Perchè ciò che appartiene a li Proverbij di Erasmo, bisogna che sia veduto qui et approvato dal M.ro S. Palazzo, e da lui proposto alla Congregatione de Cardinali sopra l'indice. I quali tutti hanno mala opinione e di Erasmo per le heresie, e del M.ro S. Palazzo morto. Onde poco è mancato, che di nuovo il libro non sia stato prohibito, dico dopo la revisione del S. Palazzo, che ha lasciati pochi amici. E se non ci era l'opera mia, non si stampavano mai i Proverbij. Ma Sirletti, e Giustiniano che mi amano e stimano, sapendo la fatica da me fatta, dubitorno di offendermi, se non si stampasse, secondo l'ordine del Concilio. E mossero con l'auttorità loro gli altri Cardinali." To Aldo Junior, Venice, 16 January 1574, *Lettere di Paolo Manuzio*, 108:312–14; letter 1660 in *L'epistolario manuziano*.

[37]On the Giunti see *I Giunti tipografi editori di Firenze 1497–1570*, ed. Decio Decia et al. (Florence: Giunti Barbèra, 1978); *I Giunti tipografi editori di Firenze 1571–1625*, ed. Luigi Silvestro Camerini (Florence: Giunti Barbèra, 1979); and William A. Pettas, *The Giunti of Florence: Merchant Publishers of the Sixteenth Century* (San Francisco: Bernard M. Rosenthal, 1980), family tree on page 1. Francesca Lucrezia was the daughter of Bernardo (d. 1597), brother of Filippo and Jacopo, and also involved in the publishing firm.

Giunti families, longtime rivals, had joined hands when Aldo Junior married Francesca Lucrezia Giunti, the niece of Filippo and Jacopo, in April 1572. Paolo Manuzio had abandoned the idea of publishing the work with the Aldine Press and had already contacted Filippo Giunti about publication. He did not say why. Perhaps he did so for financial reasons, because it was to be a large folio volume, perhaps as a gesture of support toward Aldo Junior's new relatives by marriage. Next, Aldo Junior, who was also a humanist scholar, had looked at the Paris 1570 edition of the *Adages*, which included additional adages by other scholars, and wanted to add some of them to the expurgated version. Manuzio informs him that he has eliminated this material from the text that will be published and has put it into an appendix. However, the "Appendix Proverbiorum" of non-Erasmian material was not included in the 1575 expurgated text.

The most interesting part of the letter follows. Manrique, the deceased Master of the Sacred Palace, "who left few friends," had approved the expurgated text. Then he (Manrique) had to obtain the approval of a hostile Congregation of the Index, who saw Erasmus as a heretic. But Manuzio's friends in the Congregation, Cardinals Sirleto and Giustiniani, had prevailed on the other cardinals to honor the promise made to Manuzio. Hence, publication would go forward. But Manuzio cautions Aldo Junior that any changes to the manuscript risked a fresh prohibition. If publication were blocked, Manuzio's labor would be in vain, and the benefits of publication, intellectual and financial, would not be realized.

Pius V established the Congregation of the Index on 5 March 1571 and Gregory XIII confirmed its existence on 13 September 1572.[38] At the time of Manuzio's letter, its membership consisted of seven cardinals: Sirleto; Giustiniani; the reforming bishop of Bologna, Gabriele Paleotti; the Dominican Arcangelo de' Bianchi; the Franciscan inquisitor Felice Peretti da Montalto; Pius V's nephew and chief diplomatic secretary; the Dominican Michele Bonelli; and the French archbishop of Sens, Niccolò Pellevé.[39]

The more prominent of Manuzio's two friends was Sirleto. Born in Calabria, Sirleto was the most scholarly cardinal of his generation. He served as custodian of the Vatican Library from 1554 to 1557 and participated in the

---

[38]See Ugo Rozzo, "Index de Parme 1580," and Paul F. Grendler, "Introduction historique," in *Index de Rome 1590, 1593, 1596: Avec étude des index de Parme 1580 et Munich 1582*, ed. J. M. De Bujanda et al. Index des livres interdits, 9 (Sherbrooke, Quebec: Centre d'Études de la Renaissance, and Genève: Librairie Droz, 1994), 24–25, 272–73.

[39]Paleotti (1522–c. 1597, cardinal 1565); Bianchi (cardinal 1570, d. 1580); Montalto (1521–90, cardinal 1570, elected pope 1585 as Sixtus V); Bonelli (1541–98, cardinal 1566); Pellevé (cardinal 1570, d. 1594).

1562–63 sessions of the Council of Trent. Most important, Sirleto was a scholar and skilled in Greek. He wrote about the lives of early church martyrs, worked on the Vulgate, the Tridentine Catechism, Breviary, Missal, and the *Corpus iuris canonici*. He met Manuzio as early as the 1550s, was a strong supporter of the Stamperia del Popolo Romano, and worked with him in editing church fathers.[40] Here Sirleto favors the publication of the expurgated *Adagia*. Later he would prove to be a strict censor of Carlo Sigonio, professor at the University of Bologna, who wrote early medieval church history.[41] Much less is known about Vincenzo Giustiniani. From a Genoese noble family, he became a Dominican, was general of the order in 1558, participated in the Council of Trent, wrote a logical work, and helped edit the Thomas Aquinas edition (1570–71).[42]

Manuzio returned to the subject of publication in a letter of 30 January 1574. Again he warned Aldo Junior not to try to add anything to the text of the *Adages* because the permission to print, which had been so difficult to obtain, was limited to the text that he (Manuzio) had submitted. It had been reviewed by the Master of the Sacred Palace (Manrique) and confirmed by a *motus proprius* of the pope. New licenses and new *motu proprii* would only stir up adversaries (those who did not want the *Adages* to be published?) and it would take a long time to explain.[43] That was the last reference to the *Adages* in Manuzio's correspondence. By late March, Manuzio was gravely ill. He died on 6 April 1574 before Aldo Junior could arrive from Venice.

In 1575 the Florentine Giunti Press published the book with a long, awkward, and somewhat ambiguous title page:

> Adages, which have been issued up to now, liberated by the study
> and diligence of Paolo Manuzio, with the help and advice of very
> learned theologians, from all faults which could offend the

---

[40]Barberi, *Paolo Manuzio*, ab indice; Rodríguez and Lanzetti, *El catecismo romano*, ab indice; Pio Paschini, "Guglielmo Sirleto prima del cardinalato," in Paschini, *Tre ricerche sulla storia della Chiesa nel Cinquecento* (Rome: Edizioni Liturgiche, 1945), 153–281; Georg Denzler, *Kardinal Guglielmo Sirleto (1514–85), Leben und Werk: Ein Beitrag zur Nachtridentinischen Reform*: Münchener Theologische Studien, 1. Historische Abteilung, 17 (Munich: Max Hueber, 1964). I have been unable to consult Pietro Emidio Commodaro, *Il cardinale Guglielmo Sirleto 1514–85* (Catanzaro: La Provincia di Catanzaro, 1985).

[41]See McCuaig, *Carlo Sigonio*, chap. 4.

[42]Sirleto (1514–85, cardinal 1565); Sigonio (1523–84); Giustiniani (1519–82, cardinal 1570).

[43]"Quanto a' Proverbij, ogni tuo utile mi sarà carissimo: ma credo, bisognerà far la tua giunta separata. Perchè la licenza, che qui s'è tanta difficoltà, si ristringe alla copia solo, che ho dato io, riveduta dal M.ᵣₒ S. P. e confermata da un *motu proprio* d'un Papa: e non son cose da rimescolar più con nuove licenze, e nuovi *motu proprii* per gli avversarij, che si hanno, di che sarebbe lunga cosa l'informati." Letter to Aldo Junior, Venice, 30 January 1574, *Lettere di Paolo Manuzio*, 119:317; letter 1663 in Pastorello, *L'epistolario manuziano*.

# ADAGIA
## QVAECVMQVE AD HANC DIEM EXIERVNT,

PAVLLI MANVTII STVDIO, ATQVE indultria, doctilsimorum Theologorum confilio, atque ope, ab omnibus mendis vindicata, quae pium, et veritatis Catholicae ltudiofum lectorem poterant offendere :

*Sublatis etiam falfis interpretationibus, & nonnullis, quae nihil ad propofitam rem pertinebant, longis inanibufq. digreffionibus.*

Quem laborem, a Sacrofancti CONCILII TRIDENTINI Patribus Manutio mandatum,

*GREGORIVS XIII. MOTU PROPRIO ita comprobauit, vt omnes Adagiorum libros, vna excepta editione Manutiana, prohibeat, atque condemnet.*

Cum plurimis, ac locupletifsimis INDICIBVS Græcis, & Latinis, quorum non nulli nufquam antehac imprefsi fuerunt.

CVM LICENTIA ET PRIVILEGIO.

## FLORENTIAE.
### APVD IVNTAS
M D LXXV.

Title page of the first edition (1575) of the *Adages* by Paolo Manuzio. The book is a folio-sized volume, 32.5 by 22 cm. Photo of author's copy.

learned reader and Catholic truth. Indeed, false interpretations and many long and useless digressions which do not concern the subject matter have been removed. Which labor the Fathers of the Holy Council of Trent commanded of Paolo Manuzio, Gregory XIII with *motus proprius* approved. And all books of adages with the exception of the edition of Manuzio are prohibited and condemned.[44]

Next comes the dedicatory letter by Aldo Manuzio Junior to Gregory XIII, dated 1 May 1575 from Venice. This date suggests that the work was printed and published in May or June. In addition to courteous statements and lofty sentiments, the letter states that the Council of Trent had authorized Paolo Manuzio to clean of impious material a book of old proverbs in two languages (i.e., Latin and Greek). Aldo goes on to write that his father had done this, with the aid of learned theologians, before his death. The letter does not mention any other author or compiler of the proverbs. Next comes the *Motus proprius* of 12 August 1572 of Gregory XIII. It begins by referring to the charge given to Paolo Manuzio to expurgate, so that they will not offend pious Catholics, an anonymous volume of "*Adagia*" and an anonymous book of "Apophthegmata," which was done with the counsel of Tomás Manrique, Master of the Sacred Palace. It goes on to say that Paolo Manuzio has the right to print and sell these expurgated versions of "Adagia" and "Apophthegmata" while all other versions are prohibited and condemned.

On the reverse side of the third leaf are three brief statements. The first is Locatelli's affirmation of 27 February 1573, previously discussed, that he had expurgated "the *Adages* of Erasmus." Next follows a brief statement of Paolo Manuzio, also dated 27 February 1573, from Rome. Manuzio affirms that he has received from Friar Tomás Manrique "the *Adagia* of Erasmus," expurgated of everything that could offend the Christian religion and pious readers, and that he had transmitted the text to Filippo and Iacopo Giunti in Florence.[45] These two brief mentions are the only references to Erasmus in the work of about 750 double-columned, folio-sized pages. Finally, the Inquisitor General of the Florentine state, one Francesco

---

[44]Please see the photograph of the title page of the author's copy. The book is a folio-sized volume measuring 32.5 by 22 cms.

[45]"Cum a Reverendo Fratre Thomma Manrique olim Magistro Sacri Palatij, Adagia Erasmi castigata, & ab omnibus, quae Christianam religionem, & pias lectoris aures offendere poterant expurgata, Ego Paullus Manutius receperim, illa Philippo & Iacopo Iuntis Florentiam imprimenda transmisi: In quorum fidem praesentem attestationem manu propria scripsi, & solitum meum sigillum apposui hac die xxvii. Februarij. MDLXXIII. Romae. Paullus Manutius." *Adagia quaecumque ad hanc diem exierunt.* Florentiae. Apud Iuntas MDLXXV, Sig. †3 verso.

da Pisa, gives permission to publish "these Adages expurgated by Locatelli on the request of the Master of the Sacred Palace." His permission is dated 15 March 1573 from Florence.[46] Thus, the expurgated edition of the *Adagia* appeared in print some twelve years after the Index commission of the Council of Trent decided that the *Adagia* could be permitted in expurgated form, and eleven years after the Tridentine Index authorized Paolo Manuzio to prepare and publish the expurgated version.

The expurgations were numerous and sometimes very extensive. The fate of one famous adage, "Sileni Alcibiadis" (The Sileni of Alcibiadis), demonstrates the extent and nature of the expurgations. The Silenus of Alcibiadis (mentioned in Plato's *Symposium*) was originally a wooden figurine of the demigod Silenus which could be opened to reveal an interior much more interesting than the modest exterior promised. Erasmus explained that the proverb referred to any thing or person who "at first sight looks worthless and absurd, (but) is yet admirable on a nearer and less superficial view...."[47] Erasmus then gave a series of examples of ancient Greeks who presented very modest, even homely, and vulgar exteriors, but revealed a wealth of probity and learning to those who looked more closely. Socrates was one example. Toward the end of this classical material, Erasmus added a second meaning for Silenus: Something that has great exterior beauty and attraction, but is empty or corrupt inside. This was an "inside-out Silenus."[48]

Erasmus then abruptly shifted his focus in order to apply both the positive and negative meanings of Silenus to the contemporary world, especially to clergymen. He described Christ and the Apostles as good Sileni, men who were externally humble and lowly, but full of interior piety. But he characterized current popes, prelates, princes, theologians, and doctors of theology as bad Sileni. They were clothed in external purples and silks, enjoyed titles and distinctions, but were empty of merit, or worse, were sinful. The adage became a slashing denunciation of the hypocrisy of churchmen and the leaders of contemporary society, delivered with passion and eloquence.

[46]Vidimus Adagia Reverendissimo D. D. Eustachio Locatello Reggii Episcopo, precibus Reverendi D. Thommae Manrique, olim Magistri Sacri Palatij castigata & emendata, & quia ita esse agnovimus, ut formis excuderentur iuxta mandatum eiusdem Magistri Sacri Palatij, permissimus, Florentiae die xv. Martij. MDLXXIII. Ita est Franciscus de Pisis Generalis Inquisitor Dominij Florentini." *Adagia quaecumque ad hanc diem exierunt.* Florentinae. Apud Iuntas MDLXXV, Sig. †3 verso.

[47]*The Collected Works of Erasmus,* vol. 34: *Adages II vii 1 to III iii 100,* trans. and annotated by R. A. B. Mynors (Toronto, Buffalo, and London: University of Toronto Press, 1992), 262. The entire adage is 262–82.

[48]*The Collected Works of Erasmus,* 34:268.

The expurgated version left untouched the beginning of the adage with its Greek classical material, but ended at that point.[49] It eliminated all the rest of the adage (about three-quarters of the total) with its criticism of contemporary churchmen and civil rulers. The expurgation transformed "The Sileni of Alcibiadis" into a short, uncontroversial piece of Greek erudition. Since the original adage is clearly divided into two distinct parts, a reader unacquainted with the original might not have sensed that anything was missing.

The expurgation of the bulk of *Sileni Alcibiadis* was an extreme example. Some adages were little altered, and the ancient and philological material remained unchanged throughout.[50] But it typified the approach: Erasmus the classical scholar remained, while Erasmus the sharp critic of clerical and princely abuses did not survive expurgation. At the same time, Paolo Manuzio had restored the work to its Erasmian dimension by scraping off the additional adages that, like barnacles to a ship's hull, had attached themselves to Erasmus' book after the author's death. He was still the humanist dedicated to publishing a text purged of its accretions.

The expurgated *Adagia* appeared in four more Italian printings: 1578, 1585, 1591, and 1609, always in Venice.[51] The Giunti did not reprint the work. All carried the name of Paolo Manuzio on the title page. But all four excised all the introductory material except for Aldo Junior's dedicatory letter to Gregory XIII. Hence, these subsequent editions did not mention Erasmus at all.

This study suggests several conclusions. First, while Manuzio receives the credit or blame for expurgation, and his name appeared on the volume, it is not clear how much of the expurgation he did. Certainly he worked on the text. But Locatelli and Manrique made the ultimate decisions on what to cut, and the final text had to be approved by the Congregation of the Index. Second, Manuzio's motives for doing the expurgation were probably more commercial than intellectual. He saw this as an opportunity to publish a famous book with the Aldine Press, his press. Manuzio never suggested an intellectual reason, such as protecting readers from Erasmus' errors, or respect for Erasmus' scholarship, or the desire to

---

[49]*Adagia quaecumque ad hanc diem exierunt....*Florentinae. Apud Iuntas, 1575, cols. 835 and 836. These two columns comprise about three full pages in *The Collected Works of Erasmus*, vol. 34, 262 through the first twelve lines of p. 264, and the paragraph at line16 from the bottom of p. 266 and ends at line 4 on p. 267.

[50]*Bibliotheca Belgica*, vol. 2, E123, 309–11, lists many of the cuts in comparison with the editions of Basel 1559 and Paris 1570.

[51]See *Bibliotheca Belgica*, vol. 2, E124, E127, E128, and E132. I have examined the editions of 1578 (E124) and 1591 (E128).

bring the *Adages* to a new generation of readers, for undertaking the expurgation. Third, given the hostility of high Roman churchmen to Erasmus, an expurgated version was the best that could be expected. Indeed, one wonders if the expurgated edition would have appeared at all, if not for the Tridentine commitment.

Finally, the long history of the expurgation of the *Adages* and the persons involved offer insight into the complexity of Italian Catholicism at this time. It is customary for scholars to divide sixteenth-century Catholicism into Catholic Reformation and Counter-Reformation. The former included, but was not limited to, an extensive program of scholarly renewal, embracing the editing and publication of church fathers, the Tridentine catechism, and revision of the breviary and missal. The Counter-Reformation, by contrast, prohibited and expurgated books judged heretical or overly critical of clergymen and church practices. Inevitably, modern scholars have viewed those who participated in Catholic Reform activities positively, and the censors and expurgators negatively.

But sixteenth-century churchmen defy easy classification. The same men who labored on the texts of Catholic Reform also proved to be expurgators of Erasmus and compilers of indices of prohibited books. From their point of view, publishing the church fathers and expurgating Erasmus' *Adages* were both essential actions in order to save the souls under their care.[52] This is the context of the expurgation of Erasmus' *Adages*, a revealing episode in the history of sixteenth-century Italian Catholicism.

---

[52]See John W. O'Malley, "Was Ignatius Loyola a Church Reformer? How to Look at Early Modern Catholicism," *The Catholic Historical Review* 77 (1991): 177–93.

# THE ECLECTIC STYLE IN THEORY
# AND PRACTICE
# IN ANGELO POLIZIANO'S EP. VIII.16

*Keith A. Shafer*

Epistle VIII.16 in the collected correspondence of Angelo Poliziano is the Florentine's famous letter to Paolo Cortesi on the subject of imitation.[1] Written around 1485, this letter has received some attention by scholars, most notably and recently by Thomas Greene and Martin McLaughlin.[2] No extensive literary discussion of the epistle has yet been attempted, however, despite the fact that it possesses true literary merits and is one of the important treatises in the Ciceronian debate. The brief essay in this volume will focus on the relationship between mimetic theory and practice in Ep. VIII.16, especially as it reflects Poliziano's notion of *recondita eruditio*. I shall argue that the language and sources employed by Poliziano are bound up with his preference for an eclectic style, a style founded on a multiplicity of models. Poliziano's letter not only makes a case for eclectic *imitatio*, but is itself an example thereof. Thus in Ep. VIII.16 there exists a marriage between the medium and the message. The literary approach that I propose to undertake differs from most previous scholarship on Ep. VIII.16; it is more concerned with Poliziano's method of composition than the place of the letter in the Ciceronian debate.

Below is a translation of Ep. VIII.16:

---

[1]The translation of Poliziano's letter is based on the Latin text in Eugenio Garin, ed., *Prosatori Latini del Quattrocento* (Milan: R. Ricciardi, 1952), 902 ff. The Latin text of Poliziano's Ep. VIII.16, to which I shall make frequent reference, is in the appendix on page 33.

[2]Thomas Greene, *The Light in Troy* (New Haven: Yale University Press, 1982), 150–55; Martin McLaughlin, *Literary Imitation in the Italian Renaissance* (Oxford: Oxford University Press, 1995), 202–6.

I am returning to you the letters that you carefully collected, in the reading of which, to speak freely, I am ashamed to have spent valuable time. For on the whole, except for a few, they are not at all worthy that they should be said to have been read by a learned man or to have been collected by you. I will not explain which letters I like and which I do not. I do not want anyone to be pleased or displeased in them on my account. There is, however, an issue concerning style about which I disagree with you somewhat. For, as I take it, you are accustomed to approve only the one who fashions the outline of Cicero. In my opinion, the face of a bull or lion is preferable to that of an ape, even though an ape's is more similar to a man's. Nor are those who are believed to have held the preeminent place in eloquence similar to each other, as Seneca has made known. Those who think that they are Cicero's kin because they close their periods with the words *esse videatur* are ridiculed by Quintilian. Certainly, to me, whosoever compose solely from imitation are like the parrot or the magpie, bringing forth things that they do not understand. For what they write lacks strength and life; it lacks movement, it lacks mood, it lacks native talent; it lies down, falls asleep, snores. There is nothing true in it, nothing solid, nothing effective. You do not, someone says, express Cicero. What of it? I am not Cicero; I express, as I take it, myself.

Moreover, my dear Paolo, there are some people who beg for their style in crumbs as if for bread. They do not live to the future, but day to day. And then, unless they have in front of them a book from which to draw something, they can hardly string three words together, and even these they spoil with foolish connections and shameful barbarisms. Therefore, their style is always quivering, tottering and weak and clearly cared for and nourished poorly. These men I cannot bear, daring, as they do, to pass judgment on those who are learned, that is those whose style a hidden erudition, broad and deep reading and long practice have, as it were, leavened. But to return to you, Paolo, whom I love deeply, to whom I owe much, whose talent I especially respect, I ask that you not bind yourself to that superstition that nothing of your own brings you pleasure and you never take your eyes from Cicero. Rather, when first you have read Cicero and other good authors deeply and have ruminated on them, learned them by heart and digested them, and have filled your breast with a knowledge of many subjects, and you then want to try to compose something yourself, I would desire that you swim without a float (as they say) and use your own counsel, laying aside that fretful and deeply distressed care of reproducing only Cicero and, instead, putting all your own powers to the test. For those who, awestruck, contemplate the ridiculous things that you call features, do not, believe me, adequately reproduce them; rather, they slow the progress of their own talent, as if blocking the path of a runner and, to use the Plautine phrase, *remoram faciunt*. But just as the man who will place his foot in others' prints is unable to run well, so one cannot write well who does not dare leave the prescribed rule. Finally, know that it is the sign of an infertile mind to imitate always and never produce anything independently. Farewell.

The occasion for Poliziano's writing is explained in the letter itself. Paolo Cortesi, a humanist employed in the papal curia and an intimate of Poliziano, had sent the Florentine a collection of letters written in the Ciceronian style. The Roman apparently had asked his friend to make suggestions, which Poliziano does not hesitate to make. Poliziano is utterly displeased with the letters, grousing about the time he had wasted in reading them and chastising his younger friend for the time spent in their collection. When Poliziano refers to *docto aliquo*, he may be alluding playfully to Cortesi's own *De hominibus doctis*, which discusses the stylistic vices and virtues of a number of Italian humanists. Poliziano then adds that he will not give any specific details about which letters he approves (confined to *minime paucas*) and which he does not approve, for he does not want others to be swayed by his opinion.[3] Poliziano's transition to his main argument seems harmless: *est in quo tamen a te dissentiam de stylo nonnihil.* The use of the adverb *nonnihil* is noteworthy here, since in the remainder of the letter, Poliziano depicts a wide gulf separating the two humanists on stylistic matters. *Nonnihil* is, therefore, an ironic foil to the polemic against Ciceronianism that Poliziano delivers in the balance of his letter.

A brief overview of Ep. VIII.16 will provide a context for a discussion of the wedding of theory and practice in Poliziano's eclecticism. Poliziano begins by outlining Cortesi's position as he understands it: One must, to gain the Roman's approval, reproduce the outline (*lineamenta*) of Cicero. Poliziano rejects this approach, citing an example from art (*mihi vero...similior est*) to buttress his argument. He moves quickly to a triad of

---

[3]Erasmus, who was to champion the eclectic cause, did not follow his Italian forerunner on this account. His *Ciceronianus* of 1528 named names and caused a great stir in the academic world.

rapid-fire references from antiquity; Seneca, Quintilian, and Horace all support Poliziano's eclectic approach. After some literary name-calling (the Ciceronians are *similes psittaco vel picae*), Poliziano finishes with a flourish, proclaiming his own independence: *non enim sum Cicero; me tamen, ut opinor, exprimo.*

One is struck by the negative tone of the letter to this point, a tone that Poliziano maintains with the image that follows. The Ciceronian stylist is like a beggar. Wholly dependent, he must have the source of his writing close at hand; without it, his prose is *tremula, vacillans, infirma.* Carrying on the metaphor, Poliziano labels Ciceronian prose *male pasta.* He is especially upset by the audacity of those who, despite their own ignorance, take it upon themselves to judge *de doctis.* Hitherto Poliziano has kept to the attack, putting off any positive formulation of his own for successful *imitatio.* Finally near the middle of the letter he offers his own, albeit brief, list of the ingredients for successful writing. Even here the formulation is set in a negative context; the Ciceronians lack these ingredients. A strong prose style must be fomented by three qualities: *recondita eruditio, multiplex lectio,* and *longissimus usus.* These qualities will receive particular attention following a brief analysis of the final section of Ep. VIII.16.

Poliziano continues with an address to Cortesi (*sed ut ad te redeam*). There is a marked shift in tone in this section of the letter, as Poliziano recalls his friendship with the younger scholar. He holds Cortesi in the highest regard (*quem penitus amo, cui multum debeo, cuius ingenio plurimum tribuo*). It becomes clear that, for Poliziano, Ciceronianism represents a threat to Cortesi's intellectual development. His advice in the letter, although harsh at times, is necessary to combat the dangers of rigid Ciceronian imitation. The mental strain of such rigid imitation makes the practice *sollicitudo morosa nimis et anxia.* Not only are they undernourished, but the Ciceronians suffer from a nervous disorder.[4]

At the close of the letter Poliziano argues that just as one cannot run if he must place his feet in the footsteps of another, so one cannot write well if he does not dare break away from his model. The image of the writer following in his model's footsteps is, as G. W. Pigman notes, "perhaps the most common of the commonplaces" in ancient and Renaissance discussions of style.[5] The metaphor illustrates the distance between the writer and his model. The writer's attitude determines how he copes with this

---

[4]Erasmus picks up the notion that Ciceronianism is a disease. In the *Ciceronianus* he attributes the death of Christophorus Longolius to an overzealous desire to imitate Cicero. See Erasmus, *Ciceronianus*, trans. Betty Knott, in *Collected Works of Erasmus*, vol. 28 (Toronto: University of Toronto Press, 1986), 430.

[5]G. W. Pigman, "Versions of Imitation in the Renaissance," *Renaissance Quarterly* 33 (1980), 20.

distance. Pigman's study shows that the vestigial image can be used to show deference to the model (Pigman calls this imitation) or an attempt to surpass the model (emulation).[6] In his appeal to Cortesi, Poliziano transforms the metaphor to suit his own view. His focus is not on the distance between the writer and his model, but on the footprint itself. The difficulty in following another's footprints is due to individual characteristics, such as length of gait and foot size of both leader and follower. Poliziano's imitative scheme relies heavily on the power of the individual, who, he argues, must be free to choose his own path. This is an act of courage (Poliziano uses the phrase *audet egredi*), of breaking away from the established rule and becoming self-reliant. Poliziano reiterates this idea in the last sentence of Ep. VIII.16, reminding his younger colleague that it is healthier to produce from one's own resources than to rely on imitation.

An analysis of some key passages in the letter shows that Poliziano himself draws heavily on his classical reading in making his case for an eclectic method of imitation. In calling to task the poor stylists who dare to judge the output of those well-schooled in writing, Poliziano defines the latter: *hoc est de illis quorum stylum recondita eruditio, multiplex lectio, longissimus usus diu quasi fermentavit*. The last word provides the key to the image. The verb *fermentavit* recalls the beggar image that precedes it by its reference to leavening bread. It also captures the sort of self-sufficiency that Poliziano deems necessary for the successful stylist. One must eschew reliance on outside sources and become able to increase one's output internally. The three elements of style (*recondita eruditio, multiplex lectio, longissimus usus*) are a way to achieve such self-sufficiency.

The third element, *longissimus usus*, bears little examination. Students became familiar with Latin vocabulary and syntax by constant drill. Rhetorically, *longissimus usus* is opposed to Poliziano's picture of the Ciceronians who copy words out of the master's works into their own writing. This is too simple and shallow to produce good writing, which is the product of long practice and repetition.

The second element of style is *multiplex lectio*. Thomas Greene translates the phrase "broad reading," an improvement on Izora Scott's "much reading."[7] But the idea that Poliziano expresses is more complex and defies tidy translation. *Multiplex lectio* should perhaps be defined as "deep reading

---

[6] Ibid., 16 ff. The author cites Statius' address to his book (in *Thebaid* 8.16–17) to keep far behind the *Aeneid* and venerate its footsteps as an example of imitation. For an example of emulation he refers to Petrarch, *Fam.* 22.2.20–21, wherein the author avows that he will not be prohibited from placing his foot wherever he chooses.

[7] Greene, *Light in Troy*, 150; Izora Scott, *Controversies over the Imitation of Cicero* (New York: Teachers College, Columbia University, 1910), 18.

on a variety of subjects." Poliziano's emphasis on breadth and depth of reading here is an extension of his rigorous philological method. Rudolph Pfeiffer praises the Florentine's *ardor eruditionis*, which "brought him a comprehensive knowledge not only of Latin, but also of the Greek world."[8] In Poliziano's masterwork, the *Miscellanea*, he gives the following advice to the student of ancient poetry:

> Qui poetarum interpretationem suscipit, eum non solum(quod dicitur) ad Aristophanis lucernam, sed etiam ad cleanthis oportet lucubrasse. Nec prospiciendae autem philosophorum modo familiae, sed et iureconsultorum et medicorum item et dialecticorum et quicunque doctrinae illum orbem faciunt, quae vocamus Encyclia, sed et philosophorum quoque omnium.[9]

The humanists' enterprise entailed the reconstruction of a classical past that had been lost. To understand that past and make it useful for their own present, humanists attempted to rediscover as much about antiquity as they could. Perhaps no humanist of his time understood the complexity of that process better than Poliziano. For him, stylistic imitation is a way to participate in the broad sweep of history; Ciceronianism, on the contrary, is limiting and essentially unhistorical because it refuses to accept the broad spectrum that is Latin literature. But Poliziano's eclecticism is not an enslavement to a past that can never be fully reconstructed; it is, rather, a method firmly rooted in the present, wherein the healthy stylist paints his prose from the variegated palette of Latin writing. The key element in Poliziano's scheme is choice; his eclecticism stresses the ability of the stylist to select his models from the masters of the past and to create a new style from them.

Poliziano's quarrel, it should be clarified, was not with Cicero, but rather with the use of that author as the sole model for prose composition. In a letter to Bartolomeo Scala, with whom he had a bitter debate about Latin style, Poliziano writes:

> Ad Ciceronem vero quod me revocas, auctorem quidem Latinae linguae summum, nec tamen solum, quaero quid aliis facias, quorum testimonia vim sententiae semper apud eruditissimum

---

[8]Rudolph Pfeiffer, *History of Classical Scholarship 1300–1850* (Oxford: Oxford University Press, 1976), 43.

[9]Angelo Poliziano, *Opera Omnia*, ed. Ida Maier (Turin: Bottega d'Erasmo, 1971), 229: "He who enters upon interpreting the poets should burn the midnight oil not only by the lamp of Aristophanes but that of Cleanthes as well. Not only should he be on the watch for the poets but the jurists, doctors, logicians and other writers who comprise the sphere of learning that we call the circle of arts and sciences, and even of all the philosophers, too."

quenque habuerunt? Quaero item, quid uni saltem Varroni respondeas, qui quidem sicuti Ciceroni palmam concedit orandi causas, ita Latine loquendi sibi retinet? Quaero etiam an quasi barbaros quosdam reiicias Livium, Sallustium, Quintilianum, Senecam, Plinium quoque utrunque, multos alios praeterea tot seculorum suffragiis comprobatos?[10]

Again we note Poliziano's recognition of the historical milieu; for him, all of antiquity is there to be mined for one's own writing. It should be noted, too, that the locus of authority for writers like Quintilian, Sallust, and Seneca is not Poliziano (or any contemporary stylist), but the collective voice of the ages. Poliziano recognizes his place in the historical continuum, which he, in opposition to the Ciceronians, refuses to limit. For Poliziano, a strong style is the product of a healthy and vigorous self that has been raised on a variety of sources.

The concept *recondita eruditio*, like *multiplex lectio*, proposes problems for translators; neither Scott's "deep study" nor Greene's "abstruse erudition" adequately represents Poliziano's intention. The two translators approach the idea from separate vantage points. Scott's emphasis is on the writer, composing from a storehouse of knowledge; Greene's translation stresses the product of the writer's deep study—an erudition that is difficult to understand. The translations of Scott and Greene diverge on their understanding of *recondita*, which carries ideas of storing up and hiding away. In the first sense, *recondita* serves as a foil to the beggar metaphor that Poliziano uses to represent the effeteness of the Ciceronians. We are again led to recall Poliziano's picture of the Ciceronian copying directly from his source. *Recondita eruditio* is a rejection of the superficiality of this practice; style must spring from an abundance of knowledge. Greene's idea of hidden learning can be found in the digestive metaphor that Poliziano uses in his advice to Cortesi; he tells the Roman humanist that he should chew up (*contriveris*), learn by heart (*edidiceris*), and digest (*concoxeris*) Cicero and other good authors. *Eruditio* is the source for good writing, but it must not be overt; it must be digested, transformed, and mixed with the writer's own talent to make imitation successful. In both senses *recondita eruditio* should be considered an extension of *multiplex lectio*, a way to

[10]Ibid., 58–59: "As to the fact that you recall me to Cicero, indeed the utmost author of the Latin tongue, but not the only one, I ask what you would do to the others whose attestations have always held the power of opinion for anyone very learned. Likewise, I ask what you would at least respond to Varro for one, who yields the palm of pleading cases to Cicero, but retains that of speaking Latin for himself. Furthermore, I ask whether you reject as barbarous Livy, Sallust, Quintilian, Seneca, Pliny and numerous others who have been favored by the approbation of so many ages?"

relate reading to the process of composition. When one takes the interpretations of Greene and Scott together, a clearer and deeper understanding of what Poliziano means by *recondita eruditio* emerges.

For Poliziano *recondita eruditio* is a bridge between the gathering and storing of ideas and sources (represented by *multiplex lectio*) and the practice of writing (represented by *longissimus usus*). In the former, learning is a latent source; in the latter, this hidden learning, charged with the native talent of the individual writer, is put into action. The learning is concealed in the new text by the writer so that it may be found by the reader. The stored passive knowledge connects the stylist with his models. The active hidden knowledge connects the author to the reader; it challenges the reader to recognize and appreciate the author's transformation of his model.

A few examples will illustrate Poliziano's *recondita eruditio* in practice, where one can glimpse the completed transformation of the model, its recontextualization. In the first example, Poliziano employs a seemingly innocuous citation from Horace. To support his refutation of strict Ciceronianism, Poliziano calls on three classical writers, Seneca, Quintilian, and Horace. The Senecan citation concisely reflects Poliziano's own misgivings about the historical validity and the rigidity of Ciceronianism: Those authors who were considered great stylists throughout the ages are quite dissimilar in their style of writing. Poliziano then characterizes Quintilian laughing (*ridentur a Quintiliano*) at the ineptitude of those who believe they are imitating Cicero when they end a period with *esse videatur*. He follows this with reference to Horace's castigation of imitators (*inclamat Horatius*). Poliziano refers to the well-known cry in Horace's Ep. 1.19.19: *O imitatores, servum pecus.* But he intends the reader to recall all of lines 19 and 20:

> O imitatores, servum pecus, ut mihi saepe
> bilem saepe iocum vestri movere tumultus![11]

The significance of line 19 to Poliziano's theme is obvious, but the following line is no less important. Taken together, the citations from Quintilian and Horace provide a new image; Quintilian's laughter has turned to Horace's rage. To unlock this clever little puzzle the reader must know the passage in Horace's epistles that spells out (*ut mihi saepe bilem, saepe iocum vestri movere tumultus*) what only has been alluded to. By invoking

---

[11]Horace, *Epistolae* I.XIX.19–20: "You imitators, flock of slaves! How your rumblings move me at one time to anger, at another, to laughter."

Horatian ambivalence, that combination of mocking laughter and ire, Poliziano identifies himself fully with the Roman poet.

Poliziano expresses the same mixed feelings about Ciceronianism in the letter to Bartolomeo Scala quoted above,[12] where he complains that the ignorance of some Ciceronians is so great that they find faults with words in Poliziano's writings which are in well-emended texts of Cicero:

> Saepe enim hoc usu venit, et quidem cum magno meo interdum vel risu vel stomacho ut illa ipsa in nostris scriptis potissimum reprehenderent quae in bonis emendatisque Ciceronis exemplaribus reperirentur....

Poliziano has found in Horace the perfect vehicle for expressing his own feelings. From a rhetorical point of view he has made his argument much stronger by identifying himself with the revered poet and critic; it is difficult to argue with Horace on matters of latinity. The Horatian citation exemplifies the sort of imitation that Poliziano endorses; it is veiled, erudite, and more concerned with capturing the mood of the model than the model's words.

Another example of *recondita eruditio* occurs toward the end of the letter. Poliziano's final point is that strict imitation is an impediment to one's natural abilities (*impetum quodammodo retardant ingenii sui*). Poliziano characterizes the Ciceronians as people who block a runner's path (*currentique velut obstant*). To complete this description, he borrows a brief phrase from Plautus, *remoram faciunt*. On the surface this borrowing, like the Horatian quote, appears rather harmless—simply another way of expressing *currenti veluti obstant*. But more is intended as a comparison with Plautus' original shows. The phrase comes from the comic play, *Trinummus*, in the opening scene following the prologue. Megaronides, the *senex*, is upset because he has to castigate a friend:

> It's a very disagreeable thing to have to castigate a friend whose faults deserve it; but as things are in this life, it is sometimes a necessary and salutary thing to do. That is what I have got to do today; remonstrate with a friend for something he has done wrong. I don't want to do it, but my conscience forces me to do it. There is a plague of wickedness rife in this city, destroying all the laws of morality; indeed most of them are by now a dead letter, and while morality withers, wickedness flourishes like a well

---

[12]Poliziano, *Opera Omnia*, 58–59: "For it has often happened, sometimes to my great amusement and sometimes to great ire, that they find especially objectionable those things in my writings that are found in good and emended copies of Cicero....."

watered plant. Wickedness is the cheapest thing you can find round here; you can pick a peck of it for nothing; there are far more people who think more of pleasing a few friends than of what is best for the majority. Thus what is desirable takes second place to interest, and interest everywhere is a confounded plague, and an obstacle (*remoram faciunt*) to private and public good.[13]

Poliziano, like Megaronides, does not want to correct his friend, but he must. As he did with the citations from Quintilian and Horace discussed above, Poliziano has used his classical source as the basis for expressing his own feeling, albeit in a concealed and learned way. He certainly intended Paolo to recognize the passage and realize its relationship to the current situation. The quote from Plautus also recalls the mixture of anger and laughter discussed above. Poliziano obviously has strong feelings about Ciceronianism, but he uses a speech from a Roman comedy to illustrate his feelings. By quoting Megaronides, Poliziano not only reiterates his concern about the perils of Ciceronianism, but also does it in a light-hearted way, altogether fitting for a letter to a friend.

These examples show the depth of Poliziano's imitative practice. In Ep. VIII.16 we glimpse a brilliant scholar at work, transforming his reading into something new and challenging his reader to keep pace. Poliziano's historical eclecticism is founded on three principles: *longissimus usus, multiplex lectio,* and *recondita eruditio,* that form the foundation of a strong style. His letter shows how these principles work in practice. Poliziano's familiarity with Latin literature is broad and deep (*multiplex lectio*) and is the product of diligent study (*longissimus usus*) both in his writing and reading. Ep. VIII.16 exemplifies *recondita eruditio* above all. By quoting a line from Horace, Poliziano identifies his feelings about Ciceronianism with Horace's opinion of his own imitators. This is done indirectly, by quoting one line of Horace and expecting the reader to identify the context. Similarly, he quotes two words from Plautus' *Trinummus* to lead the reader to the original text, in which Megaronides (the *senex*, as Poliziano has, perhaps, cast himself with his younger friend) is in a situation strikingly similar to Poliziano's. The task for contemporary readers of Poliziano's works is the same as that presented to Cortesi: To look beyond the surface of the text and extract the knowledge that has been so carefully hidden.

---

[13]Plautus, *The Rope and Other Plays*, trans. E. F. Watling (London: Penguin Books, 1964), 165.

Appendix

Angelo Poliziano Ep. VIII.16

Remitto epistolas diligentia tua collectas, in quibus legendis, ut libere dicam, pudet bonas horas male collocasse. Nam praeter omnino paucas, minime dignae sunt quae vel a docto aliquo lectae vel a te collectae dicantur. Quas probem, quas rursus improbem, non explico. Nolo sibi quisuam vel placeat in his, auctore me, vel displiceat. Est in quo tamen a te dissentiam de stylo nonnihil. Non enim probare soles, ut accepi, nisi qui lineamenta Ciceronis effingat. Mihi vero longe honestior tauri facies aut item leonis quam simiae videtur, quae tamen homini similior est. Nec ii, qui principatum tenuisse creduntur eloquentiae, similes inter se, quod Seneca prodidit. Ridentur a Quintiliano qui se germanos Ciceronis putabant esse, quod his verbis periodum clauderent: *esse videatur*. Inclamat Horatius imitatores, ac nihil aliud quam imitatores. Mihi certe quicumque tantum componunt ex imitatione, similes esse psittaco vel picae videntur, proferentibus quae nec intelligunt. Carent enim quae scribunt isti viribus et vita; carent actu, carent affectu, carent indole, iacent, dormiunt, stertunt. Nihil ibi verum, nihil solidum, nihil efficax. Non exprimis, inquit aliquis, Ciceronem. Quid tum? Non enim sum Cicero; me tamen, ut opinor, exprimo.

Sunt quidam praeterea, mi Paule, qui stylum quasi panem frustillatim mendicant, nec die solum vivunt, sed et in diem; tum nisi liber ille praesto sit, ex quo quid excerpant, colligere tria verba non possunt, sed haec ipsa quoque vel indocta iunctura vel barbaria inhonesta contaminant. Horum igitur oratio tremula, vacillans, infirma, videlicet male curata, male pasta, quos ferre profecto non possum; iudicare quoque de doctis impudenter audentes, hoc est de illis quorum stylum recondita eruditio, multiplex lectio, longissimus usus diu quasi fermentavit. Sed ut ad te redeam, Paule, quem penitus amo, cui multum debeo, cuius ingenium plurimum tribuo, quaeso, ne superstitione ista te alliges, ut nihil delectet quod tuum plane sit et ut oculos a Cicerone nunquam deicias. Sed cum Ciceronem, cum bonos alios multum diuque legeris, contriveris, edidiceris, concoxeris et rerum multarum cognitione pectus impleveris, ac iam componere aliquid ipse parabis, tum demum velim quod dicitur sine cortice nates, atque ipse tibi sis aliquando in consilio, sollicitudinemque denique vires universas pericliteris. Nam qui tantum ridicula ista quae vocatis liniamenta contemplantur attoniti, nec illa ipsa, mihi crede satis repraesentant, et impetum quodammodo retardant ingenii sui, currentique velut obstant et, ut utar plautino verbo, remoram faciunt. Sed ut ben currere non potest qui pedem ponere studet in alienis tantum vestigiis, ita nec bene scribere qui tamquam de praescripto non audet egredi. Postremo scias infelicis esse ingenii nihil a se promere, semper imitari. Vale.

# PROFESSIONAL FRIENDSHIPS AMONG HUMANISTS

## Collaboration or Conspiracy?

*Erika Rummel*

IN 1488 PIETRO MARTIRE, diplomat and historian at the court of Ferdinand and Isabella, received an invitation to give a lecture at the University of Salamanca. On the appointed day he entered the crowded lecture hall and boldly announced that he would speak on any subject proposed to him. The local professor of poetry, Marineo Siculo, rose and asked for an exposition of the second satire of Juvenal. Martire accepted the suggestion and for the next two hours, held forth on the subject with great eloquence. The audience, much impressed by this extemporaneous display of learning, treated Martire "like an Olympic victor." They were unaware that the professor of poetry and the visiting lecturer had agreed on the subject beforehand. Thus Martire's performance was not spontaneous after all.[1] The story raises questions about scholarly collaboration and its more sinister version, collusion. In this essay I would like to examine three types of collaboration: disguised sponsorship; open attempts by an individual to obtain patronage or render services to a fellow scholar; and cases of multiple sponsorship, involving letter-writing campaigns.

The case related above was not the only instance of collusion between Pietro Martire and Marineo Siculo. Evidence for a second case comes from a letter to Pedro Fajardo, Marqués de los Vélez, in which Marineo confesses to a theft. He tells his correspondent that on a visit to Martire's house, he strolled into the host's study and absconded with a manuscript

---

[1]The incident is described by Martire in a letter to Iñigo López de Mendoza, Count of Tendilla, in *Documentos inéditos para la historia de España*, ed. J. López de Toro (Madrid: Tip. De Archivos, 1953), 1:83–84. Cf. Erika Rummel, "Marineo Sículo: A Protagonist of Humanism in Spain," *Renaissance Quarterly* 50 (1997): 164-74.

copy of his most recent work. In Marineo's opinion, the composition, whose title he fails to mention, was worthy of publication. "I therefore send you the stolen work, illustrious Marquis," he wrote, "and advise and beg you to hand it over to the printers. In the meantime I will look up Martire myself and prudently deal with him, so that, if he has an action for theft against us, he will abandon it."[2] There is something rather odd about Marineo's cheerful self-incrimination. Other cases of purported manuscript thefts, confessed with equal alacrity by an impenitent thief, lead us to the conclusion that this was a game scholars played.

A collection of Erasmian letters, *Auctarium...selectarum epistolarum* [3] is another example of the practice. It begins with a dedicatory letter by Beatus Rhenanus, a close friend and confidant of Erasmus', who, like Marineo, confesses to "a daring deed": "I have robbed Erasmus, that incomparable champion of the noblest disciplines and of an almost extinct theology. 'What?' you will say, 'this is unheard-of. You must be joking!' No, I am serious."[4] Beatus goes on to describe how he filched certain letters from Erasmus' study. Like Marineo, he was motivated to defraud Erasmus by the desire not to defraud the reader of these literary treasures. And like Marineo, he was confident that the victim would forgive him.

A letter by the Erfurt reformer Johann Lang was published under similarly curious circumstances. It contains a prefatory letter by Eobanus Hessus, the leading humanist in the Erfurt circle, beginning with a confession:

> A few days ago, gentle reader, when I paid a casual visit to a friend and, as one does, looked at the newest material on his desk, it so happened that there fell into my hands a letter from the excellent theologian Johann Lang (you know how great a man he is). It was addressed to the great jurist Martin of Margareten, rector of the gymnasium, but had apparently not yet been sent off. When I had read it through diligently and avidly, as I usually read everything the man writes, I thought it was worthy of being immediately printed in as many copies as possible and put into the hands of scholars.... So here is the letter, dear reader, full of piety and

---

[2]Marineo Siculo, *Epistolarum familiarium libri XVII* (Valladolid, 1514), Ep. 5.15: "Hoc igitur opus furtivum, Illustrissime Marchio, ad te mitto et, ut impressoribus tradas, te hortor atque obsecro. Ego autem interim Martyrem ipsum conveniam et cum eo prudenter agam ut, si quam habet in nos furti actionem, nobis remittat."

[3]*Auctarium...selectarum epistolarum* (Basel: Froben, 1519).

[4]*Der Briefwechsel des Beatus Rhenanus*, ed. Adalbert Horawitz and Karl Hartfelder (repr. Hildesheim: Olms, 1966), 119–20: "Erasmum, incomparabilem illum optimorum studiorum et extinctae propemodum theologiae vindicem, compilavi. Hui, quid hoc novae rei est? inquies. Ludisne forsan? Imo serio loquor."

learning, made available to you, so that you might read it before it reaches the man for whom it was intended. You may blame me (if it is a culpable deed and not rather an act of charity).... Indeed I'll gladly and willingly shoulder the responsibility for any fault or crime this involves, if I may thereby provide a service to you and your studies.[5]

The letter that Eobanus had purportedly stolen was an endorsement of liberal studies, or to be more precise, an apologia in which Lang defended himself against the accusation of being an enemy of the humanities. It has the air of an official statement rather than a private communication and was no doubt intended for publication. The confessions of the three manuscript thieves are clearly spurious. The fact that they remained on good terms with their "victims" is perhaps the best indication that the crimes were staged. But why go about publication in this circuitous way? The purpose of the subterfuge is obvious. It allowed the author to play coy, while a friend looked after the publicity needed to find a publisher. Should the publication turn out to be a failure or arouse controversy, he was able to distance himself from the work, noting that it was an unauthorized edition. He could cover up deficiencies in style by saying that he had had no chance to polish it or that the printers had mutilated the text; he could defend indiscretions or controversial remarks by claiming that the text had been corrupted and the wording changed or arguing that he should not be held accountable for private musings. Of course one can cite numerous instances of unfeigned manuscript thefts and truly unauthorized printings, a fact that gave a degree of plausibility to the pretense made in the cases cited.

In these examples, then, the role of the third party in the publication process is disguised. I now turn to the type of case, in which a third party acts as the official sponsor of a publication or is openly approached by the author in the hope that he will sponsor the production. A good example is

---

[5]*Joannis Langi... epistola ad Excellentissimum D. Martinum Margaritanum* (Erfurt, 1521). Ai verso: "Paucos ante dies, humanissime lector, cum apud amicum quendam familiariter obversarer ac scrinia quaedam (ut fit) opistographorum evolverem, commodum incidit in manus meas eximii Ioannis Langi theologi (nostin qualis viri) epistola quaedam ad magnificum Martinum Margaritanum iure consultum, gymnasii principem, inscripta, nondum tamen, ut videbatur, transmissa. Quam ubi diligenter ac avide (ut eius viri soleo omnia) perlegissem, digna visa est quae statim in quam plurima exemplaria transfusa veniret in manus doctorum hominum.... Habes igitur, mi lector, epistolam pietatis ac eruditionis iuxta plenam, tibi nimirum prius legendam exhibitam quam ei cui est inscripta transmissam. Cuius rei culpam (si qua est ea ac non potius charitas)... in me reiicias licebit. Etenim huius quicquid est vel erroris vel criminis lubens volensque accusari sustineo, dummodo tibi tuisque studiis aliqua ex parte consulam."

the case of Edward Lee, an English diplomat at the court of Henry VIII. Lee studied for some years at the University of Louvain, where he got entangled in a controversy with Erasmus over the latter's edition of the New Testament. Lee published his criticism in 1520 and was answered by Erasmus that same year. Although mutual friends managed to arrange a truce between the two men, they remained resentful of each other. In 1526, while on a diplomatic mission in Spain, Lee tried to publish a second edition of his attack on Erasmus.[6] However, since the Spanish court was full of Erasmian supporters, the enterprise needed a powerful sponsor. Accordingly Lee enlisted the help of his fellow ambassador, Girolamo Ghinuzzi, who wrote on his behalf to Cardinal Wolsey. He explained that Erasmus, in his 1520 reply to Lee, had "answered only those parts in his work which appeared to be relatively easy to answer." He therefore suggested that Lee's work be reprinted in its entirety and offered to see it through the press. Apparently Wolsey did not reply to this suggestion. Two weeks later Ghinuzzi raised the question again, putting it in more urgent terms: "I would have reprinted the work, which would bring honour to both Lee and the English kingdom, if I had a copy, and I'll gladly do so, if a copy is sent to me."[7] We do not know how Wolsey reacted to this second request, but nothing came of Ghinuzzi's initiative. Presumably the project was abandoned because Erasmus heard of Lee's plan and began lobbying against it. He wrote to the imperial chancellor, Mercurio Gattinara:

> I have been informed by certain people through letters that Edward Lee, who acts as ambassador of his king at your court, is preparing to publish a book with shameless attacks on me, or has perhaps already published it. If this is true, I can only say that he would not dare to do in his native Britain what he is bold enough to do in Spain. For I enjoy great favor with the King, the Cardinal [Wolsey], and the Queen and the Archbishop of Canterbury, in short with almost all bishops.

Gattinara wrote back, reassuring him:

> So far I have heard nothing about a book by Edward Lee, although I know that he has been agitating against you for a long time and spreading some slander or other. Whatever it can be, he will never

---

[6]On this episode see Erika Rummel, "New perspectives on the controversy between Erasmus and Lee," *Netherlands Archief voor Kerkgeschiedenis* 74 (1994): 230–31.

[7]Ms BM VIT B VIII, 44: "…solum nonnullas partes eius operis suscepisse quae sibi faciliores visae sunt"; ibid., 65: "…quod quidem [i.e. the edition] pro honore et Lei et regni fecissem, si exemplar habuissem et <si> mihi mitteretur, libenter faciam."

be allowed to publish it in Spain, unless it has been duly considered and examined beforehand. For in Spain great precautions are taken against people's being allowed indiscriminately to publish whatever comes into their heads.[8]

In this case, then, the efforts of a third party on behalf of an author were blocked. Erasmus' backers were evidently more powerful than Lee's sponsor, or diplomatic interests prevailed over Lee's private ambitions.

The maneuvers of Gerard Morinck, a friend and disciple of the Louvain theologian Maarten van Dorp, provide another example of an author who casts around for support to have his work published. On Dorp's death in 1525, Morinck composed a biography to honour the memory of his mentor. He was confident that he would find a publisher: "I believe the work will certainly be printed with the help of friends, if not in Basel, then in Antwerp," he wrote.[9] Among the sponsors he had in mind was Erasmus. Morinck perhaps thought he had a claim on the humanist because he had kept him informed about the machinations of his enemies in Louvain. His calculations were wrong, however. The relations between Dorp and Erasmus had not always been cordial. At one point the two men engaged in a controversy over the merit of language studies for biblical exegesis. Dorp eventually acceded to Erasmus' arguments. Indeed his career suffered as a result of their renewed friendship since Erasmus was persona non grata in Louvain. The faculty of theology suspected that Dorp sympathized not only with Erasmus but with Luther as well and temporarily withdrew his license to teach. In the end, however, Dorp appeased the faculty and was allowed to resume his lectures.

The biography, for which Morinck had such high hopes, remained unpublished. In 1547 he commented on the matter to a friend who had asked for a copy of the manuscript, with a view to publishing it. Morinck replied that it was not ready for publication.

---

[8]P. S. Allen, ed., *Opus Epistolarum Des. Erasmi Roterodami* (rept. Oxford: Oxford University Press, 1963), Ep. 1747:76–81: "Ex quorum litteris cognoui quod Eduardus Leus, qui isthic oratorem agit sui regis nomine, librum apparat aedere contumeliosissime scriptum in me, ac fortasse iam aedidit. Quod si verum est, non auderet hoc in sua Britannia quod audet in Hispania. Nam et regem et cardinalem et reginam et archiepiscopum Cantuariensem, breviter omnes fere episcopos, habeo mihi faventissimos." Allen Ep. 1785:31–5: "De libello Eduardi Lei nihil adhuc audivi; tametsi sciam hominem nescio quid calumniae in te iamdiu moliri. Id tamen quicquid erit, nequaquam illi in Hispania edere licebit, nisi prius mature visum et examinatum sit. Id enim summo studio apud Hispanos cautum est, ne cuivis sua somnia excudere liceat."

[9]Henri de Vocht, *Monumenta Humanistica Lovaniensia* (Louvain: Líbrairie universitaire, 1934), Ep. 1 (1526), 507–8.

It needs to be licked into shape. Much has to be phrased differently; indeed the whole thing needs rewriting. When I composed it, I was influenced more by my affection for the man rather than by regard for the truth. When I reread it today, I am embarrassed and ashamed to think that I was careless enough to let it pass into the hands of certain people.

He mentions that he sent it to Erasmus to see "whether he thought it was ready for the press; he wrote back a letter that was not very complimentary.... There were some things in the biography that were not to his liking." Apparently he resented Morinck's remark that theologians could benefit from reading scholastic authors. He also objected to the statement that Dorp was "falsely suspected of Lutheranism because on his deathbed he summoned two principal theologians and stated openly that he greatly disapproved of Luther's tenets and wished to die in the Catholic faith which had been handed down from the apostles to us. Erasmus said he had letters from Dorp that proved the opposite." Morinck himself admitted that Dorp had been enthusiastic about Luther in the beginning and knew that he had exchanged letters to this effect with Oecolampadius. And of course "if a great man like Erasmus, who is in such things a veritable Lydian stone, did not much approve of my little work,...no one can expect me to make it available."[10]

These examples of authors' enlisting the help of a third party show that sponsorship could play a decisive role in getting a manuscript published. It could furthermore enhance sales of the published book. Printers liked to prefix the text with letters of endorsement by renowned scholars. Their praise had the same function as laudatory quotations on the dust jackets of modern books. Two examples will illustrate the advertising power of the names of Erasmus and Luther in the sixteenth century.

In 1534 Antonius Corvinus, advisor of Philip of Hesse and reformer of Göttingen, published a short treatise with a remarkably candid preface by Luther:

The printer extorted from me this preface to be published under my name, so that this book, which has sufficient sales potential in itself, would earn even greater approval though my endorsement. I myself greatly approve of the subject matter, the elegant style,

---

[10]Henri de Vocht, *Monumenta*, Ep. 5 (to Nicolas de Winghe), 579–82.

and the author's modesty and have no doubt that it will gain the approval of learned readers even without my testimony.[11]

Luther, in his usual style, was brutally honest about the purpose of the preface and the fact that he had not volunteered it. Clearly publishers were in the habit of pestering important men for such endorsements. Erasmus complains about the practice to Boniface Amerbach, relating the following incident: The Basel printer Nicolaus Episcopius came to his house to request a preface for a forthcoming edition of Ammianus. As he sat down to write it, a second printer, Johann Herwagen, was shown in and requested a preface for an edition of Demosthenes. Erasmus replied with some irritation that he

> had been too obliging in this matter and did not wish to prostitute [his] name in the same way in future. Herwagen was insistent. I kept saying no. In the meantime Episcopius urged me to write the letter to Goclenius about Ammianus. While I was writing it, Herwagen kept bothering me, saying "please, please." I told him to go away, adding: "You know what I think about this practice, why go on talking?" He went away.... Afterwards I sent my servant to him to soften my response."[12]

In the end Erasmus did produce the requested preface.[13] Unlike Luther, however, he was discreet. In fact, the reader would never guess from the preface how reluctant Erasmus had been to write it.

I now come to a third category of endorsements, the mobilizing of public support for an author's cause through a letter-writing campaign. The best-known example of such a campaign in the sixteenth century is *Clarorum virorum epistolae* (Tubingen: Anshelm, 1514), a collection of letters in support of Reuchlin. The renowned scholar had come under attack for his defense of Hebrew literature. Since an imperial decree had imposed silence on the parties in the controversy, the collection appeared without

---

[11] *Quatenus expediat aeditam recens Erasmi de sarcienda ecclesiae concordia rationem sequi, tantisper dum adparatur synodus, iuditium Antonii Corvini* (Wittenberg: Schirlentz, 1534), aii recto: "Extorsit mihi typographus praefationem hanc sub nomine meo edendam ut libellus hic, per sese satis vendibilis, meo velut testimonio magis probaretur quanquam re ipsa et stili elegantia tum ipsa modestia etiam mihi ipsi valde probetur, haud dubie piis et eruditis etiam sine meo testimonio multo magis probabilis futurus."

[12] Allen Ep. 2686: 9–20: "Sed rem accipe. Presente Episcopio egit mecum, ut prefarer in Demosthenem. Respondi, me in hoc nimium indulsisse typographis, posthac nolle prostituere nomen meum simili modo. Ille instabat. Pernegaui. Interim Episcopius petiit Epistolam ad Goclenium de Ammiano. Dum hanc scribo, Hervagius obturbat, oro te, oro te. Iussi illum valere, addens: Scis mentem meam; quid opus est pluribus verbis? Abiit. Nam comites illorum vrgebant. Misi post famulum, qui mitigaret responsum."

[13] It is Allen Ep. 2695 (1532).

an editor's name. It contained a preface by Philipp Melanchthon which disguised the true purpose of the publication, advertising the letters as models of style.[14] A second prefatory letter by the corrector of the press, Johann Hiltebrand, made it clear, however, that the letters had been published on Reuchlin's initiative: "Johann Reuchlin brought us the selection of letters by famous men that makes up this elegant little work." Elsewhere Reuchlin is quoted as complaining that "he was forced…to go to the public with printed letters"; that is, he had to use this roundabout method of defending himself.[15]

When Erasmus made use of this method of rallying public opinion a few years later, he, too, went about it in a covert manner. I have already mentioned the polemic with Edward Lee. In the course of this controversy a collection of letters appeared, entitled *Epistolae aliquot eruditorum* (Antwerp: Martens, 1520). Its subtitle promised to reveal "the virulence of a certain sycophant." A second, enlarged edition identified the sycophant as Edward Lee. Erasmus left readers with the impression that he had nothing to do with the collection, but two letters that remained unpublished during his lifetime make it clear that he orchestrated the campaign and carefully timed the publication. The first is a letter to Ulrich von Hutten containing hints of the intended action. "The time is not yet ripe," he wrote in July 1519, "but I shall soon recommend that [Lee] be immortalized in the writings of learned men." The following spring he wrote to Justus Jonas, instructing him to prepare a collection of letters.

> My friends are to write letters highly critical of Lee, but taking care to praise English scholars and the great men in England who support them, and bearing down on Lee and no one else; and him they are to laugh at as a foolish, boastful, deceitful little man, rather than attack him seriously. I should like to see many letters of this kind put together, so that he may be overwhelmed all the deeper. I should like them to be collected from the learned writers

[14]Melanchthon's *Briefwechsel*, ed. Heinz Scheible (Stuttgart: Frommann-Holzboog, 1991), 1:35: "…ut de plurimis quam elegantissime scribi dicique possit, literas ad Ioannem Reuchlin…scriptos multiiuga eruditione prodere voluimus."

[15]Hiltebrand's remark is cited in Ludwig Geiger, *Johann Reuchlin: Sein Leben und seine Werke* (repr. Nieuwkoop: De Graaf, 1964), 323 n.5; Reuchlin's complaint, "coactus est…publice per impressas literas propalare" in *Acta judiciorum*, is quoted in *Johannes Reuchlin (1455–1522)*, ed. Hermann Kling and Stefan Rhein (2d ed.; Sigmaringen: Thorbecke, 1994), 220.

and sent me by safe hand, and I will revise them myself and see to their publication.[16]

Officially, Erasmus continued to present himself as conciliatory. He told several of his friends that he had suppressed letters commenting on Lee because he wished to put an end to the affair: "A number of scholars in Germany have sent bundles, or more truly volumes, of letters, in which they cut Lee up into little pieces. I have kept them very dark and given them no one to read, partly because I long to see an end to this sad business, partly because I do not wish Lee to seem important enough for so many men of such standing to sharpen their pens against him," he wrote.[17]

The episodic evidence presented here shows that the art of manipulating public opinion for commercial or ideological reasons is almost as old as the printing trade itself. Whether the general readership in the sixteenth century was aware of these practices and how they reacted to them are questions that need further investigation.

[16]CWE Epp. 999:348–50 (adapted); 1088:4–12.
[17]CWE Ep. 1139:108–13.

ACKNOWLEDGMENT
I wish to thank Wilfrid Laurier University and SSHRC for the support which enabled me to present this essay at the Neo-Latin Conference in Avila, August 1997.

# FROM OUTSIDERS TO INSIDERS
## Some Reflections on the Development of a Group Identity of the German Humanists between 1450 and 1530

*Eckhard Bernstein*

HOW ARE IDEAS TRANSLATED INTO INSTITUTIONAL REFORMS? By which processes does a small group of outsiders develop into influential insiders?[1] What obstacles did German humanists face? How did they achieve a certain cohesion and identity and become a major force in German intellectual, literary, educational, and political life? I plan to look at about eighty years of German history to answer these questions. The period I have chosen, from 1450 to 1530, needs some justification. In the middle of the fifteenth century some Italian-trained humanists, like the indefatigable Peter Luder, made their first appearance in Germany. In 1456 he held his first lectures on the *studia humanitatis* in Heidelberg, repeating them in subsequent years at the universities of Erfurt and Leipzig.[2] At approximately the same time Samuel Karoch von Lichtenberg and the Italian Petrus Antonius Finariensis tried to introduce the study of ancient literature in Germany.[3] Moreover, in the early fifties of the fifteenth century,

---

[1]The first part of this article's title is adopted from Peter Gay's *Weimar Culture: The Outsider as Insider* (New York: Harper and Row, 1968).

[2]For the time of early German humanism see Eckhard Bernstein, *Die Literatur des deutschen Frühhumanismus* (Stuttgart: Metzler, 1978); on Luder see the various works by Frank Baron. His latest: "Peter Luder (ca. 1415–72)," *Dictionary of Literary Biography*, vol. 179: *German Writers of the Renaissance and Reformation 1280–1580* (Detroit, Washington, London: Bruccoli Clark Layman and Gale Research, 1997), 129–34.

[3]For Samuel Karoch von Lichtenberg see Heinz Entner, *Frühhumanismus und Schultradition in Leben und Werk des Wanderpoeten Samuel Karoch von Lichtenberg* (Berlin: Akademie Verlag, 1968). On Petrus Antonius see Veit Probst, *Petrus Antonius de Clapis (ca. 1440–1512): Ein italienischer Humanist im Dienste Friedrichs des Siegreichen von der Pfalz* (Paderborn, Munich, Vienna, Zurich: Schöningh, 1989).

Albrecht von Eyb, after spending seven years in Italy, returned to Germany, displaying his newly acquired classical Latin in four works in the spirit of Italian Renaissance humanism. This literary activity prompted Heinz Otto Burger to declare that in 1452, the year in which Eyb's "Tractatus de speciositate puellulae" was composed, "the first flag of German early humanism was raised"[4] while Heinz Entner placed Eyb's *Margarita poetica*, an anthology of humanist texts, "at the beginning of the humanist movement in Germany."[5] In establishing the beginning of German humanism at the middle of the fifteenth century rather than a century earlier, when at the Prague court of Emperor Charles IV the first tender seeds of humanism were planted, I join the majority of scholars who dismiss the Prague's chancellery's encounters with early Italian humanism as a short and isolated episode at the periphery of the empire and who prefer the term "Pre-Humanism" or "Proto-Humanism" ( *Vorhumanismus* or *Ersthumanismus)* for these first contacts.[6]

While there is near agreement about the beginning of German humanism, there is considerable confusion about its end. Whereas some scholars argue that humanism proper ended with the Reformation,[7] others maintain that humanism reached its peak in the late sixteenth century.[8] The debate need not interest us in this article because it is not essential in answering our question of the transformation of the humanists' outsider-to-insider status. For that, a look at the *first* eighty years is sufficient, because in the period between approximately 1450 and 1530 the German humanist intelligentsia emerged as a major factor in German intellectual life. The year 1530, arbitrary as it may seem, recommends itself

---

[4]Heinz Otto Burger, *Renaissance-Humanismus-Reformation: Deutsche Literatur im europäischen Kontext* (Bad Homburg, Berlin, Zurich: Verlag Gehlen, 1969), 136: "...das erste Fähnchen des deutschen Frühhumanismus wurde gehißt."

[5]Heinz Entner, "Probleme der Forschung zum deutschen Frühhumanismus," *Wissenschaftliche Zeitschrift der Ernst-Moritz-Arndt-Universität Greifswald,* Gesellschaft-und sprachwissenschaftliche Reihe 15 (1966): 87.

[6]Eckhard Bernstein, *German Humanism* (Boston: Twayne Publishers, 1983), 7.

[7]Cf. Wilhelm Scherer, *Geschichte der deutschen Literatur,* 2d ed. (Vienna: Concordia, 1949), 249: "Die Musen schweigen; die Theologie allein hat das Wort." See also Wolfgang Stammler, *Von der Mystik zum Barock,* 2d ed. (Stuttgart: Metzler, 1950), 303–4: "Für eine Generation verzichtete der Deutsche willig auf künstlerischen Lebensgehalt, weil das Religiöse ihn fest im Bann hielt. Auch die humanistischen jungen Keime und verheißungsvollen Antriebe wurden von der Lutherischen Bewegung entweder zerknickt oder mußten sich in dieselbe kirchliche Richtung umbiegen lassen."

[8]For instance, Manfred Fleischer in several books and articles, among them "Humanism and Reformation in Silesia: Imprints of Italy—Celtis, Erasmus, Luther, and Melanchthon," *The Harvest of Humanism in Central Europe: Essays in Honor of Lewis W. Spitz,* ed. Manfred P. Fleischer (St. Louis: Concordia Publishing House, 1992), 17–107.

for several reasons. By that time, lectures on classical authors and on rhetoric and ancient poetry, the primary fields of study of the humanists, were offered at many Germany universities. At some universities regular positions for the *studia humanitatis* had been established, with the reform university of Wittenberg blazing the way[9] and Cologne lagging considerably behind.[10] Also, and more importantly, through Luther's break with the old church, which can be dated with some justification to the early twenties when his three major Reformation treatises appeared, the intellectual and religious landscape of Germany had changed forever. Humanism was integrated in many cases in the curricular reforms of Melanchthon. Humanism, while by no means at its end, was profoundly modified in its character by the Reformation.

The acceptance and success of humanism was a gradual process and the result of several factors, among them the invention of printing and the growing need of the courts, the cities, and the universities for precisely those skills the humanists were thought to possess, namely a command of written and spoken Latin and an excellent general knowledge based on the study of the newly discovered ancient authors.[11] The success of humanism, however, was also the result of deliberate attempts by the humanists to advance their cause and create a shared sense of cohesion and identity. In other words, the gradual emergence of the humanists as a self-confident educational and literary elite and a major intellectual force did not happen by some magic working of the *Zeitgeist*, but was the result of conscious and well-thought-out strategies, policies, and professional moves, including a considerable amount of propaganda. It is this latter aspect, the humanists' intentional attempts of pushing their agenda and creating a sense of identity, that I am concerned with in this article.

---

[9]Cf. Maria Grossmann, *Humanism in Wittenberg, 1485–1517* (Nieuwkoop: B. de Graaf, 1975).

[10]Charles Nauert, "Humanists, Scholastics, and the Struggle to Reform the University of Cologne, 1523–1525," *Humanismus in Köln/Humanism in Cologne*, ed. James Mehl (Cologne: Böhlau, 1991). See also James H. Overfield, *Humanism and Scholasticism in Late Medieval Germany* (Princeton: Princeton University Press, 1984), 322–25.

[11]Wilhelm Kühlmann and Hermann Wiegand talk in this context of a "Funktionselite": "Humanismus," in Walther Killy, *Literaturlexikon: Autoren und Werke deutscher Sprache*, vol. 13 (Gütersloh/Munich: Bertelsmann Lexikon Verlag, 1992), 422. See also Gerhart Oestreich, "Die antike Literatur als Vorbild der praktischen Wissenschaften im 16. und 17. Jahrhundert," *Classical Influences on European Culture, A.D. 1500–1700*, ed. R. R. Bolgar (Cambridge: Cambridge University Press, 1976), 315–24.

I

First I have to demonstrate that the humanists were, at least up to the first decades of the sixteenth century, outsiders in the social spheres where they were employed, i.e., the universities, the courts, and the cities.[12] By including humanists at the courts and in the cities I adopt a more comprehensive definition of humanists as men who were trained in the *studia humanitatis* and who used their education in their professions.

Throughout the fifteenth century, the humanists, both for economic and ideological reasons, remained outsiders in the universities. For their precarious economic situation the career of Peter Luder offers an instructive example. At no time was he paid directly from any university, with the exception of Basel where he doubled as physician and lecturer in rhetoric. He lived on the meager financial contributions of the princes and from student fees. His restless life, often enough criticized by modern well-paid German professors,[13] had economic reasons. Because the pool of potential students was small and soon exhausted, Luder, like the other *Wanderhumanisten,* had to move on. In addition to their lack of integration into the university, humanist courses, even once they were established at a later stage, were taught within the framework of the faculty of arts. The arts faculty was the lowest of the four faculties into which the medieval university was organized, a faculty that had only propaedeutic function, preparing students for the three higher faculties of theology, law, and medicine. For that reason professors in the arts faculty were paid less and possessed a lower social prestige.[14]

Ideologically, humanists were opposed by the scholastics who dominated the university structures and committees. This conflict between humanism and scholasticism found expression in a number of well-known clashes between representatives of the two movements, of which the Reuchlin affair is the best known but by no means the only one. Recent scholars have become increasingly skeptical about claims such as those made by David Friedrich Strauss in the nineteenth century[15] who saw the

---

[12]Christine Treml in her study, *Humanistische Gemeinschaftsbildung: Sozio-kulturelle Untersuchung zur Entstehung eines neuen Gelehrtenstandes in der frühen Neuzeit* (Hildesheim, Zurich, New York: Georg Olms, 1989), was the first to my knowledge who has attempted a sociocultural analysis of the German humanists. Her study is based on 233 "Kurzbiographien" of humanists. Regrettably she does not name these humanists.

[13]For example Wolfgang Stammler, *Von der Mystik zum Barock*, 32: "Haltlos in Leben und Reden, sinken sie [die Wanderhumanisten] von Stufe zu Stufe und verrecken schließlich irgendwo auf der Landstraße."

[14]Overfield, *Humanism and Scholasticism*, 113.

[15]David Friedrich Strauss, *Ulrich von Hutten* (Leipzig: Brockhaus, 1858).

clash between humanism and scholasticism as a gigantic, world-historical struggle between lightness and darkness, between the forces of progress and obscurantism. James H. Overfield, who has examined six such episodes between 1500 and 1515, including the expulsions from their universities of Jacob Locher, Hermann Buschius, Johann Aesticampianus, and Tillman Conradi, argues that while personality conflicts and the combative and sensitive natures of early-sixteenth-century academics contributed to this humanist-scholastic conflict, "to dismiss these episodes as merely clashes of personality would be oversimplification."[16] Showing how, sixty years after the first appearance of humanism, the traditionalists resented the modest inroads humanists had made into the curriculum, Overfield states: "all six episodes reveal the incomplete assimilation of humanism within the German universities. The difficulties of all four humanists (Locher, Buschius, Aesticampianus, and Conradi) resulted in large measure from their *outsider-status*. Not one of them was an integral part of the academic corporation. They were part of no faculty and subject to no dean."[17] Erika Rummel comes to similar conclusions in *The Humanist-Scholastic Debate in the Renaissance and Reformation*,[18] and Charles Nauert refers to them as "marginal figures."[19]

In contrast to the universities which initially marginalized the humanists, the early modern courts offered classically trained men numerous opportunities for advancement. The reason for the growing need for these men is a well-documented process which is described by the German terms "Verschriftlichung"[20] and "Verwissenschaftlichung," i.e., the organization of a state according to rational principles combined with the introduction of Roman Law. Functions previously reserved for the nobility were increasingly assumed by bourgeois men whose specifically humanist qualifications—proficiency in Latin and a broad general knowledge derived from an intensive study of classical texts—prepared them for many positions including secretaries, emissaries, diplomats (characteristically called

---

[16]Overfield, *Humanism and Scholasticism*, 242.

[17]Ibid., 243 (italics mine).

[18](Cambridge, Mass.: Harvard University Press, 1995). She also examines the reasons for the hostility between the two camps. Next to the scholastics' misgivings about the humanist defense of classical literature and the arguments for and against the scholastic style and method she counts "personal animosity, professional envy and career ambitions, confessional divisions and resistance to change among the motives prompting the clashes" (73). See also Charles Nauert, "The Clash of Humanists and Scholastics: An Approach to Pre-Reformation Controversies," *Sixteenth Century Journal* 4 (1973): 1–18.

[19]Charles Nauert, *Humanism and the Culture of Renaissance Europe* (Cambridge: Cambridge University Press, 1995), 105.

[20]Rolf Engelsing, *Analphabetentum und Lektüre* (Stuttgart: Metzler, 1973), 6.

orators), vice-chancellors, and chancellors. At certain stages of their careers some humanists also earned their living as princely tutors, while others attached themselves to courts as propagandists, publicists, and historiographers. Among the numerous intellectuals Emperor Maximilian employed to ensure his "gedechtnus," the memory of his reign, were also a number of humanists.[21]

Although humanists in the employ of princes became more and more indispensable, at least at the beginning of this process, they often had to suffer social resentments especially from the uneducated nobles who saw their traditional positions threatened by the emergence of this "laikale Intelligenz" (lay intelligentsia).[22] Enea Silvio Piccolomini articulated the negative experiences he had made at the court of Emperor Frederick III in his famous letter to Johann von Eich, "De curialium miseriis epistola" (1444). In it he recounts in graphic detail the humiliation he and his fellow scholar-humanists, who were treated worse than cooks and stable boys, were forced to endure.[23] Thus, in spite of the growing importance of their social positions, for a long time the humanists could not shake the image of being upstarts or outsiders.[24]

The same could be said about those humanists who worked in the cities as "Stadtschreiber," legal consultants, doctors, and teachers. A host of early humanists were able to combine the study of ancient literature with these municipal tasks, ranging from Niclas von Wyle (Esslingen), Heinrich Steinhöwel (Ulm), Albrecht von Eyb (Bamberg), and Sebastian Brant (Strasbourg) to Conrad Peutinger (Augsburg) and Willibald Pirckheimer (Nuremberg). But mentioning Pirckheimer's Nuremberg reminds us of the reluctance of some of the cities to admit humanists to the inner circle of their oligarchically organized societies, although they did employ them in a variety of functions. Nuremberg laws explicitly prohibited doctors from becoming city councillors: "Nemo doctor in consilio." The reason for this skepticism towards academics was probably the fear that the increasing need for humanistically trained jurists would jeopardize the existing power structure.[25] An academic degree was not part of the "ratsfähigen Tugenden," those qualifications that allowed one to be elected to the city council, and therefore the humanist with an advanced degree constituted

---

[21]See Jan-Dirk Müller, *Gedechtnus: Literatur und Hofgesellschaft um Maximilian I* (Munich: Fink, 1982).

[22]Ibid., 48 and passim.

[23]Werner Bauer, "Humanistische Bildungsprogramme," *Deutsche Literatur: Eine Sozialgeschichte,* ed. Horst Albert Glaser (Reinbek: Rowohlt, 1991), 248.

[24]Müller, *Gedechtnus,* 42.

[25]Treml, *Humanistische Gemeinschaftsbildung,* 44.

an, albeit necessary, "Fremdkörper" in the city oligarchy. Respected and needed, humanists, at this early stage, still remained largely outsiders.

By 1530, however, humanists had begun to be successful in the universities, at the princely courts, and in the cities to implement their ideas. The process is most obvious at the universities where between 1515 and 1530 one university after the other, although with varying speed, "adopted comprehensive statute changes that implemented the major curricular goals of the humanists.... A curriculum based on the *studia humanitatis* and the mastery of ancient languages came to be established."[26] The men at whose initiative these reforms were undertaken were of course also the ones who implemented them. The former outsiders had become insiders.[27]

Without wanting to enter the complex debate of the relationship of humanism and the Reformation[28] it might suffice to point to the seminal article by Bernd Moeller, "Die deutschen Humanisten und die Anfänge der Reformation,"[29] which demonstrates the key role humanists played not only in disseminating, but also in implementing Luther's reforms in the various cities and territories of the Holy Roman Empire, as school administrators, professors, teachers, theologians, and advisers. With the shift of the church administration away from Rome to the individual German territories and the increasing "bureaucratization" of these states, the need for humanistically trained men grew, so that Luther could say: "Unzelige empter warten auf die gelerten" (Numerous offices wait for the learned).[30] By 1530 humanists had managed to make themselves indispensable in German intellectual and political life. Once again, the former outsiders, the harsh critics of the old church, had become the insiders.[31]

## II

Having demonstrated, however briefly, the growth of the humanists from a tiny minority at the margins of German intellectual life in the second part of the fifteenth century to a major force that permeated many aspects

[26]Overfield, *Humanism and Scholasticism*, 298.

[27]Nauert, *Humanism and the Culture of Renaissance Europe*, 130, speaks in this context of the "humanist triumph."

[28]For a summary see Rummel, *The Humanist-Scholastic Debate*, 126–52, with some of the relevant literature.

[29]Bernd Moeller, *Zeitschrift für Kirchengeschichte* 70 (1959), 46–61.

[30]Quoted in Heinrich Kramm, "Besitzschichten und Bildungsschichten der mitteldeutschen Städte im 16. Jahrhundert," *Vierteljahrschrift für Sozial und Wirtschaftsgeschichte* 51 (1964), 472.

[31]At the princely courts and in the cities this gradual shift from outsider to insider status was of course less spectacular because it was not accompanied by the divisive Humanist-Scholastic Debate.

of German life by the third decade of the sixteenth century,[32] we can now turn to the following question: How did the humanists achieve cohesion and identity as a group necessary for success? In order to appreciate their accomplishments we have to remind ourselves that the humanists, in their attempts to create a collective identity, faced four major obstacles: the diversity of their social background, the diversity of their professional background, considerable ideological differences, and geographical dispersion.

German humanists, as a social group, were not part of the established hierarchical class system. In fact they came from almost every social background of the time, ranging from the aristocracy to peasantry. Although there are no comprehensive studies examining the social backgrounds of the German humanists, it seems that the largest segment came from the emerging bourgeoisie. Nobles who devoted themselves to the *studia humanitatis*, men like Ulrich von Hutten, Hermann von Neuenahr, and the Adelmann von Adelmannsfelden brothers, remained exceptions, and some, like Hutten, were under considerable pressure from their peers to justify their engagement for humanism. Exceptions were also those humanists who came from the other end of the social spectrum, the peasants—notwithstanding some prominent names like Eobanus Hessus, Crotus Rubeanus, Conrad Celtis, and Euricius Cordus.

If humanists came from different social backgrounds, they also were employed in a variety of professions, unless we embrace the notion that only those can be termed humanists who are engaged in teaching the typically humanist courses. While they all shared some form of humanist

---

[32]The few studies that deal with the humanists as a sociocultural rather than an intellectual phenomenon estimate the number of humanists at the beginning of the sixteenth century at 250. James Tracy, in his article, "Humanism and the Reformation," *Reformation Europe Guide to Research*, ed. Steven Ozment (St. Louis: Center for Reformation Research, 1986), has examined those humanists in Germany, the Low Countries and Switzerland who were born between 1450 and 1510, and has arrived at the number 278. Treml, *Humanistische Gemeinschaftsbildung*, based her study on 233 biographies of humanists who lived between 1470 and 1540, leaving it open whether humanists from Switzerland and the Low Countries, were included. Since both studies are based on dictionaries (Tracy) or humanist correspondences (Treml), only those humanists are included who in one form or the other left behind some writing. According to Erich Trunz, "Der deutsche Späthumanismus als Standeskultur," *Zeitschrift für Geschichte der Erziehungund des Unterrichts* 21 (1931), 17–53; reprinted in *Deutsche Barockforschung: Dokumentation einer Epoche*, ed. Richard Alewyn, 2d ed. (Cologne, Berlin: Kiepenheuer und Witsch, 1966), 147–81, the number had risen to thirty-three thousand a century later around 1600. However, these figures are hardly comparable since this latter figure is extrapolated from university enrollment statistics, while the figures for the beginning of the sixteenth century are based on biographical information. But even if we accept the hardly realistic figure of thirty-three thousand, the "learned," i.e., humanists, represent only a tiny fraction of the total population of about twenty million, namely 0.15 percent; Trunz, "Späthumanismus," 155.

education, they were active at the courts, in the cities, and at the universities,[33] each profession requiring its own allegiance and having its own values, customs, and rituals.

A similarly wide spectrum can be found in their ideology, i.e., the degree of their commitment to the humanist cause. That commitment ranged from a wholehearted embrace of the classics by the dangerously paganistic Jakob Locher to the tepid conservative humanism of a Jakob Wimpfeling who admitted only a few safe classical authors to the reading canon of young students. Finally, the humanists were dispersed over all the corners of the far-flung Holy Roman Empire, adding to their social, professional, and ideological differences a geographical isolation.

### III

In spite of this diversity and dispersion, in spite also of the differing views held by the humanists, it is surprising that something like a collective humanist identity developed as a necessary prerequisite for their success. The German humanists, like those in other countries, were individuals, each with his own story. At the same time, they were members of an emerging new social class, a lay order[34] with, at least initially, no distinct historical definition. The process of creating and perpetuating a group identity was a deliberate one and involved six interconnected factors:

1. The use of Latin and the adoption of Latin names,
2. the creation of various "Feindbilder" with the aim of building solidarity among the humanists,
3. the founding of humanist *sodalitates,*
4. the creation of a sense of cohesion through letter writing,
5. the role of humanist friendship,
6. humanist travel as a community-building activity.

We know, of course, that the humanists almost exclusively wrote in Latin and, in many cases, adopted Latin names; we have learned that they painted their opponents in the bleakest colors; we are aware that they founded numerous *sodalitates;* we have ample evidence that they wrote letters on all occasions;[35] we are also familiar with the humanists' cult of

---

[33]Treml, *Humanistische Gemeinschaftsbildung,* 15–35.

[34]A term Mutianus Rufus occasionally uses.

[35]The correspondences of the major German humanists have been edited. There are modern editions of the correspondences of Erasmus of Rotterdam, Beatus Rhenanus, Conrad Celtis, Johann Reuchlin, Conrad Peutinger, Willibald Pirckheimer (partial), Jakob Wimpfeling, Joachim Vadianus, Mutianus Rufus, and Ulrich von Hutten.

friendship and their frequent travels. Rarely, however, has the why about the function of these activities been asked. Why did the humanists adopt Latin names? Why did they gather in humanist circles, the *sodalitates*? Why did they write so much, assuring each other of their friendship? What was the reason for maligning their adversaries? What was their purpose in taking upon themselves the hardships of traveling? In redirecting our attention to these questions, I shall argue, using the six points above as guidelines, that the humanists deliberately attempted to create a shared sense of identity, and that this proud self-perception, to a large extent, contributed to their acknowledged success, their change from outsider to insider status in sixteenth-century culture. I am, of course, aware that by examining the group identity formation of the humanists, I am entering a field which has "as yet no discrete location in the academic division of labor."[36] Yet I believe that only by looking from outside our historical-philological discipline can we hope to gain fresh insights into a field that is plagued by a tendency to ask the same questions over and over again.

1. The language of the humanists was Latin. In that idiom they communicated, wrote and spoke, composed their poems and formulated their treatises, and recorded their thoughts. With the exception of works by some early German humanists such as Niclas von Wyle, Heinrich Steinhöwel, and Albrecht von Eyb,[37] humanist literature was written in Latin. In numerous letters, poetical treatises, and speeches, they articulated the basic superiority of Latin over the vernacular. The cultivation of the language of the ancient Romans gave them a sense of collective identity because it allowed them to set themselves off against the overwhelming majority of the population. Since mastery of Latin was identified with being educated, a special culture emerged that was accessible only to a few. Those incapable of speaking or writing classically based Latin were ridiculed as barbarians or beasts. With a few exceptions, therefore, humanists and authors writing in the vernacular moved in different social circles. Willibald Pirckheimer, the well-known Nuremberg humanist, and Hans Sachs, the equally famous Meistersinger, lived for decades only a few blocks from each other in the old imperial city—a meeting of the two is not documented.[38]

---

[36]Richard C. Trexler, *Persons in Groups: Social Behavior as Identity Formation in Medieval and Renaissance Europe* (Binghamton, N.Y.: Medieval and Renaissance Texts and Studies, 1985), 3.

[37]See Bernstein, *Die Literatur des deutschen Frühhumanismus*, 41–98.

[38]A picture showing Sachs and Pirckheimer peeking out of the famous Fembo House in Nuremberg (in a recent tourist brochure) is unhistorical wishful thinking.

The need to set themselves off from the *profanum vulgus* shows itself most clearly in the Latinization, and to a lesser degree Grecization, of proper names, for it signified an initiation into an exclusive European community of scholars. And just as a novice often adopted a different name upon entering a monastery to mark the importance of his decision, so the humanists assumed a new name to celebrate their entrance into the lay order of the humanist intelligentsia. Thus Mutianus Rufus commented, not without irony, on the new name of his friend Crotus Rubeanus: "Now that you are *reborn* and are addressed as Crotus rather than Jäger, as Rubeanus rather than Dornheim, you will also lose your long ears, your tail and your rough fleece."[39]

Ironically, in addition to conferring symbolic membership in the international *respublica litteraria,* a name change could also be an attempt to mask the modest social background of a humanist. For, as stated above, a majority of the humanists came from the middle or even from the peasant classes, with their class-specific names[40] that could easily betray them as social upstarts in a new environment. Thus, adopting a Latin name concealed the humble origins and leveled the playing field.[41] In this sense the humanist name changes can be interpreted as a step towards a more democratic society, just as the shift away from the notion of a nobility of birth to one of the mind was a step toward our modern meritocracy notwithstanding the fact that the humanists considered themselves an intellectual elite.[42]

If the humanists distinguished themselves on the one hand from those who worked in the vernacular, they just as clearly set themselves off against those who wrote and spoke the wrong Latin, i.e., the Latin used throughout the Middle Ages by clerics, diplomats, and the scholastics in the universities. To this idiom they juxtaposed a Latin modeled on the authors of ancient antiquity which they claimed to have awakened from a prolonged sleep during the Middle Ages. The mastery of that language, which they elevated to a linguistic norm, became their status symbol and qualification at the same time.

---

[39]Quoted in Heinz Otto Burger, *Renaissance: Humanismus Reformation: Deutsche Literatur im europäischen Kontext* (Bad Homburg, Berlin, Zurich: Gehlen, 1969), 363 (italics mine).

[40]Thus Pickel became, for instance, *Celtis*; Köpfel, *Capito*; Fischer, *Piscator*; Müller, *Molitor*; Kürschner, *Pellicanus*; Hausschein, *Oecolampadius*.

[41]Heinrich Kramm, "Besitzschichten und Bildungsschichten" 469: "...sodaß der Namensträger, wie es zumeist geschieht, anderwärts gleichsam als Unbekannter auftaucht, nicht abgestempelt durch das alte Milieu, neu beginnt und sich gewissermaßen erleichtert den Aufstieg zu ebnen versucht." The fact that nobles generally did not change their names supports this interpretation.

[42]This argument is made by Klaus Garber, with the very title of the collection of essays, *Europäische Sozietätsbewegung und demokratische Tradition* (Tübingen: Max Niemeyer, 1996).

Command of the new humanist Latin became also the humanists' primary selling point. In 1462 Peter Luder, in a mixture of modern selling strategy and undiplomatic ridicule of the traditional Latin, tried to recruit listeners for his lecture on Terence. Using three free lectures as bait, he promised to "educate them in the human language and familiarize them with the art of style, so that they do not constantly insult the ears of other people with their kitchen-Latin [culiniarium Latinum], but through training in the right choice of words avoid that terrible barbarism...."[43] With equal tact, Conrad Celtis, thirty years later, called his scholastic colleagues at the University of Ingolstadt "geese and roaring oxen" (anseres et mugientes boves), mocking them for using "common, insignificant and corrupt words" (verba abiecta, vilia et corrupta), and reciting the "sweet Roman tongue" (suavissimam linguam Romae) in a "rough and barbarian way" (aspere et barbare).[44] It goes without saying that he offered himself to the university authorities to remedy these linguistic deficits.

Carried to extremes is this denunciation of medieval Latin in the *Epistolae obscurorum virorum*, for this satire is not only a criticism of the alleged empty terminological acrobatics of scholastic theology, but also by its very form a ridiculing of the barbarous Latin employed by the *viri obscuri*. "Barbare ridentur barbari" (In a barbarian fashion the barbarians are ridiculed)—with this formula Ulrich von Hutten summed up the style of that work.[45]

2. It is a truism of social psychology that a group often derives its sense of collective identity not only from common interests but also from a common enemy or common enemies.[46] Modern dictators know that as well as democratic leaders. Nothing lends itself better to distracting from domestic problems and creating a sense of community than shifting attention to a real or invented enemy. We have already shown how the humanists differentiated themselves linguistically from the non-Latin-speaking majority on the one hand, and from the wrong-Latin-speaking scholastics on the other. That the differences with the scholastics went far beyond the use of the correct Latin is well known and need not be rehearsed one more time. Suffice it to say that the disputes between scholastics and humanists often were typical academic quarrels, but they also represented real differences which the humanists in their efforts to set themselves off clearly

---

[43]Quoted after *Der deutsche Renaissance-Humanismus*, ed. Winfried Trillitxsch (Leipzig: Verlag Philipp Reclam jun., 1981), 151.

[44]Hans Rupprich, ed., *Der Briefwechsel des Conrad Celtis* (Munich: Beck, 1934), nos. 32, 56.

[45]Eduard Böcking, ed., *Ulrichi Hutteni opera.* 5 vols. (Leipzig: Teubner, 1859–61), 1:124.

[46]Stephen Mennel, "The Formation of We-Images: A Process Theory," *Social Theory and the Politics of Identity*, ed. Craig Calhoun (Oxford, Cambridge: Blackwell, 1994), 175–97, esp. 180f.

from the traditionalists magnified and occasionally played up as world-historical struggles. Scholastics were denounced as "barbarian thickheads" and "Scoti, Scauri, and Bardi," that is, "benighted, hobbling fools."[47] This strategy found its most visible expression in the Reuchlin affair and its literary fruit, the *Epistolae obscurorum virorum* (1515/17) written by Crotus Rubianus and Hutten.[48] Elsewhere I have attempted to show how the young Hutten, on several occasions, created the image of the implacable enmity between scholastics and humanists, how he painted his opponents in the blackest colors, establishing a valid "Feindbild."[49] We would do much better to take these quarrels with a grain of salt, to see them as what they were: attempts to influence public opinion,[50] and to construct humanist myths about the solidarity and size of the humanist community.

3. Clearly the most obvious sign of the humanists' efforts to construct their own collective identity are the *sodalitates*[51] which were founded in Germany in the last decade of the fifteenth century and the first two decades of the sixteenth century. In these circles of intellectuals held together by a basic consensus on a common educational canon, members tried to overcome their intellectual and geographical isolation regardless of their social background and their professional qualifications. Architect and initiator of these friendship circles was Conrad Celtis. The best documented *sodalitates* were those in Heidelberg, the so-called *sodalitas litteraria Rhenana*

---

[47]Quoted after Rummel, *The Humanist-Scholastic Debate*, 11.

[48]Cf. Reinhard Paul Becker, *A War of Fools: The Letters of Obscure Men: A Study of the Satire and Satirized* (Bern: Lang, 1981); Barbara Könneker, *Satire im 16. Jahrhundert: Epoche-Werke-Wirkung* (Munich: Beck, 1991); James V. Mehl, "Characterizations of the 'Obscure Men' of Cologne: A Study in Pre-Reformation Collective Authorship," *The Rhetorics of Life-Writing in Early Modern Europe: Forms of Biography from Cassandra Fedele to Louis XIV*, ed. Thomas F. Mayer and D. R. Woolf (Ann Arbor: University of Michigan Press, 1995), 163–85.

[49]"Creating Humanist Myths: Two Poems by Ulrich von Hutten," *Acta Conventus Neo-Latini Torontonensis: Proceedings of the Seventh International Congress of Neo-Latin Studies*, ed. Alexander Dalzell, Charles Fantazzi, Richard J. Schoeck (Binghamton, N.Y.: Medieval and Renaissance Texts and Studies, 1991), 249–60.

[50]Bernd Möller has argued that the humanists were the first in western culture to create a public (Öffentlichkeit), "Gutenberg's invention had not only brought innovations but it also had been noticed by intelligent contemporaries that books could be produced quickly and relatively inexpensively and texts could be standardized; rather fifty years after the invention it was realized that the new medium, in addition to knowledge, could also transport topical news, indeed opinions, able to influence buyers and readers in a new way. The readers were, quite different from readers of manuscripts, widely dispersed geographically, anonymous, unknown to author and printer. Only through reading could they be joined together. Readers, dispersed geographically, were able to share a sense of indignation or, by the same token, a sense of enjoyment" (my translation). "Erwägungen zur Bedeutung Erfurts als Kommunikationszentrum der frühen Reformation," *Erfurt: Geschichte und Gegenwart*, ed. Ulman Weiß (Weimar: Hermann Böhlaus Nachfolger, 1995), 275–82, here 277.

[51]On humanist sodalities see Treml, *Humanistische Gemeinschaftsbildung*, esp. 44–77; Heinrich Lutz, "Die Sodalitäten im oberdeutschen Humanismus des späten 15. und frühen 16. Jahrhunderts,"

(founded in 1495), and in Vienna, the *sodalitas litteraria Danubiana* (1497).
The latter name, however, seems to have referred to two different group-
ings: on the one hand to the Vienna circle, on the other to a number of loose
organizations in other cities which were also known under other names,
such as the Ölmütz group—the *Sodalitas Meyerhofiae* or *Maiorhoviana*.[52]
This imprecise terminology points to the ill-defined organizational framework of these circles. Statutes, membership lists, and bylaws did not exist in
any of these groups.

In other cities friends gathered around well-known personalities. In
Augsburg it was Conrad Peutinger, and in Nuremberg, Willibald Pirckheimer who formed the centers of their *sodalitates*. In 1501 Conrad Celtis
seems to have succeeded in founding an umbrella organization, the so-
called *Sodalitas Celtica* which obtained from the Regency Council
(Reichsregiment) in Nuremberg a printing privilege for ten years.[53] Other
*sodalitates* were later founded in Ingolstadt, Straßburg, Basel, and Schletts-
tadt. In Gotha young humanists gathered around Mutianus Rufus.

The function of the various *sodalitates* was to give an individual *sodalis*
the sense of belonging to a larger movement. To this end the sodalities
embarked on cooperative scholarly projects, such as editions of Latin
works, mutual assistance in explaining difficult philological problems, and
obtaining manuscripts. They also cultivated the social aspect by gathering
at banquets, at which wine was drunk, verses were recited, and poems
composed. Occasionally field trips were undertaken, like the one by the
Rhenish sodality in 1496 to abbot Trithemius in Sponheim near the river
Nahe.[54]

Recently critics have expressed some skepticism about the very existence of these *sodalitates*. Heinz Entner has deconstructed the myths and

---

*Humanismus im Bildungswesen des 15. und 16. Jahrhunderts*, ed. Wolfgang Reinhard (Weinheim: VCH
Verlagsgesellschaft, 1984), 45–60; Klaus Garber and Heinz Wismann, eds., *Europäische Sozietätsbewegung und demokratische Tradition*, 2 vols. (Tübingen: Max Niemeyer, 1996). See also *Pirckheimer Jahrbuch 1997, Der polnische Humanismus und die europäischen Sodalitäten* (Harrassowitz: Wiesbaden,
1997) and my article "Der Erfurter Humanistenkreis am Schnittpunkt von Humanismus und Reformation: Das Rektoratsblatt des Crotus Rubianus," 138-65.

[52]Cf. Moritz Csaky, "'Die Sodalitas litteraria Danubiana': Historische Realität oder poetische Fik-
tion des Conrad Celtis?" *Die österreichische Literatur: Ihr Profil von den Anfängen im Mittelalter bis zum
18. Jahrhundert*, ed. Herbert Zeman (Graz: Akademische Druck-und Verlagsanstalt, 1985), 739–85.

[53]Raimund Kemper, "'Sodalitas litteraria a senatu Rhomani Imperii impetrata': Zur Interpretation der Druckprivilegien in der Editio princeps der Roswitha von Gandersheim (1504) und in der
Ausgabe der Qvatvor libri Amorum Secvndvm Qvatvor latera Germanie des Conrad Celtis (1502),"
*Euphorion* 69 (1975), 119–84; Dieter Mertens, "Sodalitas Celtica impetrata? Zum Kolophon des Nürn-
berger Hroswitha-Druckes von 1501," *Euphorion* 71 (1977), 277–80.

[54]See Rupprich, ed., *Der Briefwechsel des Konrad Celtis*, 178.

legends that have surrounded Celtis' activities, coming to the conclusion that the much-touted *sodalitates*, in most cases, were nothing more than loose circles of friends that existed before Celtis graced them with his appearance and gave them a name. If Entner is correct, it would be another instance of the persuasiveness and longevity of humanist propaganda that convinced contemporaries and countless subsequent generations of the reality of these groups.[55]

4. Members of the various *sodalitates* stayed in contact through letters, and letters were central to the development of a humanist consciousness and, in the last analysis, also for the success of humanism itself.[56] Humanists were indefatigable letter writers. Although letters in the sixteenth century had many functions which in our time have been assumed by scholarly journals, newspapers, telephone, and even e-mail with its discussion groups, they can be best understood as community-creating forms of communication. By writing to each other, humanists confirmed their membership in an intellectual elite. Participation in the humanist discourse was evidence of being part of the *respublica litteraria*. Because letters were signs of one's erudition and wit, a good deal of care was employed on their composition, although the labors of writing these letters were artfully concealed by pointing to the haste with which they were dashed off. Like poetry itself, letter writing was considered a learnable skill. Manuals for letter writing were therefore written by many humanists including Celtis, Erasmus, and Juan Luis Vives. Letters from other humanist friends were collected as evidence of the popularity and social prestige one enjoyed. When Pirckheimer, after repeated requests, finally received a letter from the famous Italian humanist Giovanni Francesco Pico della Mirandola, he boasted in a letter to Celtis of a long and close friendship with the Italian, appending as proof a copy of Mirandola's letter. Celtis replaced Pirckheimer's name with his own and blithely incorporated the sought-after epistle into his own corpus of letters.[57] Humanists were not free of vanity.

5. Since humanists sought their identity in the tension between self-realization[58] and being embedded in a social circle, be it in a *sodalitas* or in

[55]"Was steckt hinter dem Wort 'sodalitas litteraria'? Ein Diskussionsbeitrag zu Conrad Celtis und seinen Freundeskreisen," Garber, *Humanistische Sozietätsbewegung*, 1069–1101.

[56]Treml, *Humanistische Gemeinschaftsbildung*, 77–81; *Der Brief im Zeitalter der Renaissance*, ed. Franz Joseph Worstbrock (Weinheim: Acta humaniora, 1983).

[57]Emil Reicke, ed., *Pirckheimers Briefwechsel* 1 (Munich: Beck, 1989), no. 58, 191; Treml, *Humanistische Gemeinschaftsbildung*, 86.

[58]For that, Hutten's letter to Willibald Pirckheimer, is the classic locus, in Böcking, ed., *Ulrichi Hutteni opera*, 1, 195–217.

a network of friends, humanist friendship became an indispensable part of their communicative mode of living. In an intellectual milieu which was, at least in the fifteenth century and at the beginning of the sixteenth century, indifferent or hostile to the humanist reform efforts, it was of vital importance to build up a network of like-minded friends. As a matter of fact, prestige within the humanist community was largely determined by the number of *amici* one could claim. Young humanists would often write notes or letters to older, and more established colleagues, asking them for a sign of their friendship in the form of a letter. With some justification Treml calls these letters "application forms" (Aufnahmeanträge) to the humanist *nobilitas litteraria*.[59] In this context, the effusive praise of friends, often criticized as insincere flattery by modern critics, must be understood as a ritual meant to integrate the friend and oneself into the new intellectual elite.[60] It is clear that the concept of friend has little to do with the modern German "Freund," a term that since the eighteenth century suggests a deep emotional bond, a "harmony of the souls."[61] For the humanist, on the other hand, an indispensable prerequisite for admission to the circles of friends was primarily a sound training in the classics, or as Mutianus Rufus put it: "Nobody was, is or will be a friend of Mutianus, unless he is sincere, full of integrity, but *above all well educated*."[62]

A telling example of the prime importance of friendship as understood by the humanists is furnished by Crotus Rubianus. After his rectorate at the University of Erfurt in the winter semester of 1521, he submitted the obligatory end-of-semester report to the university authorities. To it he appended a large, colorful drawing representing his coat of arms surrounded by the sixteen heraldic shields of his close friends. As I have shown elsewhere,[63] none of the persons but one was on the powerful Faculty Council; three of them had no relationship with the university;

---

[59]Treml, *Humanistische Gemeinschaftsbildung*, 82–83.

[60]Ibid., 95 "…der obligatorische Panegyrikus auf den Freund [wirkt] als integratives Ritual, das der Konsolidierung und Behauptung des neuen Gelehrtenstandes zugute kommt."

[61]The humanist understanding of "friend," it seems to me, comes closer to the American concept suggesting a relationship that is based on the "do-ut-des"-principle and on mutual respect and assistance. The custom of sending thousands of Christmas cards to one's "friends" as does the American president Bill Clinton (to the FOBs or Friends of Bill), is hard to understand for a central European and often cited for the alleged insincerity and superficiality of Americans. This stereotype is based on a misunderstanding: "Freund" and "friend" connote different meanings. The proper German translation of "friend" would be "Bekannter."

[62]"Nemo enim Mutiano amicus unquam fuit aut est aut erit, nisi qui rectus et integer et *apprime doctus*" (italics mine). In Karl Gillert, ed., *Der Briefwechsel des Conradus Mutianus*, Geschichtsquellen der Provinz Sachsen 29 (Halle: Otto Hendel, 1890), 40.

[63]"Der Erfurter Humanistenkreis am Schnittpunkt von Humanismus und Reformation: Das Rektoratsblatt des Crotus Rubianus," *Pirckheimer Jahrbuch 1997, Der polnische Humanismus und die*

Faculty Council; three of them had no relationship with the university; and two of them were only loosely connected to the university. By naming and honoring these men, who in a way were outsiders of the university, Crotus not only made a clear statement where his sympathies lay, but also seemed to suggest that a reform of the university could only come from *outside* that institution. But more importantly for our argument, the depiction of these men points to the humanist idea of the sodalitas and friendship. Not the colleagues at the university but the circle of friends was the intellectual and social source for Crotus' leadership at the university. Just as a humanist often had each of his books preceded by a number of poems of his friends to introduce them, so to speak, as godfathers of his own works, so Crotus called up his friends as witnesses of his activity during his rectorate.

6. When the humanists did not write to each other or cultivate friendship, they visited each other. The biographies of German humanists, beginning with Luder, Karoch von Lichtenberg, Celtis, Hutten, and Buschius, to Paul Melissus and Petrus Lotichius, demonstrate an insatiable *wanderlust* and a reluctance to settle down. For ten years Celtis, the German arch-humanist, crisscrossed Europe from the Elbe to the Tiber, from the Vistula to the Mosel; Erasmus changed places so often that he once joked that his horse should be the most educated in the world having attended so many universities. The career of Hutten provides a prime example for humanist "Reiselust." After studies in Mainz, Cologne, Erfurt, Frankfurt on the Oder, Leipzig, and Greifswald, he went to Italy (via Vienna) to study in Bologna and Padua. He returned to Germany in 1514 only to go back a year later to continue his study of law on the Appenine peninsula where he spent time in Rome, Bologna, Ferrara, and Venice, making contacts with Italian humanists. Following his return to Germany in 1517, he stopped over in Mainz, Augsburg, Ebernburg Castle, the Low Countries, Basel, and Zurich.[64]

While getting to know different countries, customs, and people was an indispensable element of the humanist way of life, even if it meant accepting the considerable hardships of early modern travel with its dirty lodgings and unsafe roads, the primary function of humanist travel was to visit friends, to keep alive or establish contacts with other humanist friends. In

---

*europäischen Sodalitäten* (Harrassowitz: Wiesbaden, 1997).

[64]On Hutten see Eckhard Bernstein, *Ulrich von Hutten mit Selbstzeugnissen und Bilddokumenten* (Rowohlt: Reinbek, 1988), and James Mehl, "Ulrich von Hutten," *Dictionary of Literary Biography*, 179, 111–23.

this sense traveling had the same function as attending conferences in our time: to establish or renew professional contacts, to plan projects, to discuss methods, and generally to create and keep alive the sense of belonging to a professional elite. For this reason a humanist often planned his traveling route according to the residences of his friends or those he hoped to make friends with.[65] Regular pilgrimages were undertaken to well-known humanists, such as Erasmus and Mutianus Rufus. This concentration on visits of fellow scholars may account also for the hard-to-understand lack of interest in other cultural expressions (like contemporary Italian art) by the humanists. "I am in the middle of Italy but still don't see anything of Italy" (Media in Italia Italiam non video), a German scholar wrote home, with the implication that he only saw humanist friends.[66]

Traveling found its literary expression in numerous travel poems, the *hodoeporica,* one of the favorite literary genres of the German humanists.[67] Within this genre, which deals with such diverse topics as travels to spas, to mines, to lovers, to Turkey and Italy, the friendship *hodoeporica,* i.e., poems describing visits to or by humanist friends, play a significant role. The function of these poems was to convey to the reader the impression of a widespread net of friends who are united by their commitment to the humanist cause and opposition to the scholastics. Characteristically, many of these poems were written when the humanists were still struggling to get a foothold in the universities, i.e., when they were outsiders. The community-creating intention becomes particularly clear in two poems by Hutten.[68] In the poem, "Ad Poetas Germanos," the last of the twenty elegies of his *Querelarum libri duo in Lossios* (1510),[69] Hutten sends his muse on a tour of Germany with the goal of mobilizing all German poets—the usual name at that time for what we now call humanists—for his cause, in this case the revenge against the Greifswald family Lötze who had allegedly harmed him. The fifty biographical sketches, done with great mastery, result in a colorful catalog of the German literary intelligentsia around 1510. But, since the journey itself is a fiction, so too is Hutten's colorful *Who's Who* of the German literary scene. It is not a mirror of reality but a myth—just wishful thinking. For in reality the German humanists were a

---

[65]Trunz, "Späthumanismus," 163: "Im Grunde genommen reiste man gar nicht von Stadt zu Stadt, sondern von Gelehrten zu Gelehrten."

[66]After Trunz, "Späthumanismus,"163.

[67]Hermann Wiegand, *Hodoeporica: Studien zur neulateinischen Reisedichtung,* Saecvla Spiritualia 12 (Baden-Baden: Valentin Koerner, 1984).

[68]I have examined these poems in some detail in my article "Creating Humanist Myths." (See n. 49.)

[69]*Ulrichi Hutteni opera,* ed. Eduard Böcking, 5 vols. (Leipzig: Teubner, 1859–1861), 3:64–81.

very heterogeneous group. Hutten's poem does not reflect a humanist sense of community but attempts to forge one.

This intention is even clearer in the second *Hodoeporicon*, the "Carmen rithmicale" from the second part of the *Epistolae obscurorum virorum* (1517). This poem describes a fictitious journey of a certain Philip Schlauraff who is sent by the Cologne theologians on a public relations tour to various humanist centers in Germany in order to enlist the help of scholars against the hated Reuchlin. Wherever Schlauraff turns, he is met with a hostile reception by the humanists. He is insulted, mocked, ridiculed, publicly embarrassed, and threatened. In addition to the threats, he also suffered physical injury: Students beat him up and pull him by the hair; he is slapped in the face and thrown down the stairs. Exhausted by so much verbal and physical abuse, Schlauraff returns to Cologne where he finds a congenial company of theologians. In this poem, Hutten tried to evoke the image of a monolithic fraternity of humanists. He essentially creates a myth of the power, influence, and strength of a movement that really did not exist to such an extent on the eve of the Reformation.[70] And the knight Hutten, who was not averse to occasionally resorting to violence, creates an identity of the humanist movement by symbolically humiliating and physically abusing his opponents.

"The first aim of any revolutionary group must be...to create and perpetuate its own group identity." The words of the social psychologist Richard Trexler when discussing quite a different group[71] is applicable mutatis mutandis to the social group we now call humanists. Without resorting to violence (notwithstanding Brother Schlauraff's unkind, but mercifully fictitious, treatment), and without guns and cannons, the humanists revolutionized our thinking and permanently and profoundly affected the literature, education, philosophy, and history of Europe. In my essay I have tried to explain the process by which they created and perpetuated their own collective group identity. While the use of Latin gave them a sense of collective identity, their vociferous opposition to the scholastics created a sense of solidarity. Furthermore, the *sodalitates* and their letter writing gave these often widely dispersed and isolated scholars a sense of belonging to larger community. Central to the development of a humanist consciousness was, finally, their cult of friendship, and their desire to travel to other, like-minded scholars. The emergence of the humanists as a major intellectual force, as insiders to the cultural, political, and ecclesiastical institutions, by the third decade of the sixteenth century, from a

---

[70]Overfield, *Humanism and Scholasticism*, 192.
[71]Trexler, "Introduction," *Persons in Groups*, 9.

handful of isolated outsiders in the middle of the fifteenth century, was the result of many factors, including Gutenberg's invention of printing, the enormous needs of the courts and cities for well-educated administrators, and dissatisfaction with the ossified universities. In this essay I have focused on one aspect, the development of a distinct "Standeskultur," group culture or identity, as the necessary prerequisite for success.

# HERMANN VON DEM BUSCHE'S POEM IN HONOR OF ERASMUS' ARRIVAL IN COLOGNE IN 1516

## James V. Mehl

ANYONE WHO READS THE ORIGINAL TEXTS of the fifteenth and sixteenth centuries knows that the humanists composed a great number and variety of occasional poems. In Italy and in the North such poems were written, literally, as the occasion demanded, whether to honor a prince's coronation, to memorialize a military victory, to introduce a published work, or, as in the case here, to pay tribute to the arrival of Europe's most famous humanist into the city of Cologne in May 1516. Such incidental poems were often short, comprising only a distich or two, while others were long elegies or odes going on for a number of pages. Many of them were published—and indeed were composed with that intention in mind—while others remained in manuscript. Taken as a group, these occasional poems constitute an important, if little studied, genre of Neo-Latin literature.[1] The call for such a study of the "literatura encomiastica Erasmiana" was made some years ago by Cornelis Reedijk. Reedijk listed the many humanists who had dedicated poems to Erasmus; in addition to Busche, the group included André de Resende, Euricius Cordus, Bartholomaeus Latomus, Johannes Stigel, Ursinus Velius, Henricus Glareanus, Germanus Brixius, Julius Caesar Scaliger, Janus Secundus, Étienne Dolet, Eobanus Hessus, Cornelius Grapheus, and Simon Grynaeus.[2] My intention here is to show, through a study of one of these praises—Hermann von dem Busche's poem written in honor of Erasmus' arrival in Cologne—how these minor literary works may shed additional light on our understanding of the lives

---

[1]See the comments of Paul Oskar Kristeller, *Renaissance Thought II: Papers on Humanism and the Arts* (New York: Harper and Row, 1965), 13–14.

[2]Cornelis Reedijk, ed., *The Poems of Desiderius Erasmus* (Leiden: Brill, 1956), 85.

of individual humanists and of the more general characteristics of humanist culture during the early sixteenth century. More specifically, I should like to explore the historical context concerning the composition of this specific poem as a means of demonstrating the nuances of humanist interaction in Germany on the eve of the Reformation.

The controversial and somewhat flamboyant humanist Hermann von dem Busche composed his "In Erasmum, Coloniam recens ingressum, Carmen" either at the time of Erasmus' arrival in Cologne sometime during the last week of May 1516, or shortly thereafter.[3] The exact time is obscured by the phrase "recens ingressum" in the poem title, which can be translated as "just entered" or "recently entered." Little is known about the actual circumstances surrounding the poem's composition and its means of presentation. Indeed, the opening verses of the forty-eight-line poem suggest that Busche may have written out the verses quickly as a means of expressing his joy (*gaudia*) upon hearing the announcement of Erasmus' arrival in the city. For Busche, who had known Erasmus personally for only about a year, this day was one of festivity and happiness, if only the reports were true: "O festum laetumque diem, si vera locutus / Si non haec vano mendax confinxerit ore." Busche then continued with a long acknowledgment of his mentor's learning and fame. The verses are filled with allusions and references to classical antiquity typical of humanist poems of this type. Busche noted that Erasmus had been praised as a man of highest distinction throughout the lands of Europe: in Italy, France, Spain, and even to the shores of Ireland and the Orcades Islands and to the remote territory of Britain. Such praises were justified because of Erasmus' charming manners, his acute mental capabilities, and his learned knowledge of the two ancient languages, Latin and Greek. In spite of the abandonment by certain "barbarians," those degenerate detractors who were ignorant, arrogant, and jealous, Busche concluded, Erasmus was appreciated by his associates for his measured seriousness (gravitas sine nube renidens) and his natural charm.

The praises and rhetorical flourishes of Busche's poem very likely escaped Erasmus' immediate notice. And it is doubtful that there was any kind of formal presentation or ceremony welcoming the famous humanist to Cologne in late May 1516. Very little is known about this particular journey by Erasmus from Basel to the Low Countries, except that he was

---

[3]I have used the copy in Erasmus, *Opera omnia*, ed. Joannes Clericus (Leiden, 1703–6), 3, pt. 1: 198–99, which is included at the end of this essay. The following analysis and citations are based upon a reading of that copy. For comparison, see also Busche's much longer published poem, *Hypanticon* (Basel, 1520), dedicated to Count-Bishop George of the Palatinate on his entry into Speyer.

quite concerned about the presence of soldiers and the threat of war along the way. In a letter to his friend Thomas More, written in early June shortly after arriving in Brussels, Erasmus mentions the presence of military bands everywhere around Kaysersberg. "In Cologne," Erasmus continues, "I found some Italian envoys and finished my journey with them. We were a party of about eighty horsemen, and even so our journey was not free from peril."[4] Hardly a "festive and happy day" for Erasmus in Cologne, as Busche described in his poem! Subsequent correspondence of Erasmus indicates that a copy of the poem had not been given to him upon his arrival in the city. About a month and a half later, ca. 13 July, Erasmus wrote to his friend in Basel, Henricus Glareanus, requesting that a copy of the poem be sent: "Let me have the poem you wrote about me, and Busche's verses too."[5] In his reply, dated 5 September 1516, Glareanus reported: "Busche's poem, which gives me the greatest pleasure, I have copied out as carefully as I can, considering I had a text that was corrupt; and so I beg you to look through it with your usual care."[6] And, again, in a letter of 13 November, Glareanus confirmed that he had sent the Busche poem, as requested.[7] Glareanus' statements suggest that Busche's poem was circulating, probably in multiple manuscript copies, during the summer and fall of 1516. It is likely that Glareanus had received his copy either directly from Busche, who may have been one of his teachers at the University of Cologne between 1508 and 1510, or from a mutual friend such as Johannes Caesarius, whom Glareanus had praised as one of his humanist teachers in Cologne.[8] While it has been mentioned in a recent biographical account that Erasmus then published the Busche poem, I have so far been unable to affirm such a publication and have relied on the copy in the 1703–6 Leiden edition of Erasmus' works.[9]

The somewhat curious circumstances surrounding the composition of this poem and the delay in its reception by Erasmus prompt several further questions. What motivated Busche to write this poem, especially if he

---

[4]Erasmus to Thomas More [Brussels] [c. 3 June 1516], in Peter G. Bietenholz et al., eds., *Collected Works of Erasmus* [cited hereafter as *CWE*] (Toronto-Buffalo-London: University of Toronto Press, 1974– ), 3:291.

[5]Erasmus to Henricus Glareanus [Antwerp, c. 13 July] 1516, ibid., 3:337.

[6]Glareanus to Erasmus, Basel, 5 September 1516, ibid., 4:73.

[7]Glareanus to Erasmus, Basel, 13 November [1516], ibid., 4:130.

[8]On Glareanus' instructors at Cologne, see Fritz Büsser, "Henricus Glareanus of Glarus," in Peter G. Bietenholz, et al., eds., *Contemporaries of Erasmus* [cited hereafter as *CE*] 3 vols. (Toronto-Buffalo-London: University of Toronto Press, 1985–87), 2:105, and James V. Mehl, "Humanism in the Home Town of the 'Obscure Men,'" in *Humanismus in Köln/Humanism in Cologne*, ed. idem (Cologne-Vienna: Böhlau Verlag, 1991), 14, 18.

[9]The claim for publication is made in *CE*, 1:233.

could not present it immediately? What was the relationship between Busche and Erasmus at this point, and how did that relationship develop over the next several years? And what does this poem signify regarding the nature of humanist culture in early-sixteenth-century Germany?

Busche's motives for composing the poem, in spite of the awkward circumstances, were several. He seized the occasion of Erasmus' arrival in Cologne as a means of strengthening an increasingly warm, if somewhat recent, friendship between the two humanists. In the company of Reuchlin and Ulrich von Hutten, Busche and Erasmus had met, probably for the first time, during the spring of 1515 in Frankfurt am Main.[10] At that meeting, their plans to print a series of satirical letters, the *Epistolae obscurorum virorum*, as a way of defending Reuchlin and the preservation of certain Hebrew books, were shared with Erasmus. Erasmus was sympathetic, at least initially, to this humanist cause, although he cautioned moderation. Busche apparently took seriously the advice of the famous humanist, especially in moderating the tone of his most important literary defense of humanistic study, the *Vallum humanitatis*, which he was then beginning to write. Erasmus later praised Busche for this work. In 1516 two antiwar poems by Busche were published with Erasmus' *Querela pacis*.[11] But Busche was increasingly anxious to solidify the friendship because his own situation in Cologne was deteriorating rapidly.

Busche's involvement, especially after 1514, in the Reuchlin affair, along with his entanglement in several other local controversies, brought a growing disenchantment with the city. In 1508, shortly after his arrival in the city, he had composed a long poem, the *Flora*, in praise of Cologne. Now, in 1516, he issued a pessimistic ode of renunciation, the *Lossage von Cöln*.[12] The dogged attacks of the Dominican Inquisitor, Jacob Hoogstraten, and other "obscurantist" opponents had persuaded him to leave the city. By the time of the writing of the Erasmus poem, Busche may not have yet negotiated to become the new headmaster at the Latin School in Wesel, just north of Cologne on the Rhine.[13] The new contract for this academic appointment was approved by the Wesel city council in early July,

---

[10]For additional biographical information on Busche, see my "Hermann von dem Busche's *Vallum humanitatis* (1518): A German Defense of the Renaissance *Studia Humanitatis*," *Renaissance Quarterly* 42 (1989), 480–506, with references to other biographical sources on 481 n. 6.

[11]As noted by Hermann Joseph Liessem, *Hermann van dem Busche: Sein Leben und seine Schriften* (Cologne, 1884–1908; rept. Nieuwkoop: De Graaf, 1965), Anhang, 37.

[12]Ibid., Anhang, 39.

[13]On this phase of Busche's career, see my "Hermannus Buschius' *Dictata utilissima*: A Textbook of Commonplaces for the Latin School," *Humanistica Lovaniensia: Journal of Neo-Latin Studies* 42 (1993): 102–25.

although he did not take up his administrative responsibilities until late September 1516. Busche was obviously aware that a recommendation from Erasmus could pave the way for a new position. Indeed, following the rescinding of his contract at Wesel in August 1517, Erasmus may have tried repeatedly to secure for Busche the chair of Latin in the Collegium Trilingue at Louvain.[14] While these efforts ultimately were unsuccessful, the two humanists maintained a close friendship during these years. After moving to Wesel, Busche visited Erasmus in the Low Countries and in England, seeking advice on several literary projects. The two met again briefly in Speyer in 1518, during Erasmus' well-reported journey down the Rhine that year.[15] In 1520 Busche supported Erasmus in his controversy with Edward Lee. But Busche's attraction to Luther and the new evangelical cause soon strained the friendship. Following Busche's public participation in a Lenten feast in Basel in April 1521, Erasmus had to offer apologies to the local bishop. Then, rather abruptly, during the summer of 1523, Erasmus broke off the relationship, having heard rumors that Busche was preparing literary attacks against him.[16]

For his part, Erasmus seems to have responded to Busche's poetical tribute almost as an afterthought. It was nearly a month and a half after his visit to Cologne that Erasmus requested a copy of the poem from his Basel friend, Glareanus. And Erasmus was just as interested in having Glareanus send his own poem as the one composed by Busche. It was in September, at the earliest, that a corrected copy of the Busche poem was forwarded to Erasmus. Erasmus apparently did not correspond directly with Busche for a copy. Indeed, the correspondence between the two was infrequent, especially when compared to the number of letters Erasmus had exchanged with Caesarius and the patron of the Cologne humanists, Graf Hermann von Neuenahr, between 1516 and 1518. In a long letter to Caesarius, dated 23 June 1516 [just after the composition of Busche's poem], Erasmus asks that "my warmest greetings" be given to "that open-hearted Maecenas of the humanities," Neuenahr.[17] There is no mention of Busche. There are only two brief letters to Busche dating from 1518. Erasmus sent one of them in April, after writing to Caesarius earlier that month:

---

[14]*CE*, 1:233.

[15]Erasmus to Beatus Rhenanus, Louvain [first half of October] 1518, in *CWE*, 6:114. See also Preserved Smith, *Erasmus: A Study of His Life, Ideals and Place in History* (New York–London: Harper and Brothers, 1923), 143–45.

[16]*CE*, 1:233–34.

[17]*CWE*, 3:321.

I hear that Busche has returned to your part of the world, and I am
delighted; this is much better than that his gifts should be hid
somewhere in obscurity [a reference to Busche's recent return to
Cologne from Wesel]. Very soon, if I mistake not, barbarism will
be entirely expelled from Cologne too, by the valor of all ranks. I
hear that my lord the count of Neuenahr is doing battle like a very
Hercules against those arrogant professors of unlearned learning,
but I wish he had somewhat more honorable opponents.[18]

The struggle against the barbarian professors in Cologne, mentioned here
by Erasmus, echoes the reference to the same band of ignorant and arrogant barbarians who opposed Erasmus, referred to earlier in Busche's
poem. The other short letter to Busche followed closely after their meeting
in Speyer in October.[19] This letter is in reference to Erasmus' attempts to
find employment for his friend at Louvain. But, in spite of this paucity of
correspondence, the two apparently maintained a close friendship
throughout this period.

While Busche saw Erasmus' arrival in Cologne in May 1516 as an
opportunity to cultivate this friendship, Erasmus probably had no knowledge of the poem composed in his honor and rather welcomed the sight of
the city's many Gothic spires because Cologne was one of the last stops on
his long journey from Basel to the Low Countries. It had been a difficult
trip, fraught with military dangers, lasting about seventeen days.[20] For
Erasmus, it was but one of many trips he had taken along the Rhine
between his homeland in the Low Countries and his printers in Basel. In
retrospect, as Preserved Smith has pointed out, this particular journey
down the Rhine in 1516 marked a transition in his primary residence. He
had spent most of the last two years in Basel working with his printers,
Amerbach and Froben. For the next five and a half years Erasmus' head-
quarters would be in the lower Rhineland, where he lived chiefly in Antwerp, Brussels, and Louvain.[21]

The prince of the humanists was at the height of his fame. The popularity of his *Moria*, his *Adagia*, and his *Enchiridion militis christiani*,
together with his recent scholarly work on the New Testament, had made
his name famous in every land of Europe, as recognized in Busche's poem.
During the spring of 1516 he had been offered academic appointments at

---

[18]*CWE*, 5:358–59. The letter to Busche is in ibid., 5:403.

[19]Ibid., 6:156.

[20]See the comments by P. S. Allen in idem, et al., eds., *Opus epistolarum Des. Erasmi Roterodami*,
12 vols. (Oxford: Clarendon Press, 1906–58), 3:240.

[21]Smith, *Erasmus: A Study*, 148.

the universities of Leipzig and Ingolstadt.[22] Although his trips up and down the Rhine often had brought meetings and even festive celebrations with fellow humanists, the slow and awkward means of travel, the unpredictable and often adverse weather conditions, and the possibilities of sickness and personal attack made such travel both difficult and dangerous, as Erasmus described in great detail in a number of his letters. And the discomforts and boorish behavior he experienced in German inns along the way served as a model for one of his most famous colloquies.[23] Erasmus' arrival in Cologne in May 1516, where he joined eighty (probably armed) horsemen in order to insure some security for the last leg of the trip, typifies the personal challenges and hardships he experienced during the journeys along the Rhine.

What can be concluded and recommended, then, based on this analysis? Busche's poem was one of many occasional poems written during the fifteenth and sixteenth centuries. It was also one of a number of poems dedicated to Erasmus. The poems written by humanists from throughout Europe to praise Erasmus were part of an important genre of Neo-Latin literature, although each poem was written under different circumstances and for specific reasons. This study of Busche's poem of 1516, therefore, may be useful as a possible model for interpreting this type of humanist literature.

The historical events and motivations surrounding the composition of this particular occasional poem provide additional insights into the lives of the two humanists, the development of their interpersonal relationship, and the characteristics of humanist culture in Germany during the early sixteenth century. The time of the poem's composition, in late May or early June 1516, was a period of transition for both men. The rigors of controversy, especially the attacks of the traditionalist theologians at the University of Cologne, had left Busche weary and disenchanted with the city. He was about to leave Cologne and was in search of a new position. Erasmus was finishing a two-year period working with his printers in Basel, then living for the next five and a half years mainly in the Low Countries. Busche's meeting with Erasmus during the previous spring marked the beginning of a warm friendship between the two. Not only did Busche apparently accept the famous humanist's advice to moderate both his lifestyle and his literary efforts, but he arranged for several of his shorter writings to be printed with Erasmus' *Querela pacis* in 1516. When Erasmus arrived in Cologne during his journey down the Rhine in May of

[22]Ibid., 146–47.
[23]Ibid., 141–43.

that year, Busche saw an opportunity to solidify their friendship and a possibility for Erasmus to assist in securing his employment.

The poem was dominated by praises of Erasmus' learning and character, embellished with classical references and allusions typical of this type of humanist literature, and even included an attack against the barbarian detractors. But apparently Erasmus paid little attention to the poem in his honor. He was glad to arrive in Cologne because he could join a larger group of horsemen as a means of providing greater personal security for the remainder of his journey to Brussels. He wished to see a copy of the poem only later, requesting a copy from their mutual friend, Glareanus. Despite an infrequent correspondence, the two maintained a warm friendship until Busche's support of the Reformation brought embarrassment and later a personal antagonism that ended the relationship by 1523. This study in microhistory, therefore, also reveals the nuances of macrohistorical themes concerning the development of humanist culture in Germany on the eve of the Reformation.

"In Erasmum, Coloniam recens ingressum, Carmen"[24]
Dic puer, Erasmum cupido quis nunciat illum
Advenisse mihi, quisnam haec mihi guadia portat?
O festum laetumque diem, si vera locutus,
Si non haec vano mendax confinxerit ore.
Quisquis is est tandem, credamne, ut venerit ille?
Ille, inquam, Erasmus, cui Roterodamica tellus
Tam debet, docto sua quam Verona Catullo:
Quam tribus Hispanis urbs inclyta debet alumnis,
Ausonio fundata duci, quam Bilbilis alta,
Cornipedum gregibus foecunda, et fortibus armis
Ingenio debet culti celeberrima civis,
Quam cantata suo debet Mevania vati,
Parthenopeque suo, sontes qui carmine Thebas
Eruit, et sylvas plectro modulatus eburno,
Magnanimum in Troas, et in Hectora movit Achillem:
Quam Sulmo tibi Naso tener, quem barbarus Ister,
Braccatique Getae, cygnea voce canentem
Tristia, fleverunt: quam Mantua prisca Maroni,
Quo duce Musarum meruit domus ipsa vocari,
Et fama pulsare polos, et sydera laude,

---

[24]Hermann von dem Busche, May 1516, as transcribed and corrected from Erasmus, *Opera omnia*, ed. Joannes Clericus (Leiden, 1703–6), 3, pt. 1, 198–99.

Omneque venturae spacium superare senectae.
Estne ille Erasmus, modo quem venisse loquuntur,
Ipsis qui solus possit certare Latinis?
Quem probat, extollitque virum clarissimus ordo,
Pontificis Romae qui limina scandit in ostro,
Quemque per Italiam passim lectissima turba,
Cordaque suspiciunt doctissima Grajugenarum,
Qui sibi quaesivit nomen, per Gallica regna,
Hispanumque Tagum, per Hibernica litora, perque
Orchadas, et nostro semotos orbe Britannos:
Terrarum Reges, quem fulvo munere jungunt;
Conciliantque sibi, quo fante, ignobile ducunt
Eloquium Pyliae quod fluxit ab ore senectae:
Quo citharam tendente, et Apollinei peragente
Officium vatis, stupet ipse ad carmina Phoebus,
Calliopeque sui gemitu reminiscitur Orphei.
Venit, certa fides, vidi, vidi ipsi cupitum
Optatumque mihi toties, occurrere vultum
Hospitis egregii, dextramque amplexus inhaese.
O blandi mores! O fandi exacta facultas!
Quanta vetustatis, linguaeque scientia docto
Quanta utriusque viro, quantum discessit ab illo
Barbaries, ruditas, ignava superbia, livor
Degener! imo alios multos secum attulit ipse
Diversos comites, gravitas sine nube renidens,
Ingenuusque lepos, Pitho, Charitesque sorores,
Pegasidesque omnes, gressus comitantur euntis,
Florenteisque rosas gestans, posita aegide Pallas.

**Rasmus von rothero**
dam ein fürst aller gelerten zů vnseren zyt/
schreibt jm bůch genāt Encomion morias/
vom predigen der bättel münch.

Ein jeden ich hie fründlich bit /
Das er mich läß vnd lach nit.
D ✳ G

## Der. VI. bundts gnosz.

# "START SPREADING THE NEWS"
## Martin Luther's First Published Song

*Paul F. Casey* †

EARLY MODERN GERMAN SONG TEXTS have failed to elicit the attention literary scholars have devoted to other contemporaneous genres, such as the drama, sermon, and narrative fiction. Not surprisingly, our initial knowledge of the genre owed much to industrious German musicologists of the mid-nineteenth century who analyzed the development of the *evangelisches Kirchenlied*. But these musicologists, like their literary colleagues, avoided investigating song texts as cultural phenomena; and beyond the musicological context they generally concentrated on the devotional or bibliographic aspects of hymns and their origins.[1] Their stated aim was to sketch the musicological evolution of the songs and not to investigate their impact on literary or popular culture.

In recent decades historians of the early modern period—especially those located in America—have focused more extensively on the song genre in the sixteenth century as a cultural expression with broad implications for the social history of the period. The work of Kyle C. Sessions is exemplary of this recent attention: it centers on the hymns composed by

---

[1]Nineteenth-century scholars have done a great deal of the solid spadework on early modern song—for example, the authoritative five-volume study by Philipp Wackernagel, *Das deutsche Kirchenlied von den ältesten Zeiten bis zu Anfang des XVII. Jahrhunderts* (Leipzig: B. G. Teubner, 1864–77), and the same author's *Bibliographie zur Geschichte des deutschen Kirchenliedes im XVI. Jarhundert* (Frankfurt: Wolf, 1855). Eduard Emil Koch, *Geschichte des Kirchenlieds und Kirchengesangs*, 2d ed. (Stuttgart: Chr. Belser'schen Verlagshandlung, 1866), an exhaustive work, covers the topic with great erudition. More recent, but equally authoritative, studies include Hans Joachim Moser, *Die evangelische Kirchenmusik in Deutschland* (Berlin/Darmstadt: Verlag Carl Merseburger, 1954). The emphasis in these works is on the role and development of the *Kirchenlied*. Only tangentially do they focus attention on other types of songs.

Luther himself, examining the songs' subject matter, idioms, and images for doctrinal content.[2]

In general, Germanists usually view song, an innately oral genre whose fluidity traditionally causes problems of categorization for textual scholars, as less worthy of serious consideration because the parameters of the genre and its influences are less easily detectable and definable, diluted as they are by a heavy admixture of popular culture. Most early modern songs first saw the light of day as broadsheets, a disposable form of print deemed unworthy of collection by most contemporaries. This situation left earlier investigators wondering how complete their set of documents was and thus uneasy as to the validity of their conclusions. But this view overlooks the fact that by the beginning of the Reformation period, codification and classification of songs was well under way. Publishers collected broadsheets into *Gesangbücher, Kirchenliedbücher, Enchiridien, Bergreihen,* and various compendia of popular folksongs, a development which made even greater strides as the Reformation became firmly established, thus validating the integrity of early modern song as a genre. In recent years, scholars such as R. W. Scribner have increasingly dealt with the symbiotic relationship between printing and song as two interlocking and complementary means of disseminating information.[3] As a result Germanists have, in recent years, devoted increased attention to song's development as a literary genre. Hans-Georg Kemper's admirably thorough and perceptive *Deutsche Lyrik der frühen Neuzeit* encompasses a detailed consideration of song's place in the development of German poetry from the Reformation to the eighteenth century.[4] Further, studies of Luther's use of language, such as *Luther und die deutsche Sprache* by Erwin Arndt and Gisela Brandt, investigate his songs in the context of his conscious need to communicate his message (*Kommunikationsnot*).[5]

Martin Luther's earliest published *Lied* exemplifies many important features of the song as a bearer of news, thus providing a seminal example of his *Kommunikationsnot*. In a literary-historical context, "Ein neues Lied

---

[2]Kyle C. Sessions, "Luther in Music and Verse," in *Pietas et Societas: New Trends in Reformation Social History: Essays in Memory of Harold J. Grimm,* ed. Kyle C. Sessions and Phillip N. Bebb (Kirksville, Mo.: Sixteenth Century Journal Publishers, 1985), 123–39. Also, Sessions, "Luther's Hymns in the Spread of the Reformation" (Ph.D. diss., Ohio State University, 1963).

[3]R. W. Scribner, *Popular Culture and Popular Movements in Reformation Germany* (London and Ronceverte: Hambleton Press, 1987), especially his essay on "Oral Culture and the Diffusion of Reformation Ideas," 49–69.

[4]Hans-Georg Kemper, *Deutsche Lyrik der frühen Neuzeit,* vol. 1, *Epochen- und Gattungsprobleme: Reformationszeit* (Tübingen: Niemeyer, 1987), is particularly relevant to my discussion.

[5]Edwin Arndt and Gisela Brandt, *Luther und die deutsche Sprache: Wie redet der Deutsche man jnn solchem fall?* (Leipzig: VEB Bibliographisches Institut, 1987), especially 106–15.

wir heben an" (1523) bears a marked resemblance to what we have come
to think of as balladic works: it narrates a story. It compels our attention
both because it is Luther's first published song—which, of course, does
not imply that he had not tried his hand previously at other, more devotional compositions—and also because, beyond the doctrinal points made
in the hymn, its subject matter suggests Luther's awareness of the propa-
gandizing and proselytizing capabilities of the song genre.[6]
As Luther developed his ideas on worship, choral song came to form
an integral part in the new, participatory divine service, to a degree
unprecedented in the traditional Roman Catholic mass. The Roman Catholic service did not exclude music—at times quite beautiful vocalizing by
soloists enhanced the service, and Latin hymns traditionally formed a part
of it—but the mass avoided singing by the congregation and, most importantly, singing in the vernacular. Evangelical believers demonstrated their
faith by raising their voices in unison to God, and they did so in German.
Luther's insistence on the vernacular church service as a means of underscoring the priesthood of all believers and his firm belief in the efficacy of
integrating song into the worship service drew popular song in its wake.[7]
No longer lost in the mists of the oral tradition of the *Volk*, vernacular
song became a legitimate and respected art form. Moreover, despite its
orality, which distinguishes its impact from that of the printed word, song
became increasingly linked to the print medium as the Reformation took
hold.

Initially at least, the broadsheet facilitated a rapid dissemination of
songs of both sacred and secular content among diverse segments of the
population. As Luther well knew from his considerable experience in the
turbulent world of the *Streitschrift*, the broadsheet was the fastest means of
reaching a targeted audience with a specific message. The concerted efforts
of printers in Augsburg, Nürnberg, Basel, Strassburg, and Wittenberg to
spread song through the broadsheet have led specialists to characterize the
sixteenth century as "die Blütezeit des Volksliedes."[8] The Reformation did
more for vernacular song in its various guises, both sacred and secular,
than for any other single genre; certainly it did more than any other force

---

[6]Sessions, "Luther in Music and Verse," 124, comments only briefly on this hymn.

[7]I shall adopt the practice of citing the Weimar edition of Luther's works, *D. Martin Luthers
Werke: Kritische Gesamtausgabe*, 100 vols. (Weimar: Hermann Böhlhaus Nachfolger, 1888–1966), in
the text and notes as *WA*, followed by volume and page numbers. In *WA* 12:218, Luther expresses the
wish "daß wir möglichst viele Lieder hätten, die das Volk während der Messe singen könnte." (That we
might have as many songs as possible, which the people could sing during the mass). All translations
into English in this essay are mine, unless otherwise noted.

[8]Rolf Wilhelm Brednich, *Die Liedpublizistik im Flugblatt des 15. bis 17. Jahrhunderts* (Baden-
Baden: Verlag Valentin Koerner, 1974), 1:16.

in the immediately preceding centuries. Martin Luther's personal involvement in the integration of the song into the new worship service and his own compositions for popular consumption not only lent the genre respectability and authority, but also encouraged others to follow his lead. His enthusiasm for music was almost limitless:

> Musica ist das beste Labsal einem betrübten Menschen, dadurch das Herze wieder zufrieden, erquickt und erfrischt wird.... Musicam habe ich allzeit lieb gehabt. Wer diese Kunst kann, der ist guter Art, zu Allem geschickt. Man muß Musicam von Noht wegen in Schulen behalten.[9]

In a letter of 1530 to Ludwig Senfl, Luther ranks music directly behind theology as an art: "Musica est insigne donum Dei et theologiae proxima." In another letter he confesses: "Wäre ich nicht Theolog, würd' ich am liebsten Musiker sein."[10] Luther's initiative almost always encouraged significant response from his adherents, so his musical compositions unleashed a wealth of musical activity: "Gedacht waren sie (his songs) als Anregung, nicht unbedingt als Vorbild für die, die es 'besser machen' könnten."[11] His impetus in the field has resulted in his justifiable designation as "the founder of the German Church Song,"[12] or as Cyriakus Spangenberg enthusiastically exaggerates, "der größte Meistersinger."[13]

But song, once it had attained a measure of respectability, assumed further significance beyond the confines of the evangelical church service and religious instruction. Luther's initial enthusiasm for the genre may have resulted from his determination to make music an integral part of the worship service, but reformers—and many composers and poets who operated on the fringes of the Reformation—soon discovered that song could be of inestimable value as well in reaching vast sections of a largely untutored public with a specific message.[14] Its orality became its strength. As a means of communicating new ideas and spreading the Word, song

---

[9]*WA Tischreden* 1:968: "Music is the best tonic for a distressed man, whereby the heart becomes satisfied, revived, and refreshed... I have always liked music. The practitioner of this art stands in good stead and is dexterous in all things. It is a matter of necessity that music be kept in the schools."

[10]*WA Tischreden* 3:3815: As quoted by Moser, 40 note 7: "Were I not a theologian, I would have liked best to have been a musician." The letter was addressed to Johann Walter.

[11]Friedrich Blume, *Geschichte der evangelischen Kirchenmusik,* 2d ed. (Kassel: Bärenreiter, 1965), 26. "They (Luther's songs) were intended as an impetus, not necessarily as a model, for those who could 'do it better.'"

[12]Koch, *Geschichte des Kirchenlieds,* 1:230. Arnold E. Berger, *Lied-, Spruch- und Fabelsichtung im Dienste der Reformation,* Deutsche Literatur in Entwicklungsreihen, 4: Reihe Reformation (Leipzig: Reclam, 1938), 20, terms Luther "der Urheber des evangelischen Kirchenliedes." Many other similar epithets occur in the literature on church song.

[13]As quoted in Blume, *Geschichte,* 26. Spangenberg termed Luther "the greatest Meistersinger."

[14]On Luther's efforts to integrate songs into the divine service, see Kemper, *Deutsche Lyrik,* 1:175:

possessed immediacy and more viability than the sermon—the other genre that flowered in the hands of the Reformers. The sermon targeted only limited numbers of auditors and, even in printed form, reached only restricted numbers of the literate. In the form of a protoballad, following a narrative line, the broadsheet song could rapidly disseminate noteworthy items, its content the more memorable for being sung: as Luther observed, "Die Noten machen den Text lebendig. Sie verjagt den Geist der Traurigkeit, wie man am Könige Saul sieht."[15] Song had a mellowing effect on audiences, making them "gelinder und sanftmüthiger, sittsamer und vernünftiger"; in sum, more receptive to its message.[16] In many respects, then, such compositions functioned as precursors of the modern newspaper as a means of "spreading the news" of recent events, unrestrained by a need for literacy in the audience.

Unexpectedly, Luther's first published song focuses not on sacred material, or even immediately on the Word as such, but on a historical, highly politicized event in distant Brussels. Hans-Georg Kemper suggests Luther's initial interest in songwriting in his fortieth year, was a response to Thomas Müntzer's having recently designed a German worship service, thus anticipating Luther in this important liturgical area.[17] But Luther's first published song is only tangentially connected with divine worship, and focuses attention, instead, on a recent martyrdom in the Netherlands.

"Ein neues Lied wir heben an" appeared in 1523 as a broadsheet (*Einzeldruck*) in Wittenberg, but all copies of this original print have apparently disappeared.[18] The song reappeared the following year, although in

---

Among those difficult to classify as reformers I think, in the first instance, of the many cantors active in Germany during the period, such as Johann Walter, who contributed greatly to the development of the church song genre and who will feature later in my discussion. Wackernagel's *Das deutsche Kirchenlied* (vol. 3) is replete with such cantor/composers. Songs on nonreligious themes were also much in evidence. See Berger's selection in *Lied-, Spruch-, und Fabeldichtung.*

[15] *WA Tischreden* 1:968. "The notes enliven the text. They banish the spirit of sadness, as one sees in the case of King Saul."

[16] Ibid., "gentler and meeker, more virtuous and reasonable."

[17] Kemper, *Deutsche Lyrik*, 1:175–76.

[18] There seems to be little doubt, however, that the original form of the song was an *Einzeldruck* (*WA* 35:10–11). All sources generally agree on its incorporation into the Wittenberg *Gesangbuch* and the Erfurt *Enchiridion* bespeaks a broadsheet precursor. Franz M. Böhme evidently used the broadsheet version of this song in his *Altdeutsches Liederbuch* (Leipzig: Reclam, 1877), 477. Brednich discusses the provenance of the song in *Die Liedpublizistik im Flugblatt des 15. bis 17. Jahrhunderts,* 1:86–87, and he, too, is convinced of an original broadsheet version. Markus Jenny summarizes the historical situation: "Obwohl von diesem allerersten Lied Luthers, entstanden wohl gleich nach Bekanntwerden des Brüsseler Ereignisses vom 1. Juli 1523, kein früher Einzeldruck auf uns gekommen ist, kann es keinem Zweifel unterliegen, daß das die Form seiner ersten Verbreitung war." ("Although no broadsheet copy of Luther's very first song, probably composed immediately after the events of 1 July 1523

two noticeably divergent forms, in both the Wittenberg *Geystlicher Gesang Buchlein*—i.e., songs intended for both the home and the church and collected or composed under Luther's guidance—and also the *Enchiridion* (1524).[19] Johann Walter (or Walther), cantor in Torgau, came to Wittenberg, perhaps at the behest of Luther, to compile the *Gesangbuch*, which constitutes one of the earliest evangelical song collections.[20] Walter is responsible for assembling, perhaps commissioning, the compositions in the collection, but the twenty-four songs composed by Luther up to the time of Pentecost 1524 make up the core of the anthology, the assortment also containing songs by Johann Agricola, Lazarus Spengler, Paul Speratus, and even one woman, Elisabeth Cruciger.[21]

Luther's songwriting activities belong largely to the short time span between the appearance of the broadsheet version of "Ein neues Lied" in the late summer of 1523 and the song's inclusion in Walter's collection in 1524, except for a few later compositions which look as if they are intended to fill in gaps. Luther developed rapidly in 1523–24 into a skilled composer of songs, which has led Friedrich Blume to term this short period of his life the "Liederjahr."[22] After a period of initial frenetic activity, however, his enthusiasm for songwriting either waned or other, more urgent matters consumed his energies. Among the twenty-four songs by

---

in Brussels became known, has come down to us, there can be no doubt that that was the means of its first circulation"). See Jenny, *Luthers Geistliche Lieder und Kirchengesänge* (Cologne/Vienna: Böhlau, 1985), 75–76.

[19]The 1524 Wittenberg collection bears the title: *Geystliche gesangk Buchlein: Tenor Wittemberg M.D.iiij (sic): Bassus Wittemberg M.D.xxiiij* (*WA* 35:315). It became known under the familiar title *Waltersches Gesangbüchlein*. According to Böhme (777), it was actually printed in Nürnberg, but this opinion is shared by no one. Böhme may have confused this *Gesangbuchlein* with the *Achtliederuch*, re-edited twice by the printer Jobst Gutknecht in Nürnberg, although he claims Wittenberg on the title page. See Sessions, "Luther in Music and Verse," 126. The Erfurt collection is entitled: *Enchiridion / Oder ein Handbuchlein / eynem yetzlichen Christen fast nutzlich / bey sich zuhaben … M.CCCCC.XXIII.* At the end: "Gedruckt zu Erffordt zeum Schwartzen / Hornn, bey der Kremer brucken / M.D.xxiiij Jar" (*WA* 35:338).

[20]The controversy as to exactly which Lutheran songbook appeared in print first need not detain us here, although it seems to fascinate scholars in the field. There are four possibilities: the *Achtlieder buch* in Nürnberg, two *Enchiridien* in Erfurt, and the *Gesangbuch* in Wittenberg. But as they all appeared in 1524, their ordering seems a quibble to our purposes. Textual evidence would indicate that the Wittenberg *Gesangbuch* was, chronologically, the last of the four. See *WA* 35:5–25 for the discussion.

[21]Ulrich Asper, *Aspekte zum Werden der deutschen Liedsätze in Johann Walters <Geistlichem Gesangbüchlein> (1524–1551)* (Baden-Baden: Verlag Valentin Koerner, 1986), 51–52. discusses the extent of Walter's role in compiling this collection and concludes that it was considerable. This conclusion seems to concur with the results of most modern scholarship.

[22]Blume, *Geschichte*, 25–26.

Luther in Walter's collection,[23] we find some of those which have become his most famous; for example, "Aus tiefer Not schrei ich zu dir" ("From Deep Trouble I Cry to Thee") and "Mitten wir im Leben sind" ("While in the Midst of Life").

As to Luther's role in the production of the Wittenberg *Gesangbuch*, two assumptions would seem reasonable: that he was instrumental in helping Johann Walter assemble the collection, and that Walter exercised a compositional influence on Luther's songs, aiding Luther in the development of his own identity as a composer.[24] The melody of Luther's first song has elicited differing musicological opinions. Wilhelm Lucke characterizes it as "of a lustrous uniqueness" and "so perfect in its form" whereas Blume states: "The melody for the martyrs' song, presumably by Luther himself, does not attain the level of his greatest songs."[25] "Ein neues lied wir heben an" bears so few traces of a neophyte's work that it seems appropriate to infer some technical assistance from Walter. Lucke ascribes the song's excellence to Luther's intense interest in both the subject matter and in the historical folksong tradition,[26] both of which are decidedly contributing factors to the song's quality. But Lucke seems to view any indication that Luther had assistance with this first song as diminishing Luther's ultimate stature as a composer. Why would he not seek Walter's advice on technical matters, when he apparently thought enough of Walter to call him from Torgau to Wittenberg to compile the collection? Not only was Walter in Wittenberg—perhaps even as early as the 1523 appearance of the broadsheet—but there is compelling evidence that Luther worked closely with the printer Joseph Klug to correct this early version before it appeared in the collection.[27]

[23] *WA* 35:25.

[24] Walter Blankenburg, "Johann Walters Chorgesangbuch von 1524 in hymnologischer Sicht," *Jahrbuch für Liturgik und Hymnologie* 18 (1973/74): 65–96, argues persuasively that Johann Walter, not Luther, is responsible for the *Gesangbuch*. Of the work Blankenburg (95) says: "Das Chorgesangbuch von 1524 hat Johann Walter selbst zusammengestellt und in den Einzelheiten erarbeitet" (Johann Walter himself compiled and worked out the details of the choral song book of 1524). Asper (51) makes a similar argument. But Luther contributed twenty-four songs and a preface to the edition, so it is difficult to envision Walter working in Wittenberg on the collection without Luther's assistance in some form. Böhme (477) speaks of the melody of Luther's first song as "unter Beihilfe Walters vollendet" (completed with Walter's assistance).

[25] *WA* 35:94; Lucke's original calls the song "von so glänzender Eigenart" and "in der Form so vollendet." Blume, *Geschichte*, 26: "Nicht auf der Höhe seiner größten Lieder steht...die wahrscheinlich von Luther selbst stammenden Weise zum Märtyrerlied."

[26] *WA* 35:94–95.

[27] The fact that Luther corrected the broadsheet is an essential part of Lucke's explanation for the divergencies between the various texts of this song, which I discuss below. See *WA* 35:94. On Johann Walter, see the entry by Walter Blankenburg in *Musik in Geschichte und Gegenwart* (Kassel: Bärenreiter, 1968), 14:192–201.

"Ein neues Lied wir heben an" (number 6 in the Wittenberg *Gesangbuch*; number 25 in the Erfurt *Enchiridion*) deals with the public burning, on the marketplace in Brussels on 1 July 1523, of two Augustinian monks from Antwerp, Heinrich Vos and Johannes van den Esschen, condemned to death for their adherence to the new evangelical teachings.[28] Originally from the monastery in Eisleben, Luther's hometown, the monks transferred to Antwerp, where they persisted in their heretical teaching. These men became the first two martyrs to the evangelical cause and the first victims in the Netherlands of the Inquisition, introduced into that region by Charles V in April 1522.[29] On 6 October 1522, Margarete von Habsburg, Charles' aunt and governor (*Statthalterin*) of the Netherlands, ordered the inhabitants of the Augustinian closter in Antwerp arrested.[30] Many were able to flee, some recanted, but three men held fast to their convictions: while Lambert Thorn requested time to consider his theological position, the other two were burned at the stake. Their deaths elicited from Luther in early August 1523 a great outpouring of sympathy to the Christians of the Netherlands in the form of a letter, whose intensity must stem, at least partially, from the victims' being fellow Augustinians.[31] Luther had expected to be the first martyr to the evangelical cause: "Ich vermeint, ich sollte ja der erste sein, der um dieses heiligen Evangeliums wegen sollte gemartert werden; aber ich bin des nit würdig gewesen!"[32] Intended for publication rather than actual transmission to the faithful in the Netherlands, the letter is remarkable for its tone of vindication: in this martyrdom Luther saw confirmation of the validity of his preaching of the

---

[28]Variants of the monks' names appear in some of the literature on the subject. Kemper, *Deutsche Lyrik*, 1:176, refers to them as "Henricus Vos" and "Johannes Esch." Hildegard Hebenstreit-Wilfert, "Märtyrerflugschriften der Reformationszeit," in *Flugschriften als Massenmedium der Reformationszeit: Beiträge zum Tübinger Symposion 1980*, ed. Hans-Joachim Köhler (Stuttgart: Klett-Cotta, 1981), 400, opts for "Heinrich Voes" and "Johann van den Esschen." In *Luther: Man between God and the Devil* (New York and London: Yale University Press, 1989), Heiko A. Oberman identifies (265) the two as Johann von Essen and Heinrich Vos and indicates that they were originally from Eisleben. I adhere to the form of the names as they appear in the protocol of Johann Pascha, the Inquisitor at their trial, which is also the form used in the Weimar edition of Luther's works (*WA*: 35:91). It is interesting how often these names become mangled in transmission. John M. Todd, *Luther: A Life* (New York: Crossroads, 1982), 251, lists them as Heinrich Vries and Johann Esch.

[29]Scholars have thoroughly investigated the details of the case. See, for example, Berger, 61, and *WA* 35:91–92.

[30]See Hebenstreit-Wilfert, 397, for a depiction of events.

[31] *WA* 12:77.

[32] *WA* 12:74. "I thought I would be the first to be martyred for this holy gospel, but I wasn't worthy of it."

gospel.[33] In composing the song, he echoed both the sentiments and the words of this letter.[34]

Written little more than a month after the event, the song is highly topical and emotional in its subject matter. Luther's musical response to the event acknowledges his tacit admission that the medium of popular song would provide the most effective means of addressing his intended audience. By the third decade of the sixteenth century, broadsheets were capable of spreading songs rapidly. The printed form, however, did not restrict their scope, since they could travel from mouth to mouth much faster than the broadsheet itself could circulate.

As one would expect of an experienced polemicist who quickly became a consummate lyricist and composer, Luther constructed his ballad as an argument aimed directly at advancing the evangelical cause. The original broadsheet title, "Ein lied von den zween Merterern Christi, zu Brüssel von den Sophisten von Löuen verbrandt," changed quickly in the Wittenberg *Gesangbuch* of 1524 into "Ein neues Lied wir heben an," doubtless because the symbolic implications in the new title better connote the novelty and innovation of Luther's religious message.[35] The revised title also associates the song firmly with the genre of the already extant *historisches Ereignislied*, a flourishing folksong tradition, in which many broadsheet song titles begin by stressing the newness of their topics, thereby demanding their audience's attention. Among such contemporary historical songs we find: "Ain news lied von dem Wirtenbergischen krieg" (1519), "Ein new Lied von der stat Rottenberg an der thawber / und von vertreibung der Juden do selbst" (1520), "Ain schön lied new gemacht von dem Türken" (1521), "Ein hüpsch neü lied von der Stat genna" (presumably "Genua"; 1522), and "Ein hubsch news lied wie drey / Fürsten wider den Frantzen gezogen seind" (1523).[36] Some songs closely parallel Luther's in the construction of the initial line: "Ein news lied von dem Hertzog von Wirttenberg" (1519) has as its opening: "Ain newes liedlein heb ich an / zusingen yetz zu dyßer frist...."[37] The retitling of the song

---

[33] *WA* 12:75.

[34] *WA* 35:93. Kemper, *Deutsche Lyrik*, 1:176 maintains that Luther enclosed a copy of his song with the letter to the Netherlands, but I can find no substantiation for this belief.

[35] The original broadsheet title continues, "Geschehen im jar MDXXII," a misprint for 1523. Cf. Böhme, 477.

[36] Brednich, *Die Liedpublizistik*, 2:70–74, contains these and many additional titles. The titles translate as follows: "A new song about the Württemberg war" (1519), "A new song about the city of Rotenburg ob der Tauber and the expulsion of the Jews there" (1520), "A beautiful and new song about the Turks" (1521), "A new and pretty song about the city of Genua" (1522), and "A new and pretty song on how three princes attacked the French" (1523).

[37] Brednich, *Die Liedpublizistik*, 2:68. "A new song about the Duke of Württemberg," whose first

enabled Luther both to stress its connection to a popular folk tradition and also to allude to the novelty of the message, for he himself was indeed singing a new song in his apocalyptical message. Moreover, the adjective "neu" contrasts pointedly with "alt," the descriptor Luther regularly connects with the devil in such expressions as "der alte Feind," so that ultimately the title suggests a tension between God and the devil, the new and the old theological positions.

Stanza 1 characterizes the event in Brussels in positive terms as evidence of the miraculous deeds of God: He has permitted the event to occur, thereby underscoring His *wundermacht*.[38] By implication, God also acknowledges Luther's evangelical position: In Brussels He accomplishes His work "durch zwen junge knaben" (two boys), whereas Luther functions as His tool in the task of awakening humankind to the imminent arrival of the Last Day. Though unstated, this implied analogy cannot have failed to impress perceptive listeners. In contending "hier geht es letztlich um eine Gottestat, nicht um eine Heldentat; hier ist Gottes Lob und Ehre im Blick, nicht Menschenruhm," the stanza captures the linkage between human deeds and divine guidance which lies at the core of Luther's theological message.[39] The second stanza names the two monks, Johannes and Heinrich, asserts their innocence, and elevates them to the status of martyrs. The initial two stanzas thus skillfully create an interest in the details of the martyrdom by supplying the event's essential components, the where-what-who that modern readers expect of newspaper reporting. The first martyr, "der erst recht wol Johannes heißt" (appropriately named Johannes), pointedly recalls John the Baptist, who served to herald the coming of Christ. In like manner, Johannes van den Esschen proclaims the Second Coming of Christ, an integral part of Luther's evangelical message with its apocalyptic context. Martyrdom was one of the most select callings in the early days of the Roman Catholic Church, and stanza 2 sets the two monks firmly among those of unshakable faith: They have merited the crown of martyrdom because they have died for the Word, as interpreted by Luther, thus vindicating his theological position. Martyrdom legitimizes the evangelical cause: "Gott gelobt und in ewikeit gebenedeyet, das

---

line runs "Now I'll begin to sing a new little song."

[38]I include Luther's song and an English translation from Ulrich S. Leupold, ed., *Luther's Works, 53: Liturgy and Hymns* (Philadelphia: Fortress Press, 1965), 214–16, at the end of this article.

[39]As quoted by Kemper, *Deutsche Lyrik,* 1:177 from Martin Rössler, "Ein neues Lied wir heben an: Protestsong Martin Luthers," in *Reformation und Praktische Theologie: Festschrift für W. Jetter,* ed. H. M. Müller and D. Rössler (Göttingen, 1983), 221: "Finally, it is here a matter of a deed by God and not an heroic deed; the focus here in on the praise and honor due God and not man's glory."

wyr erlebt haben rechte heyligen und warhafftige merterer zu sehen und zu hören, die wyr bißher so viel falscher heyligen erhebt und angebetet haben."[40] Luther further views these deaths as a welcome sign from God that his initiatives are beginning to bear fruit: "Dank sei Christus, der endlich angefangen hat, eine Frucht meiner, vielmehr seiner Verkündigung zu zeitigen in dem er neue Martyrer schafft...."[41]

The following two stanzas identify "der alte feind" as the Sophists (read: Scholastics) of Louvain and catalog their iniquities. In characterizing the Scholastics as "der alte feind," a designation for Satan found in Matt. 13:39, Luther is clearly associating them with the forces of error and evil. Despite their "sweet and sour singing" and their many attempts to pressure the two monks, the Scholastics could not wring from them a refutation of the Word. Stanza 5 describes the monks' willingness to undergo expulsion from their monastery and degradation—a process removing them from priestly orders—rather than to recant. Better to escape Satan's scoffs and mumming pranks than to submit to the hypocrisy that reigns in monasteries, a theme the sixth stanza amplifies further by castigating the mendacity of the clergy and lauding the two monks' ability to rise above human weakness (*menschentant*). In these two stanzas, the devil represents the root of evil, the opponent of the evangelical message, as indeed he does in many other works by Luther. Luther's songs in particular develop a mythology of the devil—"der alte Feind"—in which man regularly confronts entanglement in the devil's "Spiel," a term closely identified with Satan's attempts to lure mankind into sin.[42] Music itself provides a means of combating the devil: "Der schönsten und herrlichsten Gaben Gottes eine ist die Musica. Der ist der Satan sehr feind, damit man viel Anfechtunge und böse Gedanken vertreibet. Der Teufel erharret ihr nicht."[43] And in the texts of his songs, e.g., "Ein feste Burg ist unser Gott" and "Sie ist mir lieb die werde magd," Luther repeatedly sketches an "alt/ neu" dualism, a juxtaposition in which the adjective "alt" regularly alludes to the devil.[44] The world is by nature sinful, subject to deception by the

---

[40] *WA* 12:78. "God be praised and blessed eternally that we have lived to see and hear holy and true martyrs, since up to now we have elevated and worshipped so many false saints."

[41] Letter of 22/23 July 1523 to Spalatin in *WA Briefwechsel* 3:115. Cf. Oberman, *Luther*, 265. "Thanks be to Christ Who has at last begun to bring to fruition my—or, better said, His—preaching by producing new martyrs...."

[42] Patrice Veit, *Das Kirchenlied in der Reformation Martin Luthers: Eine thematische und semantische Untersuchung* (Stuttgart: Franz Steiner, 1986), 141.

[43] *WA Tischreden* 1:968. "One of the most beautiful and glorious of God's gifts is music. Satan finds it inimical because with it one can ward off temptations and evil thoughts. The devil doesn't expect it."

[44] Veit, *Das Kirchenlied*, 141.

devil—"die welt er gar betreuget" (the world he so befooleth)—and so his success at misleading the established Church comes as no surprise.

Stanza 7 describes the monks' refusal to change their minds when confronted with a written statement of traditional Christian beliefs. Men are not infallible, Luther tells us, and the Church can indeed err: "man muß allein Gott gleuben" (we should trust God alone). The eighth stanza depicts the brave death of the two monks in ecstatic terms: They go to their fates with joy in their hearts, singing God's praises, a validation that Luther's message, as he noted, had begun finally to bear fruit. That he sees martyrdom as a measure of success alerts us that at least Luther himself did not view growth in popularity as the standard by which to gauge the progress of the Reformation.[45] Stanza 8 logically concludes the narration of the auto-da-fé in Brussels: what follows draws these events into a wider symbolic and highly editorialized context.

Up to this point in the song, the texts as they appear in the Wittenberg *Gesangbuch* and the Erfurt *Enchiridion* are identical, except for nonessential textual variations due to printing conventions.[46] But at this juncture the *Gesangbuch* inserts two additional stanzas not included in the version on the original broadsheet or in the *Enchiridion*. As a result, the *Gesangbuch* version of the song contains twelve stanzas, whereas the other two renditions contain only ten. In the Weimar edition of Luther's works, Lucke argues convincingly that Luther intended these two additional stanzas as an alternative or new conclusion to the song, rather than an insertion in the text, but that through a printing error the song retained both endings.[47] From his study of the provenance of the *Gesangbuch*, Lucke argues that the printer, Joseph Klug, working from the broadsheet version, must have overlooked Luther's—perhaps faint—deletion marks on the last two stanzas.

The content of the song tends to support the view that Luther did not envision stanzas 9 and 10 as an addition. There is a contradiction inherent in the sentiments of stanza 9 and stanza 11. Stanza 9 depicts the Louvain Scholastics as ashamed of their deed, which they make every effort to hide. The text reminds us that just as Cain is unable to escape responsibility for the murder of Abel, so the perpetrators of this deed cannot go undetected or unpunished: "doch kann der geist nicht schweigen hie" (the spirit cannot

---

[45]See Oberman, *Luther,* 265.

[46]Böhme (477) describes the orthography of the *Enchiridion* as "schreckbar" and uses instead a 1545 version of the song in his collection. But as far as I can see, the orthography merely reflects printing conventions of the times, which include gemination marks above vowels in place of a concluding letter n or above an n or m to indicate a double consonant.

[47] *WA* 35:94.

be silent). Stanza 10 argues that these attempts at dissimulation are futile: The blood and ashes of the victims speak louder than words and will spread abroad knowledge of the iniquity.

Stanza 11, on the other hand, narrates the Scholastics' efforts to palliate the event. They spread the rumor that the monks had recanted at the last moment, which Luther characterizes as a brazen lie: "Noch laßen sie ir lügen nicht / den großen mort zu schmücken" (they still won't leave their lies, told to dress up the murder). Of course, starting such a rumor would not seem the most appropriate course of action if, in fact, the Scholastics sincerely regretted their deed and were serious about obscuring the whole matter. Logic cannot have it both ways: Either the Scholastics want the whole event swept under the carpet, or they want to discredit it by spreading the rumor that the monks had recanted at the last possible moment. If the monks had indeed recanted, why then did the Inquisition burn them?

Luther's original conclusion to the ten-stanza version of the song (i.e., the current stanzas 11 and 12) addresses the issue of abjuring, an issue which became crucial as the Reformation more firmly solidified. Luther refused repeatedly to recant his own beliefs at the Reichstag at Worms (1521) and elsewhere, and even on his deathbed witnesses gathered to observe his manner of dying in case he might undergo a last-minute change of heart. Heiko A. Oberman depicts this telling scene at the beginning of his *Luther: Man between God and the Devil.*[48] A deathbed recantation by Luther, or indeed any of the major Reformation figures, would have proved disastrous for the Reformation cause, as it would have thoroughly discredited the integrity of the evangelical message. Three mendicant friars, who reportedly accompanied the Brussels martyrs to the stake as confessors, apparently started the rumor of the Augustinians' capitulation. But other eyewitnesses swiftly discounted the rumor, which Otto Clemen terms "eine nichtswürdige Verleumdung."[49] With the issue of recantation dispelled, Luther opted for a new conclusion to the song. When the printer erroneously set both conclusions, Luther may have left well enough alone, perhaps because the theme of refusing to recant was personally important to him and the integrity of the Reformation. The Wittenberg *Gesangbuch* transmitted the song in its twelve-stanza length to future generations.

From a literary perspective, the concluding stanza has much to recommend it, as it encapsulates the important apocalyptical aspect of Luther's message. The metaphor of the change of seasons graphically

---

[48]Oberman, *Luther,* 3–8.

[49]Otto Clemen, "Die ersten Märtyrer des evangelischen Glaubens," *Beiträge zur Reformationsgeschichte* 1:46–47, terms the libel "a base slander." See also *WA* 35:92

associates the ossified teachings of the traditional church with the frigid climate of winter: "der somer ist hart für der tür / der winter ist vergangen / die zarten blümlein gen erfür."[50] Drawn from Revelation, where the image of the summer is one of the Kingdom fulfilled, the twelfth stanza poetically depicts the imminent arrival of the apocalypse, the fulfillment of Luther's teachings. Just as the winter melts into warmer, more nurturing weather, so the new, revitalized belief in the Word with its apocalyptical implications is about to come to full bloom like flowers in the summer. The last couplet assures us that God, who initiated this transition, will doubtless conclude it, so that faith in the power of God's Word becomes the consoling message. Ultimately, Luther sees these concluding lines as triumphantly predicting the second advent of Christ, reason enough for him to retain them in the song.

The form of the text and the musical notation tie this song closely to the German *Volkslied* of the period: Luther was operating here within a popular genre aimed at attracting as broad an audience as possible. As there is no reason to think otherwise, we assume that Luther composed the music himself, probably with some technical assistance from Johann Walter, and chose for his message a melody whose tunefulness would compel hearers' attention.[51] The sources of the melody lie in the German *Meistersang* tradition, itself derived from the late-medieval troubadour legacy, going back as far as the songs of Peire Vidal.[52] But we are safe in ascribing originality to Luther's creation insofar as most melodies of the period, like this one, rely heavily on citations to already existing compositions. Even so weighty an authority as the Weimar edition of Luther's works suggests that in this song we glimpse the Cochlaeus caricature of Luther as the folksy lute player in the tavern.[53] Luther wanted to bridge the gap between sacred and secular music and make the church song as accepted among young people as the popular tune. As he indicates in the preface to Walter's *Gesangbuch*, young people should have something worth singing about:

[50]"Summer stands just before the door, winter has ended, tender buds begin to sprout."

[51]WA 35:488; In connection with Luther's composing the music, Lucke's arguments ( WA 35:94), already summarized, make sense: The melody of the song resulted from Luther's familiarity with the folksong genre. There is general consensus that Luther composed the music. See Jenny, 14–16, for the argument.

[52]See Ursula Aarburg, "Zu den Lutherliedern im jonischen Oktavraum," *Jahrbuch für Liturgik und Hymnologie* 5 (1960): 125–31.

[53]WA 35:488; Cochlaeus trenchantly characterizes Luther as "ein zweiter Orpheus ... obschon er noch Tonsur und Kutte trug" ("a second Orpheus...although he still wore the tonsure and the cowl"), drawing all attention to himself in a pub. Cf. Adolf Herte, *Die Lutherkommentare des Johannes Cochläus: Kritische Studien zur Geschichtschreibung im Zeitalter der Glaubensspaltung* (Münster: Aschendorffschen Verlangsbuchhandlung, 1935), 283.

"die iugent, die doch sonst soll und mus ynn der Musica und andern rechten künsten erzogen werden,…da mit sie der bul lieder und fleyschlichen gesenge los worde, und an der selben stat, ettwas heylsames lernete."[54]

Luther weaves the scanty facts of the event in Brussels into a polemic to support his still not fully established theological position. In 1523–24, the evangelical Reformation was anything but assured, which may further explain Luther's apparent willingness to let the song stand as printed in the *Gesangbuch*. Martyrdom to the Word was welcome—indeed greeted jubilantly by Luther—even if his cause still lacked clear definition. At the very least, these martyrs underscored Luther's intense desire for signs of the success of his apocalyptic preaching: If educated brother Augustinians were willing to die for the saving Word before the End, Luther's message must have received the vindication he so avidly sought.

In this first hymn we also find features associated with mass media propaganda. Despite the sometimes surprising speed with which news traveled in the early sixteenth century, Luther could not have known precisely what had transpired at the auto-da-fé in Brussels. Thanks to an early, anonymous broadsheet on the event, *Der Actus und handlung / der degradation und ver / prennung der Christlichen / dreyen Ritter und Mer / terer, Augustiner or / dens geschehen zu / Brüssel* (1523), Luther originally believed that the auto-da-fé involved three monks rather than two, and wrote accordingly to Spalatin.[55] That Lambert Thorn sought a stay of execution and was not burned at the stake until three days after his fellow monks, was not immediately clear to residents of Wittenberg. Garbled in transmission, the details of the event became clear only in time, but time was what Luther lacked if he wanted to capture the imagination and fervor of his growing adherents with the news of an event he viewed as a substantiation of his message. While the sequence of the occurrence sketched in stanza 8 is probably accurate, the description of the two friars marching to their deaths, "mit freuden" and "mit Gottes lob und singen" certainly sounds like editorial embellishment of the facts. The reports speak of the victims as "standhaft" (unflinching) and "mutig" (valiant) but to describe them as facing a horrible death by fire with joy and singing may contain a measure of exaggeration for rhetorical purposes. The image does, however, connect these martyrs symbolically with those of the early Christian church, whom we often see facing death not only willingly, but joyfully.

---

[54]Wackernagel's *Bibliographie*, 543, reproduces the preface (Vorrhede). "The young should and must also be educated in music and the other arts, so that they can dispense with amorous songs and carnal music and instead learn something wholesome."

[55]*WA* 35:92.

Such a depiction legitimizes and dignifies their deaths and, by implication, the beliefs for which they sacrificed themselves. Luther's tone of jubilation at what he saw as justification of his preaching is clearly detectable in this characterization.

His use of the material casts Luther as consummate publicist, to which undertaking he also brings his considerable talent for musical composition. He spread the news of this sign of success as quickly as possible, combining all the advantages of the broadsheet with the orality of the vernacular song. Speed was his goal, and he took full advantage of all the contemporary means of assuring rapid dissemination of the news.[56] Whatever the facts of the matter, Luther saw the point: He could use this unanticipated event to broadcast the joyous message that people were willing to die for their faith in the Word. The event constituted for him a sign from God that his apocalyptic message had validity. Furthermore, this song also allowed the reformer to highlight the need for unswerving loyalty to the Word, and to underline the glorious eternal rewards attached to such loyalty. Ultimately it makes little difference whether we term this song *ein weltliches Lied, ein weltliches Volkslied, ein Ereignislied, ein historisches Lied, ein historisches Ereignislied,* or *ein Zeitungslied.*[57] Categorizing it seems less useful than our recognition that, for this sensational event, the news of which had not yet reached the general public, Luther pointedly chose the sixteenth-century medium best calculated to reach the widest possible audience in the shortest time—the printed song sheet.

This first of Luther's songs evidences the tension in the early modern period between sacred and secular music. Intent on responding to Müntzer's surprising progress in developing a German liturgy for the mass, Luther saw himself overtaken in his reform movement by more radical elements.[58] But instead of reacting by designing his own musical liturgy, Luther seized the opportunity presented by events in Brussels to exploit this sign of the success of his interpretation of the Word. Having composed his response, Luther observed the impact this song made on the general public and devoted himself, for an extended period, to further musical interpretations of his message. Ironically the popular folksong tradition, among the most unsophisticated of popular art forms, lent itself surprisingly well to disseminating the evangelical standpoint on sophisticated

[56]Leupold, *Luther's Works,* 53:212: "[Luther] availed himself of the mass media most commonly used in his day for broadcasting important news."

[57]Brednich, *Die Liedpublizistik,* 1:83f. explores these categories in detail. In the order given in the text, these categories are: The worldly song, the worldly folksong, the song which depicts an event, the historical song, the historical event song, and the newspaper song.

[58]Kemper, *Deutsche Lyrik,* 1:175.

theological issues. "Der größte Meistersinger," while flattering his performance skills, is certainly too limited an epithet for Luther, as it fails to integrate his talent as a polemicist into his role in legitimizing the song genre.
While recognizing his musical talents, we must go further and also
acknowledge his practical skills as a publicist in expanding the use of secular song to "spread the news" of his teaching. It was this talent, and not the
melodies, which led to what Luther would have viewed as the ultimate
compliment from the Jesuits: "Luthers Lieder [haben] mehr Seelen umge-
bracht, als seine Schriften und Reden."[59]

---

[59]Blume, *Geschichte*, 27, "Luther's songs have killed more souls than his writings and speeches."

## EIN NEUES LEID[1]

Ein neues lied wir heben an,
das walt Gott unser herre,
zu singen was Gott hat getan
zu seinem lob und ere
zu Brüssel in dem Niderland
wol durch zwen junge knaben
hat er sein wundermacht bekant,
die er mit seinen gaben
so reichlich hat gezieret.

Der erst recht wol Johannes heißt,
so reich an Gottes hulden.
sein bruder Heinrich, nach dem geist
ein rechter Christ on schulden,
von diser welt gescheiden sind,
sie han die kron erworben,
recht wie die rechten Gottes kind
für sein wort sind gestorben,
sein mertrer sind sie worden.

Der alte feint sie fangen ließ,
erschreckt sie lang mit dreuen;
das wort Gotts man sie leugnen hieß,
mit list auch wolt sie teuben.
von Löven der sophisten vil,
mit irer kunst verloren,
versamlet er zu disem spil.
der geist sie macht zu toren,
 sie kunden nichts gewinnen.

Sie sungen süß, sie sungen saur,
versuchten manche listen;
die knaben stunden wie ein maur,
verachten die sophisten.
den alten feint das ser verdroß,
daß er war überwunden
von solchen jungen, er so groß,
er ward vol zorn von stunden,
gedacht sie zu verbrennen.

## A NEW SONG[2]

A new song here shall be begun,
The Lord God help our singing!
Of what our God himself hath done,
Praise, honor to him bringing.
At Brussels in the Netherlands
By two boys, martyrs youthful
He showed the wonders of his hands,
Whom he with favor truthful
So richly hath adorned.

The first right fitly John was named,
So rich he in God's favor;
His brother Henry—one unblamed,
Whose salt lost not its savor.
From this world they are gone away,
The diadem they've gained;
Honest, like God's good children, they
For his word life disdained,
And have become his martyrs.

The old arch-fiend did them immure
With terrors did enwrap them.
He bade them God's dear Word abjure,
With cunning he would trap them:
From Louvain many sophists came,
In their curst nets to take them,
By him are gathered to the game:
The Spirit fools doth make them—
They could get nothing by it.

Oh! they sang sweet, and they sang sour;
Oh! they tried every double;
The boys they stood firm as a tower,
And mocked the sophists' trouble.
The ancient foe it filled with hate
That he was thus defeated
By two such youngsters—he, so great!
His wrath grew sevenfold heated,
He laid his plans to burn them.

---

[1]*Das Babstische Gesangbuch von 1545*, facsimile edition published by Bärenreiter in Kassel (1988), with modernized orthography.

[2]Ulrich S. Leupold , ed., *Luther's Works*, 53: *Liturgy and Hymns* (Philadelphia: Fortress Press, 1965) 214-16.

Sie raubten in das klosterkleid,
die weih sie in auch namen;
die knaben waren des bereit,
sie sprachen frölich amen,
sie dankten irem vater, Gott,
daß sie los solten werden
des teufels larvenspiel und spot,
darin durch falsche berden
die welt er gar betreuget.

Da schickt Gott durch sein gnad also,
daß sie, recht priester worden,
sich selbs im musten opfern do
und gen im christen orden,
der welt ganz abgestorben sein,
die heuchelei ablegen,
zum himel komen frei und rein,
die müncherei ausfegen,
und menschentant hie laßen.

Man schreib in für ein brieflein klein,
das hieß man sie selbs lesen,
die stück sie zeigten alle drein,
was ir glaub war gewesen.
der höchste irrtum dieser war:
man muß allein Gott gleuben,
der mensch leugt und treugt imerdar,
 dem sol man nichts vertrauen;
des musten sie verbrennen.

Zwei große feur sie zündten an,
die knaben sie herbrachten,
es nam groß wunder jederman,
daß sie solch pein verachten.
mit freuden sie sich gaben drein,
mit Gottes lob und singen.
der mut ward den sophisten klein
für disen neuen dingen,
daß sich Gott ließ so merken.

Their cloister-garments off they tore,
Took off their consecrations;
All this the boys were ready for,
They said Amen with patience.
To God their Father they gave thanks
That they would soon be rescued
From Satan's scoffs and mumming pranks,
With which, in falsehood masked,
The world he so befooleth.

Then gracious God did grant to them
To pass true priesthood's border,
And offer up themselves to him,
And enter Christ's own order,
Unto the world to die outright,
With falsehood made a schism,
And come to heaven all pure and white,
To monkery be the besom,
And leave men's toys behind them.

They wrote for them a paper small,
And made them read it over;
The parts they showed them therein all
Which their belief did cover.
Their greatest fault was saying this:
"In God we should trust solely;
For man is always full of lies,
We should distrust him wholly:"
So they must burn to ashes.

Two huge great fires they kindled then,
The boys they carried to them;
Great wonder seized on every man,
For with contempt they view them.
To all with joy they yielded quite,
With singing and God-praising;
The sophs had little appetite
For these new things so dazing.
Which God was thus revealing.

Der schimpf sie nu gereuet hat,
sie woltens gern schön machen.
sie türn nicht rümen sich der tat,
sie bergen fast die sachen.
die schand im herzen beißet sie,
und klagens iren genoßen;
doch kan der geist nicht schweigen hie.
des Habels blut vergoßen
es muß den Cain melden.

Die aschen wil nicht laßen ab,
sie streubt in allen landen,
hie hilft kein bach, loch, grub noch
    grab,
sie macht den feind zu schanden.
die er im leben durch den mort
zu schweigen hat gedrungen,
die muß er tot an allem ort,
mit aller stimm und zungen
gar frölich laßen singen

Noch laßen sie ir lügen nicht,
den großen mort zu schmücken.
sie geben für ein falsch gedicht,
ir gewißen tut sie drücken.
die heiligen Gotts auch nach dem tod
 von in gelestert werden;
sie sagen, in der letzten not
die knaben noch auf erden
sich solln haben umbkeret.

Die laß man liegen imerhin,
sie habens keinen fromen.
wir sollen danken Gott darin,
sein wort ist widerkomen.
der somer ist hart für der tür,
der winter ist vergangen,
die zarten blümlin gen erfür.
der das hat angefangen,
der wirt es wol vollenden. Amen.

They now repent the deed of blame,
Would gladly gloze it over;
They dare not glory in their shame,
The facts almost they cover.
In their hearts gnaweth infamy—
They to their friends deplore it;
The Spirit cannot silent be:
Good Abel's blood out-poured
Must still besmear Cain's forehead.

Leave off their ashes never will;
Into all lands they scatter;
Stream, hole, ditch, grave—nought
    keeps them still
With shame the foe they spatter.
Those whom in life with bloody hand
He drove to silence triple,
When dead, he them in every land,
In tongues of every people,
Must hear go gladly singing.

But yet their lies they will not leave,
To trim and dress the murther;
The fable false which out they gave,
Shows conscience grinds them further.
God's holy ones, e'en after death,
They still go on belying;
They say that with their latest breath,
The boys, in act of dying,
Repented and recanted.

Let them lie on for evermore—
No refuge so is reared;
For us, we thank our God therefore,
His word has reappeared.
Even at the door is summer nigh,
The winter now is ended,
The tender flowers come out and spy;
His hand when once extended
Withdraws not till he's finished. Amen.

# CHARLES V AS TRIUMPHATOR

## Bonner Mitchell

THE RENAISSANCE RECUPERATION OF THE ROMAN TRIUMPH seems a relatively minor movement when compared to the revival of the classical genres in literature or that of the Greco-Roman orders in architecture. Examples of triumphs were scattered in time and place, although they make a substantial list if one considers all of Europe for the sixteenth century. The experience was rare for its protagonists as well as for spectators. Sovereigns, for example, normally made triumphal entries into cities only soon after accession and—much more rarely—after important victories and conquests. Popes usually had a *possesso* parade after their election. In two rare sixteenth-century cases, they too were given grand entries to mark conquests. Princely states seldom saw triumphal entries except on the occasion of weddings. The scarcity of such events is, however, largely compensated for by the number of people involved, with long processions and great crowds of spectators, and by the powerful impressions made upon witnesses and participants alike. Far more people saw triumphal entries than ever attended Renaissance comedies or tragedies, and for most of them the experience was more memorable.

Of all the triumphal protagonists in the Cinquecento, Charles V was the undoubted champion. Depending upon strictness of definition, the number of his triumphal entries may be placed at close to three dozen, several times more than those of his contemporary rivals Francis I and Henry VIII. His territories were vast and he conscientiously undertook to visit most important cities at least once. In addition, he was received triumphally as a guest in London, in several French cities, and in several Italian ones not under his authority. He also met ceremonially in various cities with Henry VIII, with Francis I, and with Popes Clement VII and Paul III. Charles was proud of the breadth of his travel and is reported to have told the Estates-General in Brussels at the end of his reign that he had made nine journeys to Germany, six to Spain, seven to Italy, ten to the Low

95

Countries, four to France, two to England, and two to Africa.[1] A book would be needed to deal systematically with all his entries;[2] I shall limit myself here to looking at a selected number that illustrate the movement of classical revival in themes and decorations and also the extraordinary variety of political circumstances, i.e., the variety of Charles's relations to different polities.

Much of the pageantry of his receptions was medieval in origin, especially in the North and in the early years of the reign, but classical forms eventually became common in most places. The opportunity of receiving an *imperator* fired the imagination of the humanists whom city authorities increasingly charged with the planning of such manifestations. Classical forms were used in royal and papal entries as well, but the imperial context was unique.

Before his exaltation by the German Electors, Charles had already been given grand entries into Bruges and several other Flemish cities, and had been received as king in the Castilian capital of Valladolid. The 1515 reception in Bruges was one of the grandest of the entire century and one of the best documented.[3] There were extremely interesting architectural decorations in the streets (hereafter referred to as *apparati*), some of them related to the elaborate stage settings of late medieval theater. There were also *tableaux vivants*, in which living actors stood for historical, biblical, mythological, or allegorical figures, and sometimes held placards with explanatory words, or recited verses which the entering party paused to hear. These *tableaux* were destined to disappear from entries as classical revival progressed, although they were very expressive and might easily have been adapted to new themes.[4] A glimpse of what was to come was provided in 1515 by three Italian nations or colonies of merchants, resident in Bruges: the Genoese, the Florentines, and the Lucchesi. Each

[1]Quoted by Louis Prosper Gachard in introducing his edition of the "*Journal des voyages de Charles-Quint of Jean de Vandenesse*," in *Collection des voyages des souverains des Pays-Bas* (Brussels: F. Hayez, 1874–82), 2:xxviii.

[2]There is no such comprehensive study, but in 1956 a colloquium was held on festivals in Charles's time, and its papers edited by Jean Jacquot as *Les Fêtes de la Renaissance II: Fêtes et cérémonies au temps de Charles Quint* (Paris: C.N.R.S., 1960). Several papers in the volume (referred to hereafter as *Fêtes II*) concern specific entries, and Jacquot provides a "Panorama des fêtes et cérémonies du règne" which, although not complete, has a great amount of information.

[3]There appeared an unusually full account, with woodcuts: Rémy Du Puys, *La Triumphante et solennelle entrée faite sur le nouvel et joyeux advènement de treshault trespuissant et tresexcellent Prince Monsieur Charles, prince des Hespaignes En sa ville de Bruges lan V cens et XV le XVIII^e iour dapvril apres Pasques* (Paris: Gilles de Gourmont, 1515). Reproduced in facsimile with introd. by Sidney Anglo, in the series Renaissance Triumphs and Magnificences (Amsterdam: Theatrum Orbis Terrarum, n.d.).

[4]See the regrets of Jacquot on this subject, in "Panorama," *Fêtes II*, 475.

nation had erected a triumphal arch in what it thought to be the ancient Roman style.

When Charles arrived at Valladolid in 1517 after a difficult sea journey from Flanders and a land journey across the Asturias, the diarist Laurent Vital thought the young king's costume and accouterment more splendid (*gorgias*) and triumphant than for any of the Flemish entries, and indeed, found the whole procession to be dazzling in its splendor.[5] As for the "histories, lightings and such delightful novelties and good inventions" set up by the local citizens, however, they were quite inferior to those at home because they were not "in style," or "in the proper style" ("ilz ne sont point stillez"). Later in his account, despite the presence of some simple *apparati* at gates and intersections, Vital makes a more general observation: "Now, what the city and its inhabitants did for this entry...wasn't much, because they have no experience in such work...."[6]

After hearing of his election to the throne of Charlemagne in 1519, Charles sailed back to the Low Countries, and proceeded thence to Aachen.[7] His entry into the imperial city on 22 October involved a grand procession with brilliant costumes, but there did not seem to have been triumphal *apparati*, and the elaborate ceremonies of consecration next day were feudal in tone rather than antique, despite the presence of imperial terminology.

After two years in his northern possessions, Charles headed back to Spain in 1522. En route, he stopped off in England to court Henry VIII as an ally against Francis I. The entry into London, like that into Bruges seven years earlier, offered splendid examples of late medieval street decorations and theatrical presentations.[8] There were eight pageants, some of them again commissioned by colonies of foreign merchants, who were always expected to spend freely on such occasions. The Italians, this time, missed a chance to feature neoclassical motifs in favor of a genealogical tree. Each pageant featured live actors, who sometimes recited Latin verses to the two sovereigns. The verses probably also could be seen in written

[5]See Vital's "Relation du premier voyage de Charles-Quint en Espagne," edited by Louis Prosper Gachard and Charles Piot in *Voyages des souverains des Pays-Bas*, 3:150–55.

[6]"Or, de ce que la ville et les habitants firent à cette entrée, ce n'estoit point grant chose, à cause que en telle besoigne ne sont point accostumés...." "Relation," 154.

[7]For the pageantry in Aachen, see Hermann Heusch, "Le Sacre de Charles Quint à Aix-la-Chapelle," in *Fêtes II*, 161–68.

[8]There are numerous contemporary accounts of the occasion and several modern studies. I have used C. R. Baskerville, "William Lily's Verse for the Entry of Charles V into London, *The Huntingdon Library Bulletin* 9 (1936): 1–14; Robert Withington, *English Pageantry: An Historical Outline* (Cambridge: Harvard University Press, 1918), 174–79; and Jean Robertson, "L'Entrée de Charles Quint à Londres, en 1522," in *Fêtes II*, 169–81.

form on placards. One inscription was on display at every pageant: *Carolus Henricus Vivant. Defensor Uterq.* [ue] *Henricus Fidei. Carolus Ecclesie.*[9]

Pope Leo X had recently granted Henry the title Defender of the Faith, kept by British sovereigns to this day, while Charles was the defender of the Church as successor to Charlemagne. The inventor of the inscription, probably the poet William Lyly or his friend Sir Thomas More, found a way to present the two monarchs on an equal footing. The emperor was impressed by the pomp of his reception, although he apparently would have preferred to have the sums expended offered to him as a loan. On 6 July 1522 he embarked at Southampton for Spain.

During the six years that passed before he undertook another foreign journey, the emperor, Rey Carlos I in Spain, carried out much domestic travel, and some entailed more or less grand urban entries. The most festive occasion was provided in 1526 by his marriage to Isabel of Portugal, celebrated in Seville.[10] There were separate grand entries of the bride and the groom. Seven arches with some architectural complexity showed Charles himself and various allegorical, historical, or mythological personages. Most representations were doubtless painted rather than sculpted, but there was some sculpture. Each of the first five arches was dedicated to a virtue, and on top of each there was a figuration of the emperor as an example of that virtue. Each arch had a Latin dedication, followed by verses celebrating Charles's devotion to the relevant virtue. Spanish translations were provided on the other side of the construction. Seville's street decorations were thus of considerable sophistication and show a familiarity with classical mythology and iconography which was probably due to Italian influence.[11] Spanish entries often involved chariots as well as simple arches, but these vehicles were closer to the wagons of religious processions than to the chariots of ancient triumphs. For an entry of the emperor into Saragoza in 1533, one wagon will show the martyrdom of Saint Engracia, one the Ascension, and one the Last Judgment.[12] In fact, the true triumphal chariot, carrying the *triumphator*, found little favor in the High and Late Renaissance, after having been used

---

[9]"Long live Charles and Henry, defenders both: Henry of the Faith, Charles of the Church."

[10]For these festivities, I have used a news publication of the time reproduced completely in *I diarii di Marino Sanuto...*, ed. Rinaldo Fulin et al., 58 vols. (Venice: Visentini, 1879–1913), 41:cols. 351–58.

[11]C. A. Marsden has pointed out that the construction of truly antique triumphal arches depended upon a revived knowledge of Roman architecture gleaned from treatises such as that of Serlio (Italian publication from 1544, in Spanish translation from 1552). "Entrées et fêtes espagnoles au XVIe siècle," in *Fêtes II*, 402–3.

[12]See the manuscript account published by Jenaro Alenda y Mira, *Relaciones de solemnidades y fiestas públicas de España* (Madrid: Sucesores de Rivadeneyra, 1903), 28–31.

for entries of Alfonso I of Naples and Borso d'Este in the Quattrocento.[13] Louis XII saw chariots with classical loads of spoils for his entries into Milan in 1507 and 1509, but on the latter occasion (after victories over the Venetians) he refused to mount a chariot himself, judging, according to one chronicler, that it was a childish thing, or a toy (cosa da giuoco).[14] Whether this reaction denoted modesty or just a faulty classical education is not clear. Later Cinquecento *triumphatores* seem to have shared Louis's attitude in the matter. Certainly Charles V would have found riding in on a chariot unbecoming. He had not the megalomania of Borso d'Este; nor probably was his passion for classical revival, although present, equal to that of Alfonso I. The chariot bearing a *triumphator* would, however, have been a more authentic revival than the triumphal arches constructed of temporary materials that were soon seen all over western Europe.

On 27 July 1529, the emperor took ship at Barcelona for Italy. It was in that country that he was to be given most of his grandest and most authentically triumphal urban entries.[15] Italy was in the vanguard of classical revival, in this domain as in others. The emperor's triumphal experiences there are interesting as well for a quite different reason, i.e., for the variety of the peninsula's polities and civic traditions. It is true that he had already had experience in such variety. In Bruges and other Flemish cities he was count of Flanders and duke of Burgundy. In Spain he was king of a recently unified realm. As kaiser in Germany and Austria, he had highly differentiated relations with various principalities and free cities. In England he had been the guest of a sovereign not subject to the Empire (as he would later be also in France). Italy, however, presented political variety in a microcosm. Charles would eventually be received there in one large kingdom subject to his own Spanish crown, that of Naples and Sicily; in the unique polity of Rome and the Papal States; and in republics and princely states with varying degrees of sovereignty. It was an open question whether Italy as a whole formed part of the Empire. Most legal scholars would have said yes, but a fiercely independent republic like Venice recognized no practical imperial sovereignty. Some ruling princes held titles of nobility granted or recognized by past emperors, while other titles

---

[13]For Trecento and Quattrocento revivals of triumphal forms, see Giovanni Carandente, *I trionfi del primo Rinascimento* (Torino: Edizioni R.A.I., 1963).

[14]Giovanni Andrea Prato, *Storia di Milano…*, ed. Cesare Cantú, in *Archivio Storico Italiano* 3 (1843): 277.

[15]Rather full bibliographies of the numerous sources and studies on these entries are given in the notes of my *The Majesty of the State: Triumphal Progresses of Foreign Sovereigns in Renaissance Italy (1494–1600)* (Florence: Olschki, 1986), 133–79. Here I supply only the sources of quotations and references to a few accounts regarding whole progresses.

derived from the pope. The doges of Venice and Genoa, referred to as princes, owed their titles to election. Dante dreamed of a reunification of Italy under the German emperor Henry VII, but few people thought in those terms during the Cinquecento.

Genoa, where Charles landed, was a very old oligarchical republic, the traditional maritime rival of Venice. Its state was, however, much less stable and had suffered such serious civil strife at the beginning of the century that the citizens had actually invited King Louis XII of France to take them under his protection. Louis happily obliged, but there were four subsequent rebellions. The final regaining of autonomy had come only in 1528, when the Genoese admiral Andrea Doria switched his naval service in the Italian Wars from Francis I to Charles. Doria (who had commanded the fleet sent to fetch Charles in Barcelona) was by far the most influential citizen in Genoa but, like the early Medici, preferred to exert his influence in an unofficial way. There was a republican government with an elected doge, eight *governatori*, and a council of four hundred. Doria was jealous of the independence of his city and would not have it taken as a Spanish colony. It was instead an ally, a small one, but unusually valuable because of Doria's services and because of the imperial loans of its bankers.

The entry into Genoa on 12 August 1529 was a maritime one, the grandest ever enjoyed by the emperor (who was never to be received in Venice).[16] A special pier had been built for his landing, covered with rich cloth. After a prolonged period of artillery salutes, Charles was rowed to the pier by velvet-clad slaves, presumably Moors, whom he then freed as a sign of *magnanimitas*. He climbed onto the pier that held the first of two (or perhaps three) triumphal arches. It was covered with painted *storie*, the principal of which showed Andrea Doria holding a naked sword in one hand and, in the other, a model of Genoa, while Charles suspended a crown over the city. Thus were figured the city's debts to its chief citizen and to its imperial guest. The issue of sovereignty may seem to have been left ambiguous, but it is likely that the support of Doria's hand was meant to imply a free citizenry, while Charles's proffered crown gave imperial sanction to republican liberties.

After passing through the arch, Charles was greeted by the doge and other members of the republican *signoria*. There were further *apparati*, including a great mobile globe with an imperial eagle on top. The emperor mounted up into the city's narrow streets on a mule, with Andrea Doria walking at his side to explain decorations and landmarks along the way.

---

[16]The main account of this first Italian trip is [Luigi Gonzaga], *Cronaca del soggiorno di Carlo V in Italia (dal 26 luglio 1529 al 25 aprile 1530)*, ed. Giacinto Romano (Milan: Hoepli, 1892).

One source states that Charles stopped at the first arch and insisted upon examining and understanding all the *storie*. No doubt he also listened attentively to Doria's commentary upon the city's monuments. This kind of courteous curiosity was one of the bases of his political charm and influence.

Apartments had been prepared for him in the Palazzo dei Signori. On future visits of the emperor and his son, Phillip, in 1548, Doria insisted that they *not* stay in the Signoria but as his guests in the new Palazzo Doria. On this first visit the seaside palace was not finished. The issue was one of great importance for republics, whose elected officials were generally required to live in the public palace during their terms of office, and Genoa was particularly sensitive in the matter. On his first visit in 1502, French king Louis XII had graciously agreed to stay in a private house, but when he returned in 1507 after putting down a rebellion, he set himself up in the Palazzo dei Signori and held a court of justice there to humiliate the citizens.

The emperor had recently concluded advantageous treaties with both King Francis I and Pope Clement VIII and except for the Turkish threat, peace seemed secure. He had come to Italy to confer with the pope and hoped also to be crowned, although plans for that were not quite set. The papal coronation of an emperor, actually rather rare in the history of the Holy Roman Empire, was an event that could seize the imagination of Europe. Instead of going to Rome where wounds from the 1527 sack by his soldiers were still open, Charles preferred to meet Clement farther north, closer to his domains in Lombardy and Germany. Bologna was chosen as the site. During the preceding century the city had had alternating periods of democratic rule, local tyranny, and papal rule, and was now fairly well settled under the last, which was exercised through a legate. There was also a subordinate government of citizens.

On 4 November Charles entered the city "en armes" and wearing a helmet topped by an imperial eagle.[17] Twelve large cannon on chariots awed the population of Bologna as the big guns of Charles VIII had done the Florentines in 1494. A second major impression given by the procession, doubtless deliberate, was of the far-flung, international character of Charles's dominions. There were military detachments of various nationalities, easily distinguished by costume.

While the arches for the pope's entry had shown a number of painted scenes from biblical history (of which the most poignantly relevant

---

[17]For a pointed modern study of the well-documented pageantry in Bologna, see Vicomte Terlinden, "La Politique italienne de Charles Quint et le «triomphe» de Bologne," in *Fêtes II*, 29–44.

showed Samuel anointing David), those for Charles's several days later had more figures from medieval and ancient history. At the Porta San Felice, medallions showed the early emperors Julius Caesar, Augustus, Vespasian, and Trajan. Inscriptions pointed out the new Caesar Augustus's duties toward Christendom (Universa Res Publica Christiana) in opposition to infidel enemies (Impiis Hostibus), i.e., Lutherans and Turks. These messages received the emperor's careful attention. Two more arches along the way to the Piazza Maggiore evoked the Christian emperors Constantine and Charlemagne, along with Charles's grandfather, Ferdinand of Spain, whose intolerance of Moors and Jews was presumably a model for dealing with religious dissent in Germany.

Although the emperor clearly wanted to impress the Bolognese and ecclesiastics with his military might, he behaved personally with extreme courtesy. At the gate he exchanged his helmet for a velvet beret, which could be doffed to cheering ladies leaning from windows. As he rode through the city under a canopy carried by members of the city government, he admired sights along the way. Four special heralds in his suite tossed silver and gold coins to the populace, demonstrating imperial *liberalitas* and promoting the *hilaritas publica* essential to triumphal entries.

The pope waited before the basilica of San Petronio on a wooden construction that resembled a grandstand. He sat on a high throne, flanked by cardinals on each side. Subtle papal ceremonialists had decided that the basilica, rather than the smaller cathedral, would stand in ceremonially for St. Peter's, and that the Palazzo Communale would be the Vatican.

The two men remained at Bologna together, in political and ecclesiastical discussions, for two and a half months before the ritual of coronation was accomplished. Papal master of ceremonies Biagio da Cesena planned the proceedings after studying precedents, especially that of Frederick III in 1452. There were two separate rituals on different days. On 22 February 1530, in the chapel of the palace, Clement placed the iron crown of Lombardy on Charles's head. For this occasion, there was no grand parade. For the more important ceremony on 24 February a raised bridge had been built from the palace to San Petronio, so crowds could see the two principals pass into the basilica. The main altar had been rearranged to resemble that of St. Peter's. After the complicated and drawn-out ceremonies, the two men came outside together. Charles held the stirrup for Clement to mount his horse and then led the animal for a short distance, doubtless in imitation of the imperial services rendered to Nicholas V by Frederick III. Emperor and pope then rode side by side through the town under the same canopy, sometimes "holding each other's hand and reasoning and laughing together."[18] At the church of San Domenico, Charles went inside for ceremonies to create new knights, while Clement headed back to the palace.

The post-coronation procession was recorded in two series of similar engravings by Robert Péril and Nicolas Hogenberg, and the latter became widely available. In contrast to the dominantly military procession of the imperial entry, this one emphasized political and ecclesiastical splendor. The assigning of roles and positions within the cortège was delicate in the extreme, and there was at least one physical fight over precedence. The imperial-papal canopy was supported by three Venetian ambassadors—a great distinction for that republic—and by three highly ranked Bolognese. One source says that the latter were replaced every so often by colleagues, so the distinction could be shared.[19] The Venetians also may have been spelled along the way. A remarkably large number of political entities figured honorably in the parade. Bologna was represented not just by papal officials but also by city fathers carrying the traditional banner of "Libertas," and by students and professors from the university in academic dress. For the Roman republican government on the Campidoglio, Count Giulio Cesarini carried a banner with the august letters S.P.Q.R. Alongside dignitaries from Charles's dominions, one could see also the ambassadors of free states like France and England. It was, however, the view of pope and emperor riding together that caught the imagination of the public. Much was done to win popular goodwill. A herald again tossed gold and silver coins to the crowd. This time they had been specially struck with the legend "Carolus Quintus Imperator Augustus." Later the populace enjoyed an ox stuffed with fowl that had been roasted whole in the Piazza Maggiore and fountains that provided both red and white wine.

Many writers referred to the coronation and the following parade as a triumph. In some ways, it marked the high point of Charles's career, although he later had urban entries closer in spirit and form to the classical *triumphus*.

The emperor's reception in Mantua, after leaving Bologna, merits attention as well, first because it is an example of his being received in a vassal princely state, and second because the street *apparati* and other artistic creations were perhaps the most sophisticated in classical revival that he had so far seen. In that city several years earlier, Andrea Mantegna had done the set of drawings of Roman triumphs now at Hampton Court,

---

[18]"si pigliavano l'un l'altro per la mano, ragionando se la ridevano...." Account in *Sanuto*, 52: cols. 650–51.

[19]*Sanuto*, 52: col. 650.

which became widely known through engravings. Now Giulio Romano was the chief artist at the Gonzaga court and he was no doubt put in charge of some of the street *apparati*, which were more sculptural and architectural than those seen theretofore. The six columns of the first arch were topped by statues of Charles and five of his imperial and royal ancestors. In the main square was a tall freestanding column recalling Trajan in Rome. Such columns were genuine triumphal constructions, having been erected, like arches, to celebrate victories. There had been, of course, no time to carve spiral bas-reliefs for this one, but painted scenes with inscriptions imitated them. One alluded to Charles's antipodean subjects, presumably those in America.[20] While in town, the emperor raised the marquess to the rank of duke, establishing formally an imperial dependency far from recognized by all Italian ruling princes. During the Mantuan stay there was a series of courtly entertainments, and Charles was taken to admire Romano's newly completed Palazzo del Tè.

After leaving Mantua on 20 April, the huge imperial party passed over the Alps en route to a diet in Augsburg. At Munich, on the way, the manifestations for Charles's entry were elaborate but old-fashioned compared to those in Italian cities. Outside the city, on his approach, artillery demolished a mock castle. At the gate, or perhaps inside, he saw an extraordinary series of *tableaux vivants*, at least one of which, with mutilated bodies, seemed to allude to the religious conflicts of Germany. These *tableaux* aroused the fervent admiration of a Venetian diplomat, who said they would have been praised even by the ancients and confessed: "I would never have thought that in Germany there could be such finished [and effective] shows."[21]

Among six further visits Charles paid to Italy, one took on the character of a true triumphal progress, close in spirit as well as in form to the ancient examples. In 1535 he led a large armada to North Africa to attack the Muslim pirate Barbarossa and succeeded in taking both the fortress of La Goletta and the city of Tunis. A large number of Christian slaves were freed and Muslim prisoners were taken. The Spanish and Italian coasts and many Christian islands immediately became safer. After the expedition, Charles decided to visit his kingdom of Naples and Sicily. He landed at Trapani in western Sicily on 20 August 1535 and was on Italian soil until

---

[20]A bound old man holds a sign with the couplet: "Caesaris antipodes audito numine sacros / Ultro dignamur procubuisse pedes." Cited in report of Mario Savorgnan sent home to Venice. *Sanuto*, 53: col. 110.

[21]"et io per me confesso che mai havria pensato che in Alemagna fussero tal demonstration così ben finite et dimonstrate...." *Sanuto*, 53: col. 290.

the following summer. Genuinely moved by his victories, most Italians were in a mood to celebrate despite memories of the Sack. Charles proceeded with deliberation, taking his time as he conscientiously strove first to become acquainted with the customs and problems of dominions never before visited, and in Latium and Tuscany, to win friends and influence people. Most cities had ample time to prepare for his entries, and things were done with style. Space allows looking only at a few details of the most interesting entries. Beginning at Messina in eastern Sicily, the inscriptions of triumphal arches hail Charles as a third Africanus (after the two Scipios) for his victory over the "Carthaginians."[22] The ruins of Carthage are in fact found in Tunisia, and for humanists planning entries, the ancient parallel was irresistible. In the prevailing neoclassical mood, Messina also made an effort to revive the triumphal chariot. There was none for Charles to ride—and he would probably have refused—but two vehicles came out of the city to greet him. The smaller one was drawn by real captured Moors and held a gilded simulacrum of a classical spoil or trophy. A much larger, less classical chariot held boys who stood for virtues and a big revolving globe of the world. This complicated machine owed little to antiquity, but a chronicler found it to be "a truly imperial thing."[23]

Up the peninsula in Campania between Salerno and Naples, the modest-sized town of Cava de' Tirreni was also on the emperor's route and hoped to give him hospitality. Although, in the event, he did not spend the night, the case is instructive of local conditions and of the mood of progress. Besides being fairly well recorded in memoirs and in city archives, the incident is evoked poignantly in a literary farce that it inspired not long afterward. Citizens of Cava were often portrayed on stage, in comedies called *farse cavaiole*, as ignorant and irascible bumpkins.[24] In fact the town was relatively prosperous with renowned artisans, manufactures, and markets. Its bad reputation was doubtless due in part to the jealousy of neighbors, notably the inhabitants of Salerno. The prince of that city was in fact hoping to persuade the emperor to add the

[22]For most of the 1535–36 entries, there were special published descriptions (called *livrets* by modern scholars), listed in my *Majesty of the State*, notes for pp. 151–74. See also a general account by Vincenzo Saletta, "Il viaggio in Italia di Carlo V (1535–36)," spread over six installments in *Studi Meridionali*: 9 (1976): 286–327 and 452–79; 10 (1977): 78–114, 268–92, and 420–42; 11 (1978): 329–41.

[23]"Dico solo questo che veramente fu cosa imperiale." Cola Giacomo D'Alibrando, *Il triumpho che fece Messina nella intrata dil Imperator Carlo. V. . . .* (Messina: Petruccio Spira, 1535), fol. A5v.

[24]For the facts of the incident, I have relied mainly on Vincenzo Cazzato, "Le feste per Carlo V in Italia: Gli ingressi trionfali in tre centri minori del sud (1535–36)," in Marcello Fagiolo, ed., *La città effimera e l'universo artificiale del giardino* (Rome: Officina Edizioni, 1979), 28–30. Achille Mango edits the play in *Farse cavaiole* 1 (Rome: Bulzoni, 1973), 77–122.

autonomous town to his own feudal dominions, while the Cavesi hoped to get him to confirm their liberties instead. The prince had the emperor for four days in Salerno and Cava officials wanted to get him for at least one. They sent to Naples for information on protocol and raised a remarkable amount of money for decorations, for refreshments to offer the imperial troops and entourage, and for a gift fixed very generously at three thousand gold *scudi*. Gifts of food and money were extremely welcome to Charles, since he was nearly always short of funds while traveling with a large company. He had already arranged to spend the night farther along at Nocera after leaving Salerno but was very courteous to the city fathers who greeted him at the gate, or perhaps farther along. He admired the town and the decorations as he rode through and is said to have remarked that the prince of Salerno showed no little nerve in wanting the place added to his dominions. The officials seem not to have had the gift ready when Charles rode through, perhaps because of the suddenness of his arrival, but they took it to him in Nocera that evening and were well received.

This, in brief, is what actually seems to have happened. A much more colorful account is found in the farce, *La ricevuta dell'imperatore alla Cava*, probably written by a citizen of Salerno within a few years of the event. Here we find the city fathers in a frenzy of anxiety and bickering in anticipation of Charles's arrival, whose exact hour they do not know. A great deal of food has been prepared, and a local guard has a hard time protecting it from a stray German soldier (*lanzichinecco*) who is made to speak in pidgin Italian, or rather in pidgin Campanian-Neapolitan, since that is the dialect of the farce. The officials argue angrily among themselves about who will get to present the gift, who will carry the poles of the canopy. Then loud noises are heard from nearby, and it is ascertained that other townsmen are fighting over the canopy and the decorations. Thus is maintained the Cavesi's reputation for irascibility. The mayor sends an order for everyone to settle down and keep their hands off the decorations. Suddenly the emperor is seen riding through town without stopping. The frantic mayor cannot find the key to the place where the gift is being kept. A messenger is sent to try to persuade the great man to pause at least long enough to eat a sausage and have a glass of wine, but Charles rides on. In reaction there is great anger against him. Imperial and even Christian loyalties are forgotten. One of the officials is ready to become a Frenchman, another will become Jewish or Mohammedan. Everyone recalls the good Aragonese kings Alfonso I and Ferrante, who had had cordial relations with the Cavesi. This little German fellow (*tedeschino*) cares nothing for their feelings and has not even stopped to revere the town's relics, which include half an ear from Balaam's ass, two feathers from the Angel Gabriel, and a sneeze of the Messiah preserved in a vial. At length, the townsmen master their indignation and send a messenger who will mention the gift they had prepared. He returns crying "Viva Imperio!" The emperor has expressed regret and explained that he had hurried through town because the noise of the citizens' disputes had made him fear a party of Turks had landed. He will be glad to receive the Cava delegation in Nocera. But, says the messenger, they must be sure to take the gift, for he had perceived written on the emperor's forehead: "Omnia per pecunia fatta sunt," macaronic Latin for "All things are accomplished with money." At the play's end, the mood turns back to rage, as the city fathers vent their frustration on the fellow citizens responsible for the racket that had frightened the emperor.

Alongside the farcical portrayal of the Cavesi's incompetence and irascibility, today's reader senses an authentic evocation of the anxiety and competitive tension that must always have accompanied local preparations for an imperial visit. The suggestion of financial coercion from imperial officials, not insisted upon, is also convincing.

Three days after riding through Cava, Charles was in Naples, received there more as king than as emperor. Most of the celebratory *apparati* were grouped at the city's five ceremonial *seggi*, which had a peculiar feudal symbolism. It was the custom for new sovereigns (or old ones on a first visit) to proceed from one such seat to another, receiving the homage of five groups of local nobility, each headed by an *Electus*. On this occasion every *seggio* displayed a pair of colossal statues, e.g., Jupiter and Minerva at the Seggio della Montagna. Charles stayed five months in Naples, conscientiously familiarizing himself with the political structure and the current problems of the kingdom.

In Rome, the emperor was awaited, according to the writer Paolo Giovio, "with public joy and with private grief."[25] No one wanted to see imperial or Spanish soldiers within the walls again. On the other hand, the neoclassical possibilities of the occasion delighted humanistic minds. Like many other native Roman patricians, Pope Paul III had been educated in the school and academy of Pomponius Laetus, whose humanistic fervor had verged upon paganism. Paul decided to restore as much of the appearance of ancient Rome as possible for the emperor's entry and chose for this great project of urban renewal another native Roman humanist, Latino Giovenale Manetti (Latinus Juvenalis). Manetti, keeper of the pope's

---

[25]Paolo Giovio, "In pubblica letitia et privatu luctu." Private letter quoted by Maria Luisa Madonna, "L'ingresso di Carlo V a Roma," in Fagiolo, *La città effimera*, 63.

antiquities and a fervent archaeologist, was also one of the three *conserva-tori* of the city government that sat on the Campidoglio. That government had had its own hopes of classical revival—republican classical revival—at least since the antipapal rebellion of Cola di Rienzo in the fourteenth century. Manetti razed many medieval structures to clear an ancient Via Triumphalis from the Appian Way to the Capitolium. It was essential that the emperor be afforded grand vistas from the edge of town toward the Colosseum and the principal surviving triumphal arches: those of Constantine, Titus (then called Vespasian's), and Septimius Severus. Temporary *apparati* were also constructed, including a great arch at today's Piazza di Venezia, but the main emphasis was wisely placed on impressing Charles with the ancient grandeur of the city. As a Roman diarist of the time observed, "the jewels, the ornaments, the greatness, the reputation, and the evidence of the history of this city are the antiquities and the ruins which are contemplated with marvel and stupor and are preserved with extreme veneration...."[26] Although Charles's classical education was not so profound as it might have been, cut short by his accession to responsibilities, he was like all literate people of the time fascinated by the achievements of the Ancients, and he doubtless knew the principal monuments of Rome by reputation.

To receive him at the gate, Manetti and the two other *conservatori* had dressed themselves in togas. While the single Senator, ceremonial head of the city government, rode just ahead, they walked alongside the emperor's horse, explaining the sights to him. He perceived the Colosseum and the Arch of Constantine from afar and, once he arrived at them, could see through the Forum to the Capitolium. He seems to have ridden through the Arches of Constantine, Titus, and Septimius, although the accumulation of centuries made their openings much shallower than in antiquity or today. We are told by one source that Manetti led the emperor's horse through the last arch, and by another that Charles stopped to examine the structure closely and to make out its inscriptions.[27] The *conservatori* also must have pointed out to him the Campidoglio, which the procession skirted, and have told him that their government had its seat there. Ancient *triumphatores* had actually mounted the hill, but that would have been impractical in the circumstances. Moreover, the place was a rather

---

[26]"le gioe, li ornamenti, la grandezza, la reputazione et la fede delle istorie di questa cittade sono le antiquitate et le ruine che per meraviglia con stupore se mirano et anchora con somma veneratione se conservano...." "Il diario di Marcello Alberini," ed. D. Orano, *Archivio della R. Società Romana di Storia Patria* 19 (1896): 46.

[27]See respectively the diary of Biagio Martinelli, edited by B. Podestà in "Carlo V a Roma nell'anno 1536," *Archivio della Società Romana di Storia Patria* 1 (1877): 327–28; and Zanobio Ceffino,

sorry sight architecturally, being bereft of ancient buildings and not yet having the magnificent new ones Michelangelo was about to design. Round the hill was Antonio da San Gallo's great temporary arch, whose principal inscription dedicated it to "Charles V Augustus, Crowned by God, Great and Peaceful Emperor of the Romans."[28] The emperor proceeded to St. Peter's, first through the commercial part of town, then crossing the Tiber at Castel Sant'Angelo. The inscription on the basilica had an emphasis scarcely less neoclassical than the one at San Marco: "To Charles V Augustus, Extender of the Christian Commonwealth."[29] The allusion was presumably to North Africa and to the Spanish possessions in America.

On succeeding days Charles visited ancient monuments more carefully. While still in the city, however, he learned that Francis I had renewed hostilities. That led him to deliver one of the few ill-tempered public speeches of his career, haranguing the pontiff and cardinals about the perfidies of the French king. The state journey was subsequently speeded up so that the emperor could invade Provence. There were, however, three more triumphal entries into the Tuscan cities of Siena, Florence, and Lucca. Florence had by now lost its republican liberties and was a vassal princely state, with the first Medici duke, Alessandro, holding his title from the emperor, betrothed to Charles's daughter. Its reception was sycophantic. The little republics of Siena and Lucca, in contrast, looked to the emperor for the preservation of their liberties. Siena hailed him as "The Safeguard of Our Liberty,"[30] displaying the words next to a great imperial eagle. Charles stayed modestly in a private palace rather than in the Palazzo Pubblico. He was ceremonially visited by the Signoria and returned the visit to them at the Public Palace the next day, admiring and having explained to him some of the building's remarkable political frescoes. The city gate of Lucca had the two columns of Charles's personal device and an inscription hailing him as "The Only Hope of our Salvation."[31] Being greeted there by the *anziani* of the republican government,

---

*La triomphante entrata di Carlo. V. imperatore augusto in l'alma città di Roman…* (n.p., doubtless 1536), fol. 3r.

[28]"Carolo V Augusto a Deo Coronato / Magno et Pacifico Romanorum Imp." See [Andrea Sala], *Ordine pompe apparati et cerimonie, delle solenne intrate di Carlo. V. Imp. sempre Aug. nella città di Roma, Siena, et Fiorenza* (n.p., n.d., but 1536), Roman section reproduced in Fabrizio Cruciani, *Teatro del Rinascimento: Roma 1450–1550* (Rome: Bulzoni, 1983), 579.

[29]"Carolo V Aug. Christianae Reip. Propagatori," Sala's account in Cruciani, 579.

[30]"Praesidium Libertatis Nostrae," [Sala], *Ordine, pompe, apparati,* fol. C1v.

[31]"Nostrae Spes Una Salutis." See Nicolo Montecatini, *Entrata dell'Imperatore nella città di Lucca* (n.p., n.d., but 1536), fol. A2r.

he took the flattering and rather erudite initiative of promising to preserve the city's free status that had been sanctioned by his predecessor Emperor Charles IV in 1370. He stayed in the bishop's palace rather than in the seat of government. While walking around the impressive city walls on a later day, he delighted the citizens further by saying their city was clearly an important one, and not just "three houses and a bakery" as he had been led to believe.[32] He no doubt left the townsmen confirmed in their free imperial allegiance. Lucca, in fact, retained its independence until the upheavals of the French Revolution, while Siena was conquered by Cosimo I of Florence just two decades after the emperor's reassuring visit.

Charles's invasion of Provence was repelled and after a summit conference with Francis I at Aiguesmortes in 1538, there was an interval of peace. In 1539 the emperor was magnanimously invited to cross France as a shortcut on his way from Spain to the Low Countries. This journey, in the winter of 1539–40, entailed grand receptions in Poitiers, Orleans, Fontainebleau, and Paris.[33] Despite some neoclassical touches, a number of "mystères" played to him recall the pageants of Bruges and London decades before. The choice of themes for decorations was delicate in the extreme. One could show the two sovereigns side by side, and their two orders of merit, St. Michael and the Golden Fleece, could be evoked in association. There was, to my knowledge, no suggestion of the French king's claim of being "empereur dans son royaume."[34] In Orleans it was decided to have no inscriptions "because one or the other of the princes, or their subjects, could have inferred, or supposed, things at which one or other of the princes would not have been pleased."[35] The street arches had only abstract decorations. Charles had further entries of a more positive sort upon arriving in his home territory of Flanders.

A year later he triumphally entered his fief of Milan, which had prepared fine "architectural arches," including one with an equestrian statue of himself on its top. He continued to Lucca, where he was to confer again with Paul III. This time the question of his lodging was difficult because the Bishop's Palace had been given to the pope. The *anziani* were prepared

---

[32]"Tre case e un forno." Reported in Montecatini, *Entrata*, fol. A4r.

[33]See, besides Jacquot's summary, V. L. Saulnier, "Charles Quint traversant la France: Ce qu'en dirent les poètes français," in *Fêtes II*, 207–34.

[34]On the imperial aspirations of Renaissance French monarchs, see Frances Yates, "The Idea of the French Monarchy," in *Astraea: The Imperial Theme in the Sixteenth Century* (London and Boston: Routledge and Kegan Paul), 121–26.

[35]"pource que lung ou laultre des Princes, ou de leurs subiectz eussent peu sur icelles gloser, ou deuiner choses, ou lung ou laultre des Princes neust prins plaisir." Contemporary account *Le double et copie d'unes lettres envoyees d'Orleans…*, quoted by Jacquot in "Panorama," *Fêtes II*, 435.

to abandon the Palazzo della Signoria to him despite constitutional difficulties, but Charles implored them to remain in their apartments while he made do with just a part of the building.

Having set sail from Italy for another assault on North Africa (this one ill fortuned), the emperor stopped off en route for a visit to his dominion of Mallorca. The chief town, Palma, gave him a most elaborate entry, with several arches, and recorded it in an elegant *livret* worthy of a great city on the continent.[36]

There was much more travel before Charles's abdication from the Spanish and imperial thrones in 1556, but most of the triumphs during the last years of his reign were staged for his son Philip, who was sent across Italy, Austria, and Germany into Flanders in 1548–49. The iconography of the *apparati* for the Italian and Flemish entries on that journey reached a new level of neoclassical erudition and are therefore of great interest to cultural historians. Philip had, however, less curiosity about foreign parts than his father and much less natural courtesy. In Genoa, fully conscious of the symbolism at stake, he tried to coerce the city fathers into letting him stay in the Palazzo dei Signori.[37] By resisting valiantly and pointing out that Charles V himself had been content several times (after 1529) to stay as a private guest in the seaside Palazzo Doria, Andrea Doria saved the city's dignity. Farther along on the same progress at Mantua, a young Englishman who understood such things noted that Philip's supercilious attitude toward the duke of Ferrara and the Venetian ambassador "obtayned [for him] throughe all Italye a name of insolencye."[38] Charles, whose political wisdom had been increased through the experience of his ceremonial travels, would never have made mistakes of this kind.

The effects of the emperor's numerous triumphal entries into cities were important on more than one plane. On the purely political one, he undoubtedly won a great deal of respect and goodwill from far-flung subjects and from foreigners by the dignity of his processions and by the courteous curiosity he displayed toward entry decorations and local monuments. He also indisputably gained a great amount of useful firsthand knowledge about local institutions and conditions that he could not have acquired at court, either in Flanders or in Spain. On the artistic and

---

[36]See Joanot Gomis's Catalan description, *Libre de la benaventurada vinguda d'l Emperador y Rey Carlos en la sua ciutat d'Mallorques…* (Palma de Mallorca: Ferrando de Cansoles, 1542), very rare, reprinted anonymously, with some facsimile pages, in Palma, 1973.

[37]See Elena Parma Armoni, "Il Palazzo del Principe Andrea Doria in Genova," *L'arte* 3 (1970), 44–45.

[38]Ms. journal of Sir Thomas Hoby, future translator of *The Courtier*, quoted by Geoffrey Parker, *Philip II* (Boston-Toronto: Little, Brown and Co., 1978), 21.

literary planes, the experience of preparing for his entries—especially those of the Italian progress of 1535–36—almost certainly accelerated the progress of classical revival. In the Cinquecento, the chance of receiving a Roman emperor was a natural incentive to classicize, and the resulting stylistic development communicated itself easily thereafter to royal, papal, and even republican contexts. Something was undeniably lost in this development, for the *tableaux vivants* of Bruges in 1520, those of Munich in 1530, and the London pageants of 1522 had had an expressivity that was more direct than the doric arches with Latin inscriptions, emblems, and painted histories or allegories. Neoclassicism was, however, definitely the wave of the immediate future, in the limited domain of the triumphal entry as well as in the vaster ones of general art and letters.

# MARGUERITE DE NAVARRE AND ERASMUS
## Wives' Tales Retold

### Paula Sommers

THE RENAISSANCE DISCOURSE ON MARRIAGE incorporated a broad range of material—the admonitions of church fathers, treatises by distinguished humanists like Leon Batista Alberti, Juan Luis Vives, and Erasmus, emblems, narrative works, farces, and theological debate on the question of marriage versus chastity. With regard to the wife, beyond a necessary subordination to the husband who could help to control her weaker nature and her sexual appetites, diversity of opinion prevailed. Some writers viewed her with suspicion or condescension, confining her to the household and the distaff and limiting opportunities for education. Others were more liberal. Still others were sensitive to the plight of young girls sacrificed to the financial interests of their families. With patriarchal voices already exhibiting a range of attitudes, can one identify a particularly female point of view? Marguerite de Navarre incorporates aspects of the contemporary discourse on marriage into her courtly theatre and mystical poetry, but the *Heptameron* offers the most extensive treatment of this topic.[1] As sister of the king and role model for other *femmes de bien* she does not dare rebel against an institution sanctioned by God, nature, and

[1]For background concerning marriage in the *Heptameron* see John D. Barnard, "Sexual Oppression and Social Justice in Marguerite de Navarre's *Heptaméron*," *Journal of Medieval and Renaissance Studies*, 19.2 (Fall, 1989): 251–81; Edward Benson, "Marriage Ancestral and Conjugal in the *Heptaméron*," *Journal of Medieval and Renaissance Studies* 1:9.2 (1979): 261–75; Régine Reynolds Cornell, "Waiting in the Wings: The Characters in Marguerite de Navarre's *Théâtre profane*," in *International Colloquium Celebrating the 500th Anniversary of the Birth of Marguerite de Navarre*, ed. Régine Reynolds Cornell (Birmingham, Ala.: Summa Publications, 1995); Raymond Lebègue, "*La Fidélité conjugale dans L'Heptaméron*," in *La Nouvelle française au xvie siècle*, ed. Lionelle Sozzi (Geneva: Slatkine, 1981), 425–33, and Emile Telle, *L'Oeuvre de Marguerite d'Angoulème, Reine de Navarre et La Querelle des Femmes* (1937; reprint, Geneva: Slatkine, 1969).

tradition. Through divergence from analogs authored by male writers, she, nevertheless, questions some of the attitudes recommended for women in contemporary conduct books. Novella 38, her version of a story that appeared frequently in didactic literature as an example of the ways in which wives could tame their wandering husbands and preserve marital harmony, is a particularly striking example of this strategy of feminist retelling and reversal.[2]

In the preface to the *Heptameron*, de Navarre acknowledges her debt to Boccaccio's *Decameron* while demonstrating her capacity for original imitation.[3] Her storytellers (five men and five women) are trapped in the Pyrenees by floods and take refuge at a monastery where, after attendance at mass and daily scriptural readings, they pass the time by trading tales. Novella 38 is set in Tours and tells of a young bourgeoise whose husband has fallen in love with his *métayère*. Noting he always returns from his assignations in bad health, the wife visits the farm and provides the

---

[2]A selective bibliography on early women writers and the writing strategies they pursue include basic sources like Ruth Kelso, *Doctrine for the Lady of the Renaissance* (Urbana: University of Illinois Press, 1956) and Constance Jordan, *Renaissance Feminism: Literary Text and Political Models* (Ithaca: Cornell University Press, 1990). For selected sources on Marguerite de Navarre see Gary Ferguson, "Gendered Oppositions in Marguerite de Navarre's *Heptameron*: The Rhetoric of Seduction and Resistance in Narrative and Society" in *Renaissance Women Writers*, ed. Anne R. Larsen and Colette H. Winn (Detroit: Wayne State University Press, 1994), 143–59; Ann Rosalind Jones, "Surprising Fame: Renaissance Gender Ideologies and Women's Lyric," in *The Poetics of Gender*, ed. Nancy K. Miller (New York: Columbia University Press, 1986), 174–95, and the recent anthology of articles *Critical Tales: New Studies of the Heptameron and Early Modern Culture*, ed. John Lyons and Mary B. McKinley (Philadelphia: University of Pennsylvania Press, 1993). For a more explicit protest against the married state published more than twenty years after the first version of the *Heptameron* see Olympe Liébaut, *Les miseres de la femme mariée* (Paris: Pierre Mesnier, 1587). There is a modern edition by Llana Zinguer, *Misères et grandeur de la femme au xvie siècle* (Geneva: Slatkine, 1982).

[3]For discussion of de Navarre's relationship with the Italian subtext see Rudolf Baehr, "Marguerite de Navarre und Boccaccio: Tradition und Selbstandigkeit im *Heptaméron*," *Sprachkunst: Beitrage zur Literaturwissenschaft* 10 (1979): 5–23; P. B. Diffley, "From Translation to Imitation and Beyond: A Reassessment of Boccaccio's Role in Marguerite de Navarre's *Heptameron*," *Modern Language Review* 90.2 (1995): 345–62; Lance K. Donaldson-Evans, "The Narrative of Desire: Boccaccio and the French *Decameron* of the 15th and 16th Centuries," *Neophilologus* 77.4 (1993): 541–52; Susan Noakes, "The *Heptameron* Prologue and the Anxiety of Influence," *Studi sul Boccaccio* 20 (1991–92): 267–77; Glyn P. Norton, "The Emilio Ferretti Letter: A Critical Preface for Marguerite de Navarre," *Journal of Medieval and Renaissance Studies* 4 (1974): 287–300; Sylvie F. L. Richards, "Thrice-Told Tales: Embedded Narratives in the *Decameron* and the *Heptameron*," in *The Force of Vision, III: Powers of Narration: Literary Theory*, ed. Earl Miner et al. (Tokyo: International Comparative Literature Society, 1995); Mihoko Suzuki, "Gender, Power and the Female Reader: Boccaccio's *Decameron* and Marguerite de Navarre's *Heptameron*," *Comparative Literature Studies* 30.3 (1993): 231–52; Marcel Tetel, "Ambiguité chez Boccace et Marguerite de Navarre," in *Il Boccaccio nella cultural francese*, ed. Carlo Pellegrini (Florence: Olschki, 1971), 557–65, and Elizabeth C. Wright, "Marguerite Reads Giovanni: Gender and Narration in the *Heptameron* and the *Decameron*," *Renaissance and Reformation* 15.1 (1991): 21–36. For a more specific approach to de Navarre's feminism, see Patricia Cholakian, *Rape and Writing in the Heptameron of Marguerite de Navarre* (Carbondale: Southern Illinois University Press, 1991).

mistress with everything needed for his comfort: furniture, fine bed-clothes, and silver dishes. Upon discovering his wife's generosity, the husband abandons his extraconjugal diversion. Early versions of this story in French, Germanic, and Flemish folklore linked the husband's mistress with a mysterious *wildfrau*, a woman of wood and forest and strange powers, but by the fourteenth century she had become a less intimidating figure.[4]

Works suggested as potential sources for novella 38—the anonymous *Mesnagier de Paris*, Pierre de Lesnauderie's *La Louange de Mariaige et Recueil des hystoires des bonnes, vertueuses et illustres femmes* (1523) and Erasmus' *Coniugium* (1523)—all ground the story in realistic detail.[5] The author of the *Mesnagier* states that the bourgeois Thomas Quentin was having an affair with "une pauvre fille." De Lesnauderie identifies the husband as the Sieur de Darembon, the wife as the daughter of the count of Villars, and the mistress as a young widow, Jehanne Ramée. The latter, more victim than seductress, yields to the husband's attentions partly out of fear. When the Sieur de Darembon learns of the generosity with which his wife has furnished Jehanne's humble bedroom, he decides to find a husband for the pretty widow and return to his wife. Erasmus dispenses with proper names and aristocratic status in the *exemplum* that he includes in his colloquy. His realism is a function of the psychology that fuels the animated dialogue that he creates for his well-defined interlocutors, Eulalia and Xantippe.[6]

Like Erasmus and the *Mesnagier*, de Navarre situates her characters in a bourgeois milieu. As an anonymous *métayère*, the mistress in tale 38 is

---

[4]Background on the *wildfrau* tradition can be found in Virgil B. Heltzel, "Traces of a *Wildfrau* story in Erasmus," *Philological Quarterly* 8 (1929): 348–54.

[5]Discussion of sources for novella 38 includes works by Georgina E. Brereton, "*Le Ménagier de Paris*: Source de la XXXVIIIe Nouvelle de *L'Heptaméron*," *Bibliothèque d'Humanisme et Renaissance* 16 (1954): 207; Pierre Jourda, *Marguerite d'Angoulême, Duchesse d'Alençon, Reine de Navarre* (1492–1549): *Etude biographique et littéraire* (Paris: Champion, 1930), 2:700, 738; Jean-Claude Margolin, *Recherches Erasmiennes, Travaux d'Humanisme et Renaissance* 105 (Geneva: Droz, 1969), 98–127, and Emile Telle, "Une autre source de la nouvelle 38 de *L'Heptaméron*," *Romanic Review* 34 (1934): 375–77. Brereton observes that a copy of the *Mesnagier de Paris* is listed in the inventory of works in the library of Francis I at Blois. Margolin mentions the *Mesnagier* as well as the *Coniugium*. Telle argues that de Lesnauderie's *Louange* is a more direct source of inspiration than the *Coniugium*, given numerous similarities to novella 38. Close to Lesnauderie is another version of the tale included in the *Parement et Triomphe des Dames* by Olivier de La Marche (1495).

[6]It is because of these interlocutors, however, that Telle views the *Coniugium* as an example of the sympathy for women that the Dutch humanist displays throughout the *Colloquies*. The translation that follows is mine as are all English translations unless otherwise noted: "Sur un ton enjoué et d'un optimisme volontairement forcé, par le truchement d'une femme et non d'un homme, notons-le, d'une femme qui a bien compris la leçon des paraphrases sur Saint Paul et Saint Pierre, le réformateur

less interesting than de Lesnauderie's young widow, but she is more than the purely functional character who appears in the *Coniugium* because de Navarre shows some interest in her feelings. The pain the young woman experiences is expressed in the tears of embarrassment that she sheds when the husband asks about the luxury she is suddenly able to offer him. Tears, moreover, substitute for voice. In novella 38 Marguerite de Navarre resists the penchant for dialogue she often indulges in where female protagonists play a significant role.[7] The *Mesnagier* records in great detail the gentle speech with which the wife obtains the cooperation of the mistress. Indeed, the wife's words are important indications of her desire to preserve both her husband's health and the family reputation:

> My dear, I must protect my husband's reputation.... I beg you to speak of him in public as little as possible to avoid shame for him, for myself and for our chldren and I ask you to conceal everything for your part... For my part, since he loves you, it is my intention to love, help and assist you in everything you will have to do.[8]

Erasmus' wife, in an effort to avoid scandal and deal tactfully with the mistress, introduces herself as her husband's sister.[9] The *Coniugium* also

---

fait un cours sur la vie de mariage qui ne pouvait qu'intéresser toutes les Griseldis de son temps, et toutes les mal mariées à venir...." *Erasme et le septième sacrement* (Geneva: Droz, 1954), 313. "In a lively tone, with a rather forced optimism, through the agency of a woman and not a man, of a woman, let us observe, who has understood his paraphrases of Saints Paul and Peter, the reformer gives lessons on married life that could not fail to interest all the Griseldas of his time and all the unhappily married women to come...." For additional discussion of Erasmus' views on women see Franz Bierlaire, *Les Colloques d'Erasme: Réforme des études, réforme des moeurs, et réforme de l'église au xvie siècle* (Paris: Les Belles Lettres, 1978), 166–79; Jordan (above, n. 1), 50–64; Margolin (above, n. 5, 111, 115–16); Elizabeth McCutcheon, "Erasmus' Representations of Women and Their Discourses," *Erasmus of Rotterdam Yearbook* 12 (1992): 64–68; Erika Rummel, "A Human Affair: Erasmus and Rabelais as Marriage Counsellors," *Canadian Catholic Review* 9.5 (1991): 177–79, and Elisabeth Schneider, *Das Bild der Frau im Werk des Erasmus von Rotterdam* (Basel: Helbing and Lichtenhahn, 1995).

[7]Among important female protagonists who speak at length in order to state their point of view are the *mal-mariée*, of novella 15, Floride (n. 10) and Rolandine (n. 21). De Lesnauderie, it should be noted, also chooses not to emphasize the wife's speaking to her husband or his mistress.

[8]"M'amye, je suis tenue de garder mon mary de blasme.... je vous prye que de luy vous parliez en compagnie le moins que vous pourrez, pour eschever son blasme, le mien et celuy de nos enfans, et que le celiez de vostre part.... Car puis que ainsi est qu'il vous ayme, mon intencion est de vous aimer, secourir et aidier de ce que vous avrez a faire...." *Le Mesnagier de Paris*, ed. Georgina E. Brereton and Janet M. Ferrier (Paris: Livre de Poche, 1994), 402.

[9]Margolin (above, n. 5, p. 115) emphasizes both the mannerist approach of Erasmus with regard to the *Coniugium* and the fact that the sister's disguise does not seem to be a part of narrative tradition.

records her gracious reply to the husband's demand for an explanation of her generosity.

De Navarre's representation of the silent bourgeoise rather than the speaking wife is one of a series of details that convey her revisionist attitude to this traditional story. Tale 38 is, in effect, one of the shortest narratives in the *Heptameron*. It is also set in a context that questions the unqualified admiration normally accorded the generous wife. In this respect *Heptameron* 38 is closer to the *Coniugium* than other versions of the story. Both Erasmus and de Navarre make use of a female narrator and provide for some negative reaction from the fictional (and female) naratee(s). In fact, what distinguishes de Navarre from the Dutch humanist is the use that she chooses to make of the critical female voice.

While Erasmus may deviate from the didactic tradition by situating the story of the generous wife in a dialogue involving female interlocutors, Eulalia and Xantippe engage in a discussion with sharply limited parameters. A dedicated reader of Scripture, Erasmus could scarcely redefine the position of women in marriage, and that position was one of subordination. Xantippe, wronged by a husband who squanders her dowry, drinks too much, and threatens to beat her, is allowed to express anger, but she is potentially as shrewish as the ill-reputed wife of Socrates. She greets her husband with torrents of abuse when he finally returns home and she threatens to render blow for blow should he attempt to strike her. It is for her benefit that Eulalia tells the story of the generous wife.

Xantippe at first rejects Eulalia's *exemplum*. Given the unhappy situation in which she finds herself, her reaction is understandable, but it confirms the aggressive character that she has already—wrongfully—displayed in quarreling with her husband. Fortunately, Eulalia is able to supplement the story she tells with the example of her own, tactfully managed husband. Eulalia's rewards are evident from the very beginning of the conversation with Xantippe:

Eul.     Maybe this new dress flatters my figure.

Xan.     Of course it does, I haven't seen anything prettier for a long time.... Where did you get such a marvelous gift?

Eul.     Where should honest wives get them except from their husbands?[10]

Since Xantippe is dissatisfied with her own clothing, the dress emblematizes the differences between the two women. It also symbolizes

[10]The English translation is by Craig R. Thompson, *Colloquies of Erasmus* (Chicago: University of

the wife's economic dependence upon the husband and the material rewards that flow from her submissiveness. It is clearly up to Xantippe to modify her behavior and, in doing so, tame her husband. The rewards of sweet, feminine manipulation will be both psychological and material: restoration of the marriage bond, and fine, new clothing.

Marguerite de Navarre's fictional narrator Longarine concludes novella 38 with a moral statement that endorses the principles expressed by Eulalia/Erasmus. Indeed, her use of water imagery is perfectly compatible with the sweet or soft strategy that Eulalia recommends to Xantippe:

> Believe me, Ladies, there are few husbands who cannot be won round by a wife who is patient and loving. If they cannot, then they must be harder than rock, for even rock is in the end worn down by the soft, gentle flow of water.[11]

In the discussion that follows novella 38, however, only the pious Oisille, whose scriptural readings enlighten the group at the beginning of every day, agrees with Longarine. Xantippe's voice is displaced and given new credibility when Parlamante, a woman of irreproachable character and social poise, challenges Longarine's edifying message: "That woman had no heart and no backbone."[12]

Parlamante's objections are seconded by her cynical husband Hircan, who suggests that the wife was making her husband comfortable so that she could stay at home with a lover.[13]

While Hircan's response is a function of his conviction that women's sexual desire equals men's and that any reserve or abstinence must be due to deception, Parlamante's condemnation of the generous wife reflects, in

---

Chicago Press, 1965), 116. The Latin quotation is from *Opera Omnia Desiderii Erasmi Roterdami*, ed. L. E. Halkin et al. (Amsterdam: North Holland Publishing Company, 1969), 1:330: "Eul. Fortasse nova vestis commendat formam. Xan. Recte coniectas. Nihil iam diu vidi elegantius.... Unde tibi tam egregium munus? Eul. Unde decet honestas matronas accipere, nisi a maritis suis?" All further translations of Erasmus in this article are from Thompson and all Latin citations from the *Opera Omnia*.

[11]The English translation is that of P. A. Chilton, *The Heptameron* (London: Penguin Books, 1984), 121. The French is taken from *L'Heptaméron*, ed. Michel François (Paris: Garnier, 1963), 217. Further citations in French and English will be from these sources respectively: "Croyez, mes dames, qu'il y a bien peu de mariz que patience et amour de la femme ne puisse gainguner à la longue, ou ilz sont plus durs qu'une pierre que l'eaue foible et molle, par longueur de temps, vient à caver."

[12] 363. "Voylà une femme sans cueur, sans fiel et sans foie" (271).

[13]Critics seeking to identify the various narrators with members of the court have suggested that Parlamante is Marguerite de Navarre herself. For detailed discussion of the storytellers, their identities and their narrative function see Régine Reynolds Cornell, *Les devisants de l'Heptaméron: Dix personnages en quête d'audience* (Washington: Washington University Press, 1977), and Betty J. Davis, *The Storytellers in Marguerite de Navarre's* Heptameron (Lexington, Ky.: French Forum Press, 1978).

part, her response to the preceding story. In effect, Erasmus in the *Coniugium* and Marguerite de Navarre in her thirty-eighth novella are both working with paired examples. In Eulalia's conversation with Xantippe the story of the wife whose generosity leads the husband to give up his country mistress is complemented by the even more generous wife of Gilbert the Dutchman. Gilbert's wealthy, but elderly wife, recognizing her husband's need for sexual pleasures that she cannot fulfill, invites his young mistress into her home and does everything she can to accommodate her without causing ill will or scandal. The kind treatment of a distant mistress, therefore, yields to kind (and ever more generous) treatment of the mistress-in-the-home. Eulalia's discourse thus reveals a positive rhetorical progression in which examples complement and reinforce one another.

Marguerite de Navarre's story of the bourgeoise is the second, rather than the first, in a negative progression. It is preceded by the tale of Madame de Loué, whose husband, after a good many years of marital fidelity, spends his nights in the servants' quarters with a chambermaid. Madame de Loué, cited by the fictional narrator Dagoucin as a model of patience, seems to conform to the pattern of sweet submission advocated by Eulalia and integrated into didactic tradition. Rather than reproach her husband for his infidelity, she resorts to symbolic communication, greeting him every night as he returns from his rendezvous with a bowl of water so that he may wash his hands.[14] Symbolism, unfortunately, proves to be ineffective, and time does not appear to be working in the interest of the wife. The husband persists in frequenting the maid. Finally, tired of a repentance that never comes and offended by unmerited neglect, Madame de Loué lays aside her bowl of water, closes her *livre d'heures,* and goes to confront the husband and his mistress—an action that is not endorsed by marriage manuals. When she finds them sleeping together she sets fire to a bundle of straw, awakens her husband before the situation becomes too dangerous and warns him that she can no longer endure his behavior. The burning straw may be read variously as a sign of her anger, of a desire to punish the husband, or as a symbol of the wife's passionate love and frustration. What is clear is that she has broken the rules that require wifely patience, silence, and submission. While the fictional narrator glosses over

---

[14]Sylvie L. F. Richards, "The Burning Bed: Infidelity and the Virtuous Woman in *Heptameron* xxxvii" *Romance Notes* 34.3 (1994): 313, also notes the significance of the handwashing gesture and emphasizes the empowerment of the wife: "The 37th tale is not a story about changing husbands; it is a story about a wife changing herself, moving away from the confines of the pre/scriptive to the active plane of writing herself into the diegesis." Also see my article "Fire and Water: Marital Strategy and The '*Femme de Bien*' in Marguerite de Navarre's *Heptameron,*" *Women Writers in Pre-revolutionary France,* ed. Colette H. Winn and Donna Kuizenga (New York: Garland, 1997), 5–15.

the apparent irregularities in her conduct, the fictional audience, with the exception of the evangelically oriented Oisille, seizes upon the problematic aspects of the novella. Nommerfide cites Madame de Loué as an example of impatience. Parlamante and Longarine do not agree with her interpretation of the story, but they do question the patriarchal insistence on patience for wives whose husbands betray their marriage vows. Longarine's response to Madame de Loué's predicament recalls the intense outrage expressed by Xantippe: "Husbands like that ought to be burnt and their ashes used for the washing."[15] Her reaction is, however, mitigated by positive memories of her own marital relationship and by the statement that she would, in Madame de Loué's circumstances, have burned herself to death along with the husband. Indeed, in refusing to live without her husband, Longarine, even in anger, recognizes the fundamental unity of the married couple. Her protest is combined with affirmation of social and religious standards that are a constant feature of the didactic discourse on marriage. As Vives states in his *De Institutione Feminae Christianae:* "If friendship makes a single soul out of two, how much more should we esteem marriage which far surpasses all other friendships? For it is said to make out of two, not merely a soul or body but a complete being."[16]

In the *Coniugium* paired stories lead from the example of the generous wife to the story of Gilbert the Dutchman and his aged spouse. The progression emphasizes increasingly heroic manifestations of wifely virtue. Both stories, moreover, are set in a master, or rather, mistress-pupil dialogue in which a positively coded Eulalia convinces a negatively coded, but not unsympathetic Xantippe to cooperate with her in attempting to save her marriage. In the *Heptameron* paired stories also progress from a lesser to a greater example of feminine patience, but after the discussion inspired by novella 37, the impeccably virtuous heroine of novella 38 lacks credibility. This results partly from the dialogical interaction of the *devisants* and partly from the rhetorical presentation of the respective protagonists. Madame de Loué has a name and a distinguished social status. She also occupies more narrative space than the heroine of novella 38. The reader is

[15]360–61. "de telz marys que ceulx-là, les cendres en seroient bonnes à faire la buée" (269).

[16]"Quod si amicitia ex duobus animis unum reddit, quanto id a conjugio verius efficaciusque praestari convenit, quod unum reliquas omnes amicitias longissimè antecellit? Idcirco non unum modo, vel animum, vel corpus, ex duobus facere dicitur, sed unum prorsus hominem...." Joannis Ludovici Vivis Valentini, *Opera omnia,* ed. Gregorio Majansio (1745; repr., London: Gregg Press, 1964), 4:184. Contemporaries could also have consulted the French translation by Pierre de Changy, *Livre de l'institution de la femme chrestienne* (1542: repr., Geneva: Slatkine, 1970), 155. "Si l'amytié de deux personnes rend ung cueur & un vouloir entre eulx par plus forte & efficace raison, le fera mariage qui precelle et excede toutes autres amytiez, & faict de deux corps ung." They would have been familiar, moreover, with the Pauline tradition that inspires Vives—Eph. 5:22–31.

informed of her mental anguish and witnesses the gradual erosion of her patience. Her piety is demonstrated by prayerful reading of the Book of Hours. Her concern for her children is evident. Finally, she has a voice. Driven by desperation, she speaks directly to her husband. Her discourse, while conditioned by references to her devotion to him and her moral weakness, is sufficiently threatening:

> Monsieur, I have been trying for the past year to save you from your wicked ways. I have tried to exercise patience and kindness, to show you that in washing the outside, you should be also inwardly cleansed. But when I say that it was all to no avail, I decided to employ that element which shall bring an end to all things.... I do not know if I shall have it in my power a second time to save you from danger.[17]

The bourgeoise, as representative of perfect Christian virtue, displays no inner struggle, needs no voice, and inhabits a transcendent plane with which the *devisants*, always excepting Oisille, who no longer has to deal with the realities of conjugal love, cannot identify.

Marguerite de Navarre's retelling and recontextualization of the story of the generous wife is, to some degree, a deconstructive exercise. Perfect charity is beyond reproach, but Madame de Loué's slow and painful groping towards the resolution of her marital problems is closer to the norms of human experience as they are portrayed in the majority of the queen's novellas. This does not mean that she disagrees with Erasmus. The Dutch humanist produced a rich bibliography of works that deal with marriage as did Marguerite herself in her novellas and occasionally in her poetry and theatre.[18] Both Erasmus and Marguerite de Navarre, in this larger context, subscribe to a Pauline view of marriage that incorporates the idea of spiritual equality, mutuality, and the responsible supremacy of the husband who is the head of his wife as Christ is head of the church. With regard to the generous wife, however, the differences are clearly drawn. Erasmus' interlocutors are ventriloquized figures in a didactic dialogue.

---

[17]359. "Monsieur, j'ay essayé ung an durant à vous retirer de cest malheurté, par doulceur et patience, et vous monstrer que, en lavant le dehors, vous deviez nectoier le dedans; mais, quant j'ay veu que tout ce que je faisois estoit de nulle valleur, j'ay mis peyne de me ayder de l'element quid doibt mectre fin à toutes choses.... je ne sçay si une second fois je vous pourrois retirer du dangier, comme j'ai faict" (267).

[18]Erasmus' *Declamatio in genere suasoria de laude matrimonii*, translated by de Navarre's protégé Antoine de Berquin in 1525 (*Déclamation des louenges de mariage*) was condemned by the Sorbonne. This translation, along with other controversial issues, led to Berquin's execution in 1528. For a survey of Erasmus' writing on marriage see Telle. See also Margaret Mann Phillips, "Marguerite de Navarre et Erasme: Une réconsidération," *Revue de Littérature Comparée* 52 (1978): 194–201.

The story of the generous wife functions as a rhetorical example in that dialogue. De Navarre's interlocutors, aristocratic, drawn from both sexes, differing in degree of age and intimacy, function collectively as a means of scrutinizing and problematizing the tales they exchange. The story of the generous wife is probed and tested like all the others.[19] If it is found wanting, it is because the more articulate *devisantes* will not accept the degree of self-denial the exemplum demands. At a certain point, they are conscious of a personal dignity that cannot be sacrificed. They are not, then, simply mirrors for their husbands' moods and wants. Significantly, this traditional image of wifely submission finds a place in Eulalia's discourse: "As a mirror, if it's a good one, always gives back the image of the person looking at it, so should a wife reflect her husband's mood, not being gay when he's sad or merry when he's upset."[20] There are no such mirrors among the female narrators or protagonists of the *Heptameron*. Mirrors have, in fact, quite another role in de Navarre's writing.[21] Assimilated to Scripture or to the crucified body of Christ, they are sources of truth and identity, not images of wifely subservience.

The didactic tradition represented by the *Mesnagier*, the *Louanges de Mariage*, and the *Coniugium* assigns the wife of a philandering husband the full duty of preserving the marriage. In her retelling of the story Marguerite de Navarre accepts the moral empowerment of the wife, but the pairing of novella 38 with the barely restrained violence of novella 37 and the critical responses of her narrators distance the virtuous bourgeoise from her fictional audience and her intended readers. While the behavior of the bourgeoise is not impossible, it lacks psychological realism. In novella 38 sweet persuasion and self-sacrifice—the remedies of traditional discourse for married women—are being called into question. They function well in an idealistic context, but their practical value is not guaranteed.

De Navarre's rewriting of analogs is less radical than the overtly feminist stance adopted by Helisenne de Crenne in her *Epistres Invectives* and

---

[19]See John D. Lyons, *Exemplum: The Rhetoric of Example in Early Modern France and Italy* (Princeton: Princeton University Press, 1989), for discussion of nonexemplarity in the *Heptameron*.

[20]119. "Quemadmodum enim speculum, si probum est, semper reddit imaginem intuentis, ita decet matremfamilias ad affectum mariti congruere, ne sit alacris illi moerente aut hilaris illo commoto" (305).

[21]The wife-as-mirror is a common motif. Plutarch's *Coniugalia praecepta* provides a particularly apt illustration of its use as a means of subordinating the wife to the husband: "Just as a mirror, although embellished with gold and precious stones, is good for nothing unless it shows a true likeness, so there is no advantage in a rich wife unless she makes her life true to her husband's and her character in accord with his." From the *Moralia*, trans. Frank Cale Babbit, Loeb Classical Library (Cambridge, Mass.: Harvard University Press, 1962), 2:307.

Louise Labé in her *Euvres* but it, nevertheless, constitutes a subtle critique of excesses within the patriarchal tradition and shows how, through fiction, de Navarre dialogues with contemporary humanists interested in the reaffirmation and regulation of marriage.

# L'HEPTAMERON

# DES NOVVEL-

## LES DE TRESILLV-

### STRE ET TRESEXCELLENTE

#### PRINCESSE MARGVERITE DE VALOIS

Royne de Nauarre,

*Remis en son ordre, confus au parauant en sa premiere impres-
sion: & dedié à tresillustre & tresvertueuse Prin-
cesse Ieanne de Foix Royne de Nauarre,
par Claude Gruget Parisien.*

A PARIS.

Pour Gilles Robinot, tenant sa boutique au Palais, en la Gale-
rie par ou on va à la Chancellerie.
1 5 5 9.

## Auec priuilege du Roy.

# RABELAIS'S PANURGE AS HOMO RHETORICUS

*Barbara C. Bowen*

THE GENERAL READER, especially one who has not actually read *Gargantua and Pantagruel* but is familiar with its reputation as a saga of giants whose main occupations are lavish eating, drinking, wenching, and laughing, may not expect Rabelais's work to have any connection with rhetoric. Of the four books we know Rabelais wrote, the first two are action-packed mock epics, full of battles and assorted adventures; the *Tiers Livre* appears mainly concerned with Panurge's dilemma over whether or not he should marry; and the *Quart Livre* is (among other things) a quest in the form of a sea voyage, complete with traditional violent storm, allegorical monsters, and a real whale. What role could rhetoric play in all this?

Sometimes, moreover, Rabelais as narrator seems to be actively disparaging rhetoric. Friar John refers to his frequent swearing as "couleurs de rhetoricque Ciceroniane,"[1] while for Carpalim "couleur de Rhetoricque" means flowery discourse used to seduce ladies (TL 34). The hilarious nonsense speeches of the plaintiffs Baisecul and Humevesne whom Pantagruel reconciles with a third nonsense speech (P 10–13) can be read as a parody of judicial rhetoric, as can Janotus de Bragmardo's confused and confusing request for the return of the bells (G 19). Rabelais's hero Friar John is essentially a doer rather than a speaker, which might suggest that Rabelais's endorses the "deeds are more efficacious than words" of rhetoric's traditional opponents. We may even wonder whether Rabelais should be aligned with the many celebrated detractors

---

[1] G 39. All Rabelais quotations are from the Pléiade edition of Rabelais's *Oeuvres complètes*, ed. Mireille Huchon (Paris: Gallimard, 1994). Standard abbreviations for the four books are G (*Gargantua*, Book I in English editions), P (*Pantagruel*, Book II), TL (*Tiers Livre*, Book III) and QL (*Quart Livre*, Book IV).

of rhetoric, from Socrates to Montaigne via Cornelius Agrippa, who called it "the art of fauninge flatterie."[2]

The specialist reader is aware that Rabelais, like his hero Erasmus before him, in fact takes a typically humanist view of rhetoric, and that since the pioneering work of M. A. Screech forty years ago,[3] numerous critics have stressed the central place of rhetoric in Rabelais's comic humanist universe. Paul Smith sees the Prologue to *Pantagruel* as already fundamentally indebted to rhetorical precepts.[4] Gargantua's famous letter to his son on education (P 8) replaces the scholastic emphasis on grammar as the foundation of liberal studies by stressing languages and style.[5] The uselessness of Gargantua's bad old education is dramatically demonstrated to his father Grandgousier by the young page Eudémon's rhetorical encomium (G 15),[6] and the good new humanist education includes attention to *pronuntiatio* as well as much solid erudition. In all four books we find extended rhetorical *exercices de style*, including formal speeches (G 15, 31, 50; TL 43), Ciceronian letters (P 8, G 29, QL 3 and 4), a sermon (G 45), two laments (G 3 and 28), paradoxical encomia (TL 3–4, 49–52), enigmas (G 2 and 58), an *explication de texte* (G 38), a facetious ecphrasis (QL 2), and numerous examples of what the French call *blason*: rhetorically structured praise or blame of, for instance, women's genitalia (P 15), Gargantua's toilet-paper substitutes (G 13), the abbey of Thélème (G 51–57), testicles (TL 26), fools (TL 38), Dindenault's marvelous sheep (QL 6–7), and the frozen words (QL 55–56).[7]

Of the four books, it is the third which is most largely preoccupied with rhetoric.[8] It begins and ends with a paradoxical encomium, of debts

[2]*Of the Vanitie and Vncertaintie of Artes and Sciences*, trans. James Sanford, ed. Catherine M. Dunn (Northridge, Calif.: California State University Press, 1974), 43.

[3]In particular in *The Rabelaisian Marriage* (London: Arnold, 1958).

[4]"Le Prologue du *Pantagruel*: Une lecture," *Neophilologus* 68 (1984): 161–69, here 162.

[5]See Edwin M. Duval, "The Medieval Curriculum, The Scholastic University, and Gargantua's Program of Studies (*Pantagruel*, 8)," *Rabelais's Incomparable Book*, ed. Raymond C. La Charité (Lexington: French Forum Monographs, 1986), 30–44.

[6]See G. J. Brault, "The Significance of Eudemon's Praise of Gargantua (*Rabelais*, 1:15)," *Kentucky Romance Quarterly* 18 (1971): 307–17.

[7]Some recent critics have attempted to paint a more somber picture of Renaissance rhetoric, as fundamentally iconoclastic (W. Scott Blanchard, *Scholar's Bedlam: Menippean Satire in the Renaissance* [Lewisburg: Bucknell University Press, 1995]) or subversive (Wayne A. Rebhorn, *The Emperor of Men's Minds: Literature and the Renaissance Discourse of Rhetoric* [Ithaca: Cornell University Press, 1995]). Even if they are right, and not overextrapolating from isolated instances, I would still maintain that Rabelais does not share these views. His rhetoric, when properly used by *viri boni*, is entirely good.

[8]The debate over Rabelais's authorship of the Fifth Book is still, in my opinion, open, so I am not taking it into account here.

and the plant Pantagruélion respectively, and its central figure, Panurge, is the walking antithesis, not just of the good Stoic and the good Evangelical Christian, but of the good orator, as Screech was the first to demonstrate. Panurge willfully confuses what Thomas Wilson would call an infinite (general) question: "Is it better to marry or not?" with a definite (specific) one: "Is it better for me, Panurge, at this time to marry or not?"[9] After every specialist consultation designed to resolve his dilemma, Pantagruel interprets the advice as unfavorable, while Panurge sees it as favorable, providing a series of comic illustrations of the wily orator who can always make the worse case appear the better case. For instance, in chapter 13 Panurge recounts his dream of a pretty young wife kissing and embracing him and planting two horns in his forehead, after which he is suddenly transformed into a tambourine and she into an owl. To Pantagruel this means that Panurge will be cuckolded, beaten, and robbed by his wife—his conclusion about other oracles besides this one. For Panurge, "on the contrary" (his favorite phrase), the horns mean a cornucopia of good things, the tambourine that he will be as happy as a drum at a wedding feast, and the owl that his wife will be pretty and affectionate.

Most critics have seen a striking difference between this dishonest-orator Panurge of the Third Book, and his persona in the first book published by Rabelais, *Pantagruel*, which is Book II in collective editions. In this first book, Panurge remains close to his literary ancestors Margutte (in Pulci's *Morgante*) and Cingar (in Folengo's *Baldus*); he is a trickster specializing in ingenious practical devices and gratuitous villainy, whereas in the Third Book he does nothing but talk. I believe that his change of personality has been exaggerated, and that in *Pantagruel* he is already an accomplished orator as well as a practical joker; the embodiment, in fact, of Wayne Rebhorn's trickster as *homo rhetoricus*.[10] An excellent illustration of this, I think, is the episode of the Great Lady of Paris, which I propose to concentrate on in this article.

∽

As chapter 21[11] of *Pantagruel* opens, the giant Pantagruel and his companions are in Paris, where Pantagruel is pursuing his humanist education.

[9] *The Arte of Rhetorique* (1553), ed. Robert Hood Bowers (Gainesville: Scholars' Facsimiles and Reprints, 1962).

[10] Wayne A. Rebhorn, "'The Emperour of Mens Minds:' The Renaissance Trickster as *homo rhetoricus*," *Creative Imitation: New Essays on Renaissance Literature in Honor of Thomas M. Greene*, ed. David Quint et al. (Binghamton: Medieval and Renaissance Texts and Studies, 1992), 31–65. Rebhorn does not discuss Panurge.

[11] Chapter 14 in the first edition, chapter 21 in all collective editions.

Panurge, the disreputable trickster, has just triumphed, in a hilarious debate conducted entirely in sign language, over a learned Englishman called Thaumaste, and has thereby become a well-known figure and very pleased with himself. He decides, at the beginning of chapter 21, to set his sights on one of the great ladies of Paris (the French "venir au dessus de" indicates that he wants both to dominate her and to bed her). His declaration is couched at first in very down-to-earth language, then in a mixture of obscenities and high-flown metaphors. He continues his pursuit next day in church and after dinner at her house, but the lady still resists his advances with feigned indignation, even when he tries to bribe her, so he runs off, apparently defeated.

In the next chapter, Panurge concocts a powerful drug from the sexual organs of a bitch in heat, and scatters it over the lady's clothes in church during the celebration of Corpus Christi, with the result that "more than" (!) 600,014 dogs climb on her and piss all over her (piss and shit on her, in the first edition). The spectators are astonished, the chambermaids laugh, and even Pantagruel finds the spectacle "very fine and novel."

Relatively few critics have discussed these two chapters in detail. For Bakhtin[12] the lady's humiliation is typically carnivalesque debasement; to feminist critics,[13] naturally enough, it is a striking example of Rabelais's antifeminism; and Florence Weinberg wonders if the transformation of the dogs' urine into a cleansing river might be intended to suggest Christian redemption.[14] Most strikingly, François Rigolot, in two articles of different title but almost identical content,[15] sees the humiliated lady as a figure for the tormented Christ. All these interpretations are entertaining, but none of them seems to me to address the most obvious aspect of the text (and Rigolot's strikes me as frankly indefensible).

Panurge's first sentence to the lady runs as follows (in the Donald Frame translation[16]): "My lady, it would be most useful for the whole commonwealth, pleasurable for you, honorable to your line, and necessary for me,

---

[12]Mikhail Bakhtin, *Rabelais and His World*, trans. Helene Iswolsky (Cambridge: M.I.T. Press, 1968), 229–31.

[13]For instance, Carla Freccero, "Damning Haughty Dames: Panurge and the Haulte Dame de Paris (*Pantagruel* 14)," *Journal of Medieval and Renaissance Studies* 15 (1985): 57–67.

[14]An opinion expressed in long-ago discussion, and in a letter to me of 7 June 1995.

[15]François Rigolot, "Rabelais, Misogyny, and Christian Charity: Biblical Intertextuality and the Renaissance Crisis of Exemplarity," *Publications of the Modern Language Society of America* 109 (1994): 225–37; "The Three Temptations of Panurge: Women's Vilification and Christian Humanist Discourse," *François Rabelais: Critical Assessments*, ed. Jean-Claude Carron (Baltimore: Johns Hopkins University Press, 1995), 83–102.

[16]*The Complete Works of François Rabelais*, trans. Donald M. Frame (Berkeley: University of California Press, 1991). All quotations from Rabelais in English are from this edition.

that you should be covered by my breed; and take my word for it, for experience will demonstrate it to you." This is at first sight puzzling; in what way could their union be useful to the commonwealth? how would an affair with the penniless vagabond Panurge be honorable to the lady's line? But the four terms—useful, pleasurable, honorable, and necessary—are the four topics essential to any set rhetorical theme: *utile, iucundum, honestum,* and *necessarium,*[17] or as a contemporary English jingle put it: "Four things to praise all topics amply go: Virtue and use, pleasure and goodness show."[18]

Panurge appears then to be opening a formal oration, which will go on to explore each of the four topics in detail. His ability to manipulate rhetorical techniques is already evident in the insinuation that while the *necessarium* applies to him, all the *iucundum* will be for the lady!

The apparently serious beginning to this sentence renders all the more comic Panurge's sudden descent, not just into vulgarity, but into the impersonality of animal husbandry: The French words "couvrir" and "race" are used of horses and dogs, not of human beings. But the end of the sentence reverts to a rhetorical context; arguments from experience are routinely used in formal debate.

The lady's outraged rejection focuses less on Panurge's desire than on its expression: "You crazy wretch, have you any right to talk to me that way? Whom do you think you're talking to..." implying that she is offended by the form rather than the content of the proposition; she ends by threatening to have his arms and legs cut off. Panurge, far from being disconcerted or discouraged, comes back with a second declaration, which is worth quoting in full:

> Or (dist il) ce me seroit bien tout un d'avoir bras et jambes couppez, en condition que nous fissons vous et moy un transon de chere lie, jouans des manequins à basses marches: car (monstrant sa longue braguette) voicy maistre Jean Jeudy: qui vous sonneroit une antiquaille, dont vous sentirez jusques à la moelle des os. Il est galland et vous sçait tant bien trouver les alibitz forains et petitz poullains grenez en la ratouere, que après luy n'y a que espousseter.[19]

The initial impression of lyricism, in this paragraph, is belied by a closer look at its dazzling succession of metaphors, from banqueting (chere

---

[17]See Carol Clark, *The Vulgar Rabelais* (Glasgow: Pressgang, 1983), 128.

[18]Quoted by Anthony Grafton and Lisa Jardine, *From Humanism to the Humanities: Education and the Liberal Arts in Fifteenth- and Sixteenth-Century Europe* (Cambridge: Harvard University Press, 1986), 17.

[19]"Well, now," said he, "it would be all the same to me to have my arms and legs cut off, on

lie, only loosely translated by Frame's "roll in the hay"), weaving (manne-
quins à basses marches, no English equivalent), music (sonneroit une anti-
quaille), law (alibitz forains, not translated), rat-catching (ratouere), and
housekeeping (espousseter). The last two, particularly homely, metaphors
stress that Panurge's mind is more on practical action than on high-flown
words. The personification of Panurge's penis is both charming and hilarious, and his ability to convey a vulgar message via an apparently high-
flown style is brilliant.

Surprisingly, the lady's response to this is if anything milder: "Be off,
you wretch, be off. If you *say* one more *word* to me, I'll call my men and
have you beaten to a pulp right here" (my italics; presumably a less horrible punishment than her previous suggestion). So Panurge, too, changes
his tune, and launches into a fulsome panegyric, couched presumably in
the kind of neo-Petrarchan language the lady wants to hear. The entire
order of the universe would have to be perverted before such beauty as
hers could contain a drop of malice; her beauty is such that Nature gave it
to her to prove how all-powerful she is; she is composed of honey, sugar,
and celestial manna; Paris should have awarded the golden apple to her,
since she outdoes Juno in magnificence, Minerva in prudence, and Venus
in elegance.

So far so good, but a sixteenth-century reader knew that medieval and
Renaissance mythographers saw the Judgment of Paris *topos* as a moral
condemnation of Paris, "cet effeminé pasteur de Phrygie" as Montaigne
calls him.[20] In preferring Venus, that is to say, in choosing the sensual life
rather than the active or contemplative, he made a foolish choice, which is
why in Cranach's painting of the *topos,* the little Cupid firing at Paris has
asses' ears. Might this not imply to an erudite reader that the haughty lady
would be an even worse choice?

Panurge's lyrical *copia* in this passage suggests that he could go on like
this indefinitely, but his next sentence reverts to the bathos technique: "O
celestial gods and goddesses, how happy will be the man to whom you
grant that boon to embrace this lady, to kiss her—and to rub his bacon
with her." I do not know whether "to rub bacon" is a standard American

---

condition that you and I should have a nice roll in the hay together, playing the stiff lowdown in-and-
out game; for (showing his long codpiece) here is Master Johnny Jumpup, who will sound you an antic
dance that you'll feel to the marrow of your bones. He's a lusty one, and so expert at finding out the little out-of-the-way spots and swellings in and around the crotch and in the rat-trap that after him
there's no need for dusting."

[20] *Essais*, 1:26 (De l'institution des enfans).

phrase, or whether Frame invented it to translate "frotter son lart avec elle," which is a common sixteenth-century French vulgarism; in any case, the sudden bathetic descent from lyricism to vulgarity would have been more shocking, and thus more comic, to contemporary readers than it is to us. This sentence always reminds me of Jeeves' telling Bertie Wooster that full many a glorious morning had he seen flatter the mountaintops with sovereign eye, and then turn into a rather nasty afternoon.[21]

Shortly after this, Panurge leaves, "without worrying very much about the refusal he had had." The next day he accosts the lady in church, and his opening words to her emphasize the earthy nature of his desire: he is so in love with her that he can neither piss nor shit. He produces a very rude spoonerism on "A Beaumont le Vicomte" (brilliantly translated by Frame[22]), and plays on the secondary, obscene sense of the word knife. He also takes away her rosary beads, which causes her some anxiety until she reflects that she can tell her husband they were stolen in church.

After dinner the same day, Panurge visits the lady for the last time, and tries to bribe her by asking if she wouldn't like a gift of paternosters "in nicely enameled gold in the shape of great spheres or nice love-knots, or else all massive like gold ingots? Or do you want them of ebony, or big hyacinths, great cut garnets, with markers of fine turquoise or of lovely marked topazes…," expensive velvet and satin, or assorted jewelry. To support his *persona* of generous giver to whom money is no object, he jingles the tokens in his purse as though they were gold coins. These promises "made her mouth water"—she is obviously greedy—but she persists in her refusal. When Panurge tries to embrace her, "she started screaming, however not too loud"—she is obviously a hypocrite. He then insults her, threatens to have her "ridden by the dogs," and runs off rapidly, "for fear of blows, of which by nature he was afraid."

Panurge's revenge, the subject of chapter 22, is elaborately thought out. We are told in detail how, the day before the feast of Corpus Christi, he gets hold of a bitch in heat (designated by a scientific term, "une lycisque orgoose"), feeds her, and the next morning kills her and removes her sexual organs (designated by a periphrasis, "ce que sçavent les Geomantiens Gregoys") and chops them fine, to compose what will henceforth be referred to as "la drogue."

At the beginning of the chapter, we learn that for this feast day all the women wear their most beautiful clothes, and Panurge's lady "had put on

[21]P. G. Wodehouse, *The Code of the Woosters*, ch. 4.
[22]Rabelais's French: "*A beaumont le viconte / A beau con le vit monte*," Frame's English: "*A creek rises for a handsome punt / A prick rises for a handsome cunt.*"

a very beautiful gown of crimson satin, and a very precious white velvet petticoat." Panurge goes up to her in church, and to distract her attention while he is scattering the drug over her clothes, presents her with a *rondeau*, which, while quite clear in content, is not obscene or insulting; it ends: "For nothing do I ask, but that in turn / You tumble blithely into bed with me / For this one time." He also tells her that he hopes the love pangs he is suffering will be deducted from his pains in purgatory, and asks her to pray God to give him "patience in my plight." When the dogs, attracted by the smell of the drug, run up and start climbing all over her, Panurge at first pretends to chase them off, and then retires into the role of spectator, while "those nasty dogs pissed all over her clothes, to the point where a big greyhound pissed on her head, the others in her sleeves, the others on her crupper; and the little ones pissed on her shoes, so that all the women around her had much to do to save her. And Panurge kept right on laughing, and said to one of the lords of the city: 'I think that lady is in heat, or else some greyhound has covered her recently.'"

This is a particularly cogent remark; in a sense Panurge is punishing the lady because she is not in heat—because unlike him, she apparently feels no animal desire. He is reminding her, brutally, of the realities behind the flowery, courtly or neo-Petrarchan language she thinks suitors should use. Even so, his revenge often strikes modern readers as unnecessarily cruel and protracted, since the disgraceful scene continues during the Corpus Christi procession, where we are given the specific number of the dogs—"plus de six cens mille et quatorze," and told that she provides entertainment for large numbers of people; Pantagruel "saw the show, which he found very fine and novel," and "everybody stopped at this spectacle, watching the antics of those dogs...." Nobody, as far as we can tell, either sympathizes with the lady or condemns Panurge for the ferocity of his practical joke.

∽

We do not need modern Freudians to point out to us the close connections between oral emission and anal or genital emission. Plutarch had already, in the *De garrulitate*, drawn attention to the similarities between garrulousness and barren seed, and the analogy between penis and tongue is not uncommon in Renaissance literature; in act 1, scene 1 of Webster's *Duchess of Malfi*, Ferdinand states that "woemen like that part, which (like the Lamprey) / Hath nev'r a bone in it," and when the Duchess professes to be shocked he defends himself with: "Nay, / I meane the Tongue...." But I fail to see a connection between the violence of Panurge's revenge and any supposed sexual frustration on his part. The structure of the whole episode seems to me to indicate clearly that from the start Panurge knows exactly what he is doing, and manipulates both language and action in a specific direction. His initial sly reference to the four topics serves to alert the reader that this episode will be about rhetoric; his alternation of neo-Petrarchan bombast and down-to-earth crudity points up the lady's foolish preoccupation with words, as does her own repetition of verbs of speaking; and the climactic spectacle of the poor lady harassed by all the dogs in Paris is a theatrical performance stage-managed by an artful director.

Panurge, who has already "put his codpiece to good use," as we are told at the beginning of the episode, and indeed boasted, in chapter 15, that he has bedded 417 women of Paris in the nine days of his residence in the city (so much for the likelihood of sexual frustration), is not about to be cast down by the refusal of one "great lady." He would have to be remarkably stupid to assume that his gross verbal approach to the lady would cause her to fall into his arms, and Panurge is certainly not stupid. I propose that, on the contrary, he deliberately uses an approach which he knows cannot succeed, because his real objective is a pretext for the revenge that will follow the lady's refusal. He surely gets much more pleasure, in chapter 22, from the spectacle of the lady's distress and humiliation, than he would have from sleeping with her. As we saw in chapter 16, his favorite practical jokes are always those which hurt and/or humiliate their victims.

If this interpretation is correct, must we conclude that Panurge is a sexually perverted character? I think not; but he is certainly an extremely disagreeable personality, as other cruel tricks besides this one attest, which makes it odd indeed that Pantagruel, the virtuous giant, has such affection for him. But perhaps, as Edwin Duval and others have suggested, we are dealing here with the Christian concept of *caritas*—the nastier our neighbor is, the more truly Christian it will be to love him as we love ourselves.[23] These are intriguing questions, and outside the very modest scope of this article, which has been to propose that in Rabelais's first book we already meet the Panurge-as-dishonest-orator who will be the central character of another book, thirteen years later.

[23]See Edwin M. Duval, *The Design of Rabelais's Pantagruel* (New Haven: Yale University Press, 1991).

# HUMANISM AND CHURCH REFORM IN FRANCE

## The Role of Parisian-Trained Provincial College Masters before 1562

*Gwendolyn Blotevogel*

THE TWIN CHILDREN OF THE FRENCH RENAISSANCE, humanist studies and church reform, were born in the early sixteenth century. As the intellectual center of northern France, the University of Paris provided the seedbed for these new and exciting currents of thought, despite its predominantly scholastic curriculum and the orthodoxy of its theology faculty. By the start of the Wars of Religion in 1562, the twin offspring of Paris had reached the provinces, brought by college masters who were recruited from the Paris arts faculty to teach humanist subjects in provincial colleges. Provincial town councils recruited these masters for their ability to teach the *belles lettres* (i.e., classical literature) to bourgeois youth; many of the masters also brought with them unexpected and often unwelcome ideas advocating church reform.

In sixteenth-century Paris, the medieval scholastic curriculum continued to form the basis of statutory graduation requirements in the arts faculty at the University of Paris. The last revisions of the statutes of the arts faculty before the sixteenth century were the 1452 reforms made by Cardinal d'Estouteville under papal mandate. These statute revisions outlined the texts to be studied before determinance (graduation), and licensing (to teach). They indicate a thoroughly scholastic course of study based on Aristotelian works including the *Organon, De Anima, Physics,* and *Nichomachean Ethics.* The designated grammar book was the medieval, scholastic *Doctrinale* of Alexander of Villedieu. From a strictly statutory standpoint, the University of Paris was a medieval institution until the last decade of the sixteenth century, when Henry IV ordered that the statutes mandate humanist studies.[1]

Before these 1598 statute revisions, the humanist subjects of literature and poetry were relegated to the status of extraordinary studies, outside of the arts curriculum entirely.[2] As French scholars began to explore the world beyond the Alps, returning from Italy after having been exposed to the new humanist studies, they challenged the scholastic curriculum. There was therefore a dynamic tension between the powerful Paris theology faculty, which advocated a specialized scholastic arts course designed to prepare students for rigorous studies in theology, and humanists within the arts faculty who emphasized the importance of grammar and rhetoric. These humanists believed that rhetoric rather than logic should be the goal of arts study because it taught one to be persuasive and to conduct oneself appropriately in the affairs of the world. They opposed the barbarous Latin of the schools in favor of a more elegant style; instead of asking students to puzzle over subtle logical problems designed to train them for theological debate, they asked students to write sensibly and persuasively.[3] In short, humanist interests reflected the changing world in which educated men had a place outside of the clergy, in the royal courts or the mercantile economy. The statute reforms of 1598 brought humanist texts and a study of humanist subjects into the mainstream of the Paris arts curriculum. This statute change reflects a humanist curriculum which had been reality for some time.[4]

If the 1598 statutes formalized a humanist education which had been developed outside the regular arts curriculum at Paris, how were humanist studies taught in Paris before 1598? Mark Curtis's 1959 study tracing the sources of humanism at the English universities of Oxford and Cambridge may point to a possible answer. He finds that although university statutes mandated a scholastic education within the university, the developing

---

[1]Statutory requirements are outlined in Augustin Renaudet, *Préréforme et humanisme à Paris pendant les premières guerres d'Italie (1494–1517)* 2d ed. (Paris: D'Argenas, 1953), 28. See also L.B.W. Brockliss, "The University of Paris in the Sixteenth and Seventeenth Centuries" (Ph.D. diss., Cambridge University, 1976). On d'Estouteville's reforms, see André Tuilier, *Histoire de l'Université de Paris et de la Sorbonne* (Paris: Nouvelle Librairie de France, 1995), 1:242–49.

[2]Arthur Tilley, *The Dawn of the French Renaissance* (1918; repr. New York: Russell and Russell, 1968), 212–13.

[3]E. J. Ashworth, "Changes in Logic Textbooks from 1500 to 1650: The New Aristotelianism," in *Aristotelismus und Renaissance: In Memoriam Charles B. Schmitt*, ed. Eckhard Kessler, Charles H. Lohr, and Walter Sparn (Wiesbaden: Harrassowitz, 1988), 84.

[4]Tuilier, *French Renaissance,* 435–73.

college system was able to provide extrastatutory humanist studies.[5] Although studies comparable to Mark Curtis's have not been completed for Paris, there is evidence that the colleges also provided a home for humanist studies in Paris.[6]

Throughout the Middle Ages, education at the University of Paris was organized through the nations. As in England, Parisian colleges were originally designed to house poor scholarship students from the provinces who were sent to the university to study theology in the hope that they would return to their homes to serve as clergy. In the early sixteenth century, however, the colleges began to take on teaching responsibilities.[7] Gradually, masters began to associate themselves with certain colleges and use the space within these boarding houses as classrooms. Larger, well-endowed colleges began to hire régents. Eventually, some colleges were able to offer a full course of studies within their walls.[8] These *Collèges de Plein Exercice* became the teaching centers of the arts faculty; students living in the smaller colleges which did not offer a full course of studies attended these larger colleges for their classwork. Thus, colleges in Paris developed a cooperative teaching system; arts instruction became structured around a "system of intercollegiate lectures."[9]

Michael Ruelos believes that this collegiate system was receptive to the innovative ideas current in the intellectual world of sixteenth-century France. The decentralized instruction provided by the colleges offered a safe haven for the introduction of humanist subjects. Although the statutory graduation requirements were prescribed, all masters had the right to teach as they wished so long as they avoided banned and heretical books. Colleges provided them with a stable base of students with whom they could share their love for poetry and classical authors.[10] Thus despite resistance from the traditional elements of the university (most notably

---

[5]Mark H. Curtis, *Oxford and Cambridge in Transition, 1558–1642* (Oxford: Clarendon, 1959). For more recent studies confirming Curtis's conclusions, see *The History of the University of Oxford,* vol. 3: *The Collegiate University,* ed. James McConica (Oxford: Clarendon Press, 1986).

[6]Michel Reulos, "L'Université et les Collèges," in *Association Guillaume Budè Bulletin,* 3d ser. (1953), detailed below, provides some insight into humanist activity in Paris colleges, but the study is far from exhaustive.

[7]Gordon Leff, *Paris and Oxford Universities in the Thirteenth and Fourteenth Centuries: An Institutional and Intellectual History* (New York: John Wiley & Sons, Inc., 1968), 69–70; see also Tuilier, 150–51.

[8]Reulos, "L'Université et les Collèges," 38.

[9]Hastings Rashdall, *The Universities of Europe in the Middle Ages,* ed. F. M. Powicke and A. B. Emden, 3 vols. (Oxford: Clarendon Press, 1936), 1:528–29. See also Reulos, 38–40, and Roger Chartier, Dominique Julia, and Marie-Madeleine Compère, *L'Education en France des XVIe au XVIIIe Siècles* (Paris: Société d'Edition D'Enseignement, 1976), 151–52.

[10]Reulos, "L'Université et les Collèges," 35.

the theology faculty), which sometimes opposed humanist methodologi-
cal innovations, the colleges were malleable institutions, easily able to
introduce students to humanist thought and method and thus permit the
spread of humanism in Paris.[11] The "souplesse" of the colleges and the
courses which masters could offer in them were an invitation to curricular
innovation.[12]

Another important feature of the college system was the formal structure of studies which developed as a result of the centralization of teaching
in the colleges. Before the colleges became the center of arts study, students often attended courses in random order according to convenience;
furthermore, the content of courses was not well defined by the university
statutes and was largely left up to the masters. Generally, the university did
not concern itself with regulating the use of texts so long as the material
did not contain religious heresy.[13] The statutes were, of course, a guide to
studies, but they contained only a minimum required reading list; they did
not forbid other studies. The colleges offered something unique: instead of
gaining an education from disparate places throughout Paris, within the
colleges a student could move from elementary training in grammar to
advanced courses in rhetoric and logic through an organized sequence of
courses.

This standardization began in the larger colleges which gradually organized their curricula into a series of graded classes, each taught by a separate regent and attended by students at the same level of advancement in
their studies. The colleges with a full range of studies were the *Collèges de
Plein Exercice*. This organized series of courses was first introduced in Paris
by Jan Standonck in 1509 at the College of Montaigu. The structure came
to be known as the *Modus Parisiensis*. It did not dictate course content, but
was rather a discipline which organized and regularized the lives and the
schedule of studies followed by students at Parisian colleges.[14] The liberal
arts, from the most basic grammar to the most advanced lessons in philosophy, were covered in a sequential order so students working together in
the same class would have the same background and thus the same ability
to comprehend the subject at hand. In describing his own education in the
year 1542 at the College of Bourgogne in Paris, one student, Henri de Mesmes, describes some of the principal features of sixteenth-century college

---

[11]Reulos, "L'Université et les Collèges," 38.
[12]Ibid., 40.
[13]Ibid., 38–39.
[14]Chartier, *L'Education en France*, 157–58.

life in Paris: public disputation, familiarity with classical examples of virtue, a frugal life, and a strict daily schedule.[15]

The colleges provided a place and a structure for humanist studies at the University of Paris, but the *Collège de France,* founded in 1530 by Francis I, marks the first official institutionalization of humanist studies in Paris. Although the college had neither buildings of its own nor the right to grant degrees, the professors appointed to teach humanist subjects had a powerful influence over the development of studies in sixteenth-century Paris. The *Collège de France* provided a center for the progress of humanist scholarship and teaching in Paris, often openly opposing the narrow, increasingly stagnant scholastic curriculum of the university.[16] The study of Greek, for example, did not become a part of the curriculum of the *Collèges de Plein Exercice,* where Latin grammar still reigned supreme, but it was available as an extraordinary study through the *Collège de France.*[17]

It is therefore clear that by 1530 humanist subjects were studied in Paris within the arts curriculum. In the early years of the century, humanists encountered little resistance from the powerful theology faculty which by the sixteenth century dominated the other faculties at Paris. It was not until the Reformation threatened the established moral and ecclesiastical order that the theology faculty actively and systematically opposed humanist studies. Recent research by James Farge into the proceedings of the theology faculty confirms that the faculty did not generally concern itself with pedagogical differences of opinion between the scholastics and the humanists until after the 1521 condemnation of Martin Luther.[18] Scholars on both sides of the debate held to the common sixteenth-century belief that education was a means of instilling moral fortitude into the youth of France. Two of the leading humanist educational reformers, Erasmus and Ramus, held that the practical purpose of education was to instill proper morals and foster an appreciation for great moral examples from the classical Latin world. Such examples were to provide a blueprint for a student's own individual excellence. Thus the role of the university was to preserve a moral Christian culture. While scholastic theologians

---

[15]De Mesmes describes his Paris college experience as follows: "J'appris a répeter, disputer et haranguer en public, pris connaissance d'honnêtes enfants dont aucune vivent aujourd'hui, appris la vie frugale de la scolarité et à régler mes heures"; Chartier, 158–59.

[16]David T. Pottinger, *The French Book Trade in the Anciene Regime, 1500–1791* (Cambridge, Mass.: Harvard University Press, 1958), 15. See also Peter Bietenholz, *Basel and France in the Sixteenth Century: The Basel Humanists and Printing in Their Contacts with Francophone Culture* (Geneva: Librairie Droz, 1971), 178.

[17]Chartier, *L'Education en France,* 157.

[18]James Farge, *Orthodoxy and Reform in Early Reformation France: The Faculty of Theology of Paris, 1500–1543* (Leiden: E. J. Brill, 1985), 170.

generally agreed with Erasmus and Ramus in their conception of the university as the preserver of high moral culture, they did not agree that the ancient world provided the best examples. Preservation of the existing social order, specifically of the Roman church, was the way to ensure proper morality. There was, therefore, more at stake in the question of whether to teach scholastic grammar and logic or humanist subjects than simple pedagogical method or the matter of which subjects would be more useful. The moral and religious character of a whole generation of students was held in the balance.[19]

Thus the independence of the faculties at the University of Paris allowed humanism to grow in the arts faculty, but only until it became clear that humanist studies might threaten the status quo. In the 1530s (ironically, the decade which opened with the foundation of the *Collège de France* by Francis I) the theology faculty and the king (still Francis I) began to attack Lutheranism; humanist studies suffered as a result. In 1533, the University of Paris condemned Lutheran books, and early in 1535 the king personally warned the faculties to make sure their students were properly indoctrinated. That is, he wished to make sure the new reforming ideas were not taught.[20] In July 1534, just a few months before the Affair of the Placards whereby Protestants were condemned for publicly denouncing the pope and the Catholic mass, the university passed a statute which was designed to legislate proper moral behavior in the students. Many of the statute's provisions were not unique or new, merely repeating medieval rules on student discipline. For example, students were forbidden to carry arms, visit taverns or theaters, and fight in the streets; they were also admonished to wear their academic garb and avoid reading unauthorized literature. The primary concern of the statute, however, was in response to humanist teaching. It sought to restore order to the Paris curriculum by reinforcing the supremacy of Aristotle and the scholastic method over the grammar and rhetoric of the humanists.[21] The humanists were perceived to be the promoters of academic and religious heresy.

These reactions to the teaching of humanist subjects came too late to stop its spread. By 1530 humanist-trained masters from Paris were already teaching in provincial colleges, and the demand for them only increased as the century wore on. Colleges were beginning to replace universities as the educational centers of France because bourgeois townsmen, seeking

---

[19]Donald R. Kelly, *The Beginning of Ideology: Consciousness and Society in the French Reformation* (Cambridge: Cambridge University Press, 1981), 137–38.

[20]Ibid., 17.

[21]Ibid., 133–34.

lucrative careers outside the church for their sons, found their local college more suited to their needs.[22] The rising bourgeois class, the "gentry" as George Huppert labels them,[23] was the primary driving force behind the foundation of these provincial colleges.[24] This new social group was interested in learning and in providing a classical education which would not only bring its offspring lucrative legal and court careers but would also make them into *gens de bien*—well-educated and socially responsible young adults. In order to create these *gens de bien*, it was necessary that the provincial schools offer a special type of education, more advanced than the catechism and *abécédaire* of the early municipal schools and separate from the Latin education provided by the church to educate the clergy.[25] Students needed to be exposed to literary examples of good men who were doing brave and altruistic deeds. The source for these examples, of course, was classical literature.

Humanist studies formed the nucleus of the provincial college curriculum. In Condom, for example, the town consuls ordinarily tried to keep three masters to teach in the local college: a master of arts, called an *arcien* or *artiste*, a poet, and a grammarian. The grammarian was charged with preparing the primary students to graduate to the *belles lettres* under the tutelage of the *artiste* and the poet.[26] Thus in Condom, humanist subjects were taught in a graded series of courses in the tradition of the *Modus Parisiensis*.[27] The founders of colleges in other provincial towns were still more specific about the subjects to be taught. In Toulouse, the statutes listed the specific authors to be studied. "Said principal shall have read to the said classes the works of Cicero, Quintillian, Virgil, Horace, Persius,

---

[22]Jacques LeGoff, "La conception française de l'université à l'époque de la Renaissance," in *Les Universités Européennes du XIVe au XVIIIe Siècle*, L'Institut d'Histoire de la Faculté des Lettres de l'Université de Genève, 4 (Geneva: Librairie Droz, 1967), 98–99.

[23]See George Huppert, *Les Bourgeois Gentilshommes* (Chicago: University of Chicago Press, 1977), esp. chap. 7.

[24]George Huppert, *Public Schools in Renaissance France* (Urbana: University of Illinois Press, 1984). The old argument made by Chartier et al., *L'Education en France*, and by François Dainville, *La Naissance de L'Humanisme Moderne*, vol. 1 (Paris: Beauchesne et ses fils, 1940), that these schools were set up by Calvinists or Jesuits interested in inculcating Reformed or Catholic values throughout France no longer holds up in light of the foundation dates of many of the schools (before the Reformed church or the Jesuits even existed in France) and the business reflected in town council meetings which discussed the foundation of these schools. An argument similar to Huppert's based on the same types of sources, has been made for Italian community schools in Paul Grendler, *Schooling in Renaissance Italy: Literacy and Learning, 1300–1600* (Baltimore: Johns Hopkins University Press, 1989).

[25]For an account of the availability and arrangement of education for laymen in the fifteenth and early sixteenth century in French provincial towns, see Huppert, *Public Schools*, chap.1.

[26]J. Gardère, "Les écoles de Condom" *Revue de Gascogne: Bulletin Mensuel de la Société Historique de Gascogne*, 26 (1885), 422.

[27]See the discussion of the *Modus Parisiensis*, above, p. 136-37.

Juvenal, Ovid, Titus Livius, the commentaries of Caesar, Valerius Maximus, Lorenzo Valla [*Elegantiae linguae latinae*], Terrence, Dépautre [*Commentarii grammatici*], Cato, and the dialectics of George of Trebizonde, Caesar, Aristotle, and other authors." They were also to teach Greek, rhetoric, and philosophy "according to the ability of the scholars."[28] Clearly the authors of the statutes for the *Collège de L'Esquile* in Toulouse sought a humanist curriculum.

Eventually almost every town of any size got its own local college. In most cases, the education was offered free for all youth whose families were citizens of the municipality; noncitizens were usually allowed to attend for a fee.[29] The goal of these schools was to provide what the independent masters and cathedral schools could not—a quality, secular education close to home for the town's youth.

Students in provincial colleges, like Henri de Mesmes in Paris, lived very regulated lives, though most were not subjected to the round-the-clock supervision of the Paris collegians because they did not live in the colleges but returned home every night. The virtues of "order, regularity, hard work," which had been celebrated by the ancients, were highly regarded.[30] Essentially the provincial colleges sought to model the Parisian structure, the *Modus Parisiensis*. In Toulouse, for example, the principal of L'Esquile, the town's college, was ordered to organize his regent masters to teach specific classical authors "at certain times and at the sound of the bell...in imitation of the colleges of Paris."[31] The education sought by the provincial college founders, which was a classical moral education set in a highly regulated and organized structure, already existed in Paris with the humanists teaching in the Parisian colleges structured according to the *Modus Parisiensis*. Therefore, in recruiting masters, most communities demonstrated a strong preference for graduates of the University of Paris.

Largely because of the reform movement at Paris, an increasing number of regent masters who came from Paris to the provinces to teach in

---

[28]"Item ledit principal fera lire aux dites classes les oeuvres de Cicéron, Quintillien, Virgile, Horace, Perse, Juvénal, Ovide, Tite Lives, les commentaires de César, Vallère plus grand, Laurens Valle, Térence, Dispautère, Cathon et la dialectique de Trapézonas, César et Aristote et autres auteurs, comme les classes le requerront, ensemble quelques lectures en grec, rhétorique, philosophie, suivant la capacité des escoliers." From the original town council minutes transcribed in: M. Abbe Corraze, "L'Esquile, Collège des Capitouls," *Memoires de l'Academie des Sciences Inscriptions et Belles-Lettres de Toulouse*, 12th ser., 15 (1937): 180.

[29]See Huppert, *Les Bourgeois Gentilhommes*, chap. 7, and Huppert, *Public Schools in Renaissance France*, for more complete accounts of the foundation of these schools.

[30]Huppert, *Public Schools*, 75.

[31]"par heures certanes et au son de la cloche...à l'imitation des collièges de Paris"; Corraze, "L'Esquile," 180.

provincial schools were advocates of church reform. Many masters who studied humanist subjects had also been introduced to reformed ideas— and, later, specifically Calvinist ideas—in Paris and became the most active and vocal propagators of the faith in the provinces.[32] Individual teachers can be singled out as active supporters and evangelizers for the Reformed church. The humanist Mathurin Cordier, for example, who taught in several Paris colleges and later in several provincial schools, began openly and deliberately as early as the 1520s to encourage religious reform through his teaching.[33] Therefore, provincial colleges which were interested in hiring the proponents of the new humanist learning were also opening themselves to the new ideas of religious reform.

Education had long been viewed as a tool for religious indoctrination. The quantity of church documents intended for use in the schools indicates that beginning in the early sixteenth century, Catholic schoolteachers were to use their time with students to indoctrinate their youthful charges with the catechism. Jean Gerson's manual, *Opus tripartutum,* was recommended by the bishop of Paris in 1506 for use by masters. In 1511 the bishop of Meaux, in the synod statutes, insisted that curés make masters teach the rudiments of the faith. Advocates for church reform likewise used the tool of education to spread the word.[34] In fact, they relied even more on education to instill Christian values and to evangelize because they believed that all Christians should have some familiarity with the Bible and should be able to read it intelligently.[35] At first these reforming ideas encouraged merely a reformulation of certain Roman Catholic traditions and doctrines in the Erasmian tradition; eventually the reforming ideas which seeped into provincial villages would become a catalyst for the acceptance and active support of the Reformation in the provinces and would lead to the civil wars in France known as the Wars of Religion.

The Protestants used education as a means for religious indoctrination to great profit. In Luther's letter "to the Magistrates of German towns inviting them to open and maintain Christian schools," towns were instructed to use their resources wisely; part of this wise stewardship included sponsoring schools. Thus education in Lutheran Germany shared the bourgeois goal of creating socially responsible citizens who were prepared to be the political and business leaders of the future, but

---

[32]François LeBrun, Marc Venard, and Jean Quéniant, *Histoire Générale de L'Enseignement et de L'Education en France,* vol. 2: *De Gutenberg aux Lumières* (Paris: Nouvelle Librairie de France, 1981), 152.

[33]Kelly, *Consciousness and Society,* 152.

[34]LeBrun, *Histoire Générale,* 251.

[35]Ibid., 252.

they also were designed, especially at the elementary level, to provide a tool for religious indoctrination.[36] Frenchmen with reforming zeal likewise hoped to use the provincial colleges to indoctrinate the youth into the religious principles which they picked up in Paris.

There was a philosophical foundation for the proliferation of humanists interested in church reform. The humanist emphasis on the study of classical languages and ancient texts brought a desire to study the Bible in its original languages, Hebrew and Greek. In addition, the humanist concern for social welfare and the goal of shaping the world through persuasion threatened the authority of the church. *Gens de bien* were encouraged to create a better world based upon the classical ideals they learned about through their study of classical literature, rather than through submission to the church.[37]

Provincial college masters from Paris who were interested in church reform during the first half of the sixteenth century can be found teaching humanist subjects in many colleges in southwest France. In some towns, these men were persecuted or exiled because of their reforming goals. Other towns welcomed a solution to problems within the church. In most cases, however, reform-minded masters were greeted with mixed feelings by the town council, the local church, and individual citizens.

In 1537 four masters of the college in Agen were denounced by the inquisitor, Louis de Rochette, because they were familiar with reforming doctrines and attacked the Catholic faith in their teaching.[38] Three of these masters, Pierre Allard, Nicole Maurel, and Jean de Lagarde, were put in prison. The fourth, Philibert Sarrazin, was forced to flee, though it is possible that he did so because he had been warned by the inquisitor (who may have secretly been a Protestant sympathizer) of the impending sentence.[39] They were allowed to return to teaching in 1538, apparently without having renounced their reformed ways and with the approval of some village parents. At least one of these reform-minded masters, Sarrazin, had been educated in Paris and may have met Calvin during his stay in the capital.[40] He later served as Calvin's physician.[41]

[36]LeBrun, *Histoire Générale*, 184.

[37]Kelly, *Consciousness and Society*, 141–42.

[38]M. O. Fallières and Chanoine Durengues, publishers and annotators, "Enquête sur les Commencements du Protestantisme en Agenais," *Recueil des Travaux de la Société d'Agriculture, Sciences et Arts d'Agen*, ser. 2, vol. 16 (1913–15), 221.

[39]Ibid., 215, n.1.

[40]Ibid., 296–97, n.1.

[41]Jules Bonnet, *Letters of John Calvin* (New York: Burt Franklin repr., 1972), vol. 4, 358-60.

Other colleges, either because of their size or their importance, seem to have attracted masters who were destined to become national leaders in the reformation of the French church. The *Collège de Guyenne* in Bordeaux is one such college.[42] The college itself was structured on the Parisian model.[43] The college founders assured conformity with the *Modus Parisiensis* by hiring masters from Paris, beginning in 1532 with its first principal, the former principal of the Parisian College of Liseux, Jehan de Tartas. The city's contract with Tartas designated a humanist course of studies, including several classical languages. Tartas was responsible for bringing to Guyenne twenty professors to begin the work of educating the young men of Bordeaux. Among these twenty were several important humanists and reformers including Charles de Sainte-Marthe, a talented poet who was attracted to church reform. Sainte-Marthe clearly became a church reformer when he left Bordeaux to study in Poitiers, where he found a close follower of Calvin, Jehan Vernou, and was quickly converted to reformed thinking about the church. We have a copy of at least one letter from Saint-Marthe to Calvin himself.[44]

As the college principal in Guyenne, Tartas seems to have been difficult to get along with,[45] so his stay in Bordeaux was short. His successor, the second principal of the *Collège de Guyenne*, André de Gouvea, was also from Paris where he served as the principal of the *Collège de Sainte-Barbe*. Though not a reformer himself, he brought with him from Paris several masters sympathetic to church reform. Among them were André Zébédée, a well-known reformer who knew John Calvin and later became a Reformed minister in Nyon,[46] and Nicholas de Grouchy, a former colleague of Gouvea's at the *Collège de Sainte-Barbe* in Paris, who held a secret sympathy for the reform movement.[47] Guillaume de Guerente also studied in Paris and had Protestant leanings.[48]

The most influential reformer brought to Guyenne by Gouvea was Mathurin Cordier, who had two passions in life: religious piety and teaching. His educational and religious writings facilitated the spread of both

[42]Ernest Gaullieur, *Histoire du Collège de Guyenne D'Après un Grand Nombre de Documents Inédits* (Paris: Sandoz et Fischbacher, 1874), provides a detailed study of the college history as well as biographical sketches of the masters in Bordeaux.

[43]Ibid., 28

[44]Ibid., 76–77. See the article on Sainte-Marthe in Eugene Haag and Emile Haag, *La France Protestante* 2d ed. (Paris: Librairie Fischbacher, 1884).

[45]At least he was according to his contemporary, Robert Britannus; Ibid., 67–68.

[46]Ibid., 83–84. See also P.-Daniel Bourchenin, *Etude sur les Académies protestantes en France au XVIe et au XVIIe siècle* (Paris: Grissart, 1882).

[47]See the entry for Nicholas de Grouchy in Haag, *La France Protestante*, 1st ed. , vol. 5, 373.

[48]Gaullieur, *Histoire du Collège*, 90–91.

humanist studies and church reform throughout France and beyond. Cordier brought both his expert teaching in humanist subjects and his reformed ideas not only to the *Collège de Guyenne* but also to provincial colleges in Reims, Liseux, and Nevers.[49] His passion for teaching is obvious in his career path. He began his teaching career at the University of Paris in the upper-level classes, but requested to be transferred to teach grammar because he was distressed that his students in the upper-level courses did not have a firm grasp of good Latin grammar.[50]

Cordier attended the University of Paris as an arts student and taught in several Paris colleges including La Marche, Sainte-Barbe, and Navarre. He was an enthusiastic supporter of the structural reforms initiated by Standonck at the *Collège de Montaigu*. His efforts to imitate Standonck's reforms in the Paris colleges where he was regent served to spread the *Modus Parisiensis* to several Paris colleges.[51] As significant as this contribution is, it was his writings which make Cordier a significant educational reformer. The list of the textbooks he wrote is long and includes some of the most popular grammar books used in the sixteenth century. *De corrupti sermonis emendatione libellus*, an elementary textbook of philology, including morals and piety, and his *Colloquia*, which covered Latin conversation and provided moral guidance, were the most popular.[52]

Cordier's religious piety was manifested in his efforts to advance church reform and eventually to serve as a leader in the Reformed church. It is possible that Cordier served as an inspiration to his most famous student, John Calvin, in his search for religious truth. Calvin was one of his grammar students at the *Collège de la Marche* in Paris in 1523–24.[53] He certainly worked for church reform from its earliest days in France, for in 1534 he was implicated in the Affaire des Placards and had to flee Paris.[54]

Mathurin Alamande, master at the college in Lectoure (1530–31), is another example of the Parisian-trained arts graduate who spread humanist studies and agitation for church reform to the provinces through both his work in the provincial colleges and his writings.[55] His *Genethliacon* is

---

[49]Emile Puech, *Un Professeur du XVIe Siècle: Mathurin Cordier, Sa Vie et Son Oeuvre* (1896; Geneva: Slatkine Reprints, 1970), 5.

[50]Gaullieur, *Histoire du Collège*, 96.

[51]Chartier, *L'Education en France*, 153.

[52]Kelly, *Consciousness and Society*, 155.

[53]Gaullieur, *Histoire du Collège*, 96.

[54]Kelly, *Consciousness and Society*, 14.

[55]For a brief overview of Alamande's life and work, see A. Claudin, *Mathurin Alamande: Poète et Littérateur de Saint-Jean D'Angély* (Paris: Librairie A. Claudin, 1891).

the work of a humanist poet, while his *Odes Virginales,* also a humanist work, demonstrates his religious passion. It contains "poems and religious hymns, moral letters, and theological treatises."[56] Although he does not seem to have been directly involved with church reform, his writings on morality and his correspondence with Jacques Lefèvre d'Etaples demonstrate his interest in religious matters, specifically in ensuring the survival of piety within the church.[57]

Paris arts graduates like Cordier, Alamande, and Saint-Marthe were recruited to provincial colleges to mold the youth of southwest France into *gens de bien.* That is, they were to teach them not only the skills necessary to allow them to pursue lucrative careers, but also the moral training they would need to become socially responsible young adults. The humanist training these masters received in Paris, along with the discipline and order they learned while attending Parisian colleges, gave them the qualifications desired by the bourgeois who hired them. But the work these men did to encourage religious reform in the provinces indicates that many of the masters who were trained in Paris in humanist subjects also adopted an enthusiasm for reforming the church. Thus Paris was not simply the training center of elite humanists; it was also a breeding ground for Reformed ideas. These masters represented Renaissance and Reformation values both in education and in religion. Thus even as they rejected the impractical and narrow course of scholastic studies advocated by the theologians, they also rejected the authority which these churchmen tried to protect. They were products of the reforming Renaissance culture of the sixteenth century, and they brought the revolution in education and in religion from its French epicenter in Paris to the provinces. Had Parisian-trained college masters not been hired to teach the humanities in the provinces during the first half of the sixteenth century, bringing with them calls for church reform, it is possible that the Wars of Religion in the second half of the century might never have been fought for lack of reforming zeal in the provinces.

---

[56]See the entry for Alamande in the *Dictionnaire de Biographie Française.*
[57]For a transcription of the letter to D'Etaples, see Claudin, *Mathurin Alamande,* 10–12.

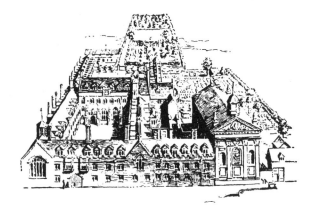

# INVESTIGATION OF A RENAISSANCE-HUMANIST CURRICULUM AT THE ACADEMY OF SAUMUR

*Janet Glenn Gray*

THE PROTESTANT ACADEMY WAS ESSENTIAL TO THE CALVINISTS. It was the lifeline of the church—the sine qua non of the religious reform movement. The academy was perceived primarily as an institution to educate sons of the faithful in the faith of the Scriptures and to produce enough pastors to ensure the permanence of the churches.[1] The Reformed wanted their own educational institutions because municipal schools, in their view, did not provide a biblical emphasis, while Jesuit schools sometimes opposed the ideas of individual humanists and religious reformers. Moreover, the academy was to provide for *gens de bien*, men educated to render leadership in civil government. Calvin saw to it that a statement on education was included in Geneva's new ecclesiastical ordinances (1541). *Docteurs*, whose importance was second only to ministers, were responsible for lecturing in theology:

> but since one is not able to profit in such lessons unless one is first of all instructed in humane languages and science, and also since it is necessary to prepare for the upcoming generations in order not to leave the church a desert for our children, it is imperative that we establish a college to instruct the children to prepare them for both the ministry and civil government.[2]

Emile G. Léonard has suggested that the Calvinist academies were not comparable to their educational rivals in depth of studies nor in the time

---

[1]John Quick, *Synodicon in Gallia reformata*, 2 vols. (London: T. Parkhurst and J. Robinson, 1692), 1:xxvi–xxvii.

[2]Cited in W. Stanford Reid, "Calvin and the Founding of the Academy of Geneva," *Westminster Theological Journal* 18 (1955): 8.

involved in pursuing those studies.[3] An investigation of the curriculum of a leading Reformed academy, the Academy of Saumur, however, contradicts his assertions. My purpose here is to examine the late seventeenth-century programs of study at the Academy of Saumur, which themselves had developed from earlier humanistic curricula. I shall focus on the curriculum as a means of demonstrating how a later development of Renaissance humanistic education was taught at a Reformed French Academy.

The Academy of Saumur was in many respects a Renaissance institution in the tradition of the *studia humanitatis* in that it inherited and taught a humanist curriculum based on rhetoric and eloquence in both its secondary and university divisions.[4] Theological studies at Saumur stressed solid scholarship with a historical dimension, critical work on biblical texts, and freedom in approaches to theology, science, and philosophy, both practical and ethical. At Saumur the academic approach was more in line with Renaissance freedoms as opposed to some of the other Protestant academies, which tended to stress consistent systems with solid biblical teaching, with an overzealous attitude toward looking for deviations that might lead to heresies.[5] Those academies sometimes fostered a spirit of exclusiveness, stiff-necked dogmatism, and condemnation as well as a legalistic tone. Yet, in all of the Reformed academies, educational emphasis was on the imitation of classical models, especially on persuasive expression that would move a person's will through both the spoken and written word. The orator would be an instructor of life, not of the empty intellectualism that humanist critics decried in scholastic education. At the same time, basic instruction was retained in the traditional medieval Trivium of grammar, dialectic, and rhetoric, as a foundation for learning the structure of language, constructing and using argument, detecting fallacies, and expressing oneself logically and effectively. It was the medieval pattern of the Quadrivium—music, arithmetic, geometry, and astronomy—that was either dropped or de-emphasized in the humanistic curriculum.

On the level of secondary education, the actual course of study at Saumur differed little in the texts used from the classical education offered at municipal schools and Jesuit schools during the sixteenth and seventeenth centuries. Parents who sent students to Jesuit and Protestant schools

[3]Emile G. Léonard, "Les académies protestantes dans le destin du protestantisme," *Foi education* 47 (1959): 61–75.

[4]Hanna H. Gray, "Renaissance Humanism: The Pursuit of Eloquence," *Journal of the History of Ideas* 24 (1963): 500.

[5]See Brian G. Armstrong, *Calvinism and the Amyraut Heresy* (Madison: University of Wisconsin Press, 1969), 165.

expected more of a Christian emphasis on education and living. Students at municipal schools were mainly sons of the bourgeois, along with those of the impoverished lower nobility. Ideas presented by ancient Greek and Roman writers on freedom of reason, development, and rewards based on merit had a sounding in municipal colleges. A school plan in 1565 by Master Massé for the municipal school at Auch called for six classes, which included beginning Greek and Latin, the study of humanist grammarians, such as Lorenzo Valla, Thomas Linacre, Nicolas Clénard, and Paul Pellisson, and the ancient masters—Cicero, Virgil, Ovid, Horace, Quintilian, Sallust, Livy, and Persius.[6] The Salmurians did not use the same grammarians, but did study most of the same ancient masters, with the exception of Persius. George Huppert has noted the proliferation during the second half of the sixteenth century of full-scale colleges in France with a tendency toward large staffs, big budgets, and sometimes advanced subjects, such as Greek.[7] By the seventeenth century many of these municipal schools were in financial trouble due to an oversupply of them and to competition from denominational secondary schools like those established by the Jesuits and Protestants.

After the Jesuits returned to France in 1604, they began to introduce the *Ratio studiorum* (1599) into their schools. Jesuit schools at first consisted of two divisions: the *studia inferiora*, an elementary course for students up to the age of ten, and the *studia superiora*, a philosophical course, lasting two or three years. A student could then enter a theological program of four to six years. At the secondary level there were three grammar classes based on skills and concepts mastered. The last two levels were humanities and rhetoric. Third grammar classes read Virgil's *Aeneid* or *Eclogues* and Ovid's *Epistulae ex Ponto*. Students worked with grammar manuals of exercises and drills (e.g., Guarino da Verona's *Regulae*, Cicero's *Epistulae ad familiares*, and Juan Luis Vives' *Colloquia*). Books such as Sallust's *Bellum Iugurthinum*, Caesar's *Commentaries*, Horace's *Ars poetica*, or perhaps Cicero's *De Amicitia* or selections from the *Epistulae ad Atticum* were used. Quintilian was also studied. The practice and composition of oratorical works occupied students at the highest level; they were often required to deliver an oration or turn in a composition every week. Students were to read Isocrates' *Ad Nicolas*, some of Aesop's fables in Greek,

---

[6]George Huppert, *Public Schools in Renaissance France* (Urbana and Chicago: University of Illinois Press, 1984), xvi–xvii. See also Roger Chartier, Dominique Julia, and Marie-Madeleine Compère, *L'Éducation en France du xvi^e au xvii^e siècle* (Paris: Société d'Édition d'Enseignement Supérieur, 1976), 53–55.

[7]Huppert, *Public Schools*, xvi–xvii.

and something from Pindar, Demosthenes, or some other author. The major difference between the Italian program and the Ratio studiorum was the new emphasis on Greek, which Jesuits had integrated into their curriculum.[8] Except for grammar manuals and Vives' *Colloquia*, the same ancient authors were used at the Academy of Saumur.

Johann Sturm, who founded the Academy of Strasbourg in 1538, relates the similarity of his program with the Jesuits, "I have seen the authors which the Jesuits explain, the exercises which they employ, and their method of instruction, which is so near our own that they seem to have derived from our own sources."[9] But there were differences, especially with theological courses at the university level. The Jesuits emphasized the philosophy of Thomas Aquinas, canon law, and scholastic and practical theology, as opposed to the Protestant emphases on instruction in vernacular and classical languages and on newer translations of the Bible. By comparison, theology courses at the Reformed academies stressed Calvin's *Institutes*, exegetical studies, and preaching.

In practice, advanced learning in all of the Reformed academies meant an awareness of the classics, including ethics, language, rhetoric, eloquence, and philosophy. Instruction was divided into the *école classique*—the lower division of six classes headed by a principal who supervised the teachers (régents)—and the *école publique*—the upper division of the faculty of arts, which would prepare students for two years beyond the secondary level. There was also a faculty of theology to instruct the first, second, and third classes of theology. In official reference, the academy was the upper division, corresponding to a university, but in general reference to a Protestant academic structure in a city, the academy was understood as the secondary and university levels together. A rector was the chief administrator.[10] Professorships were established for the faculty levels in philosophy (including logic, physics, and metaphysics), theology, law, mathematics, Greek, Hebrew, eloquence, and exercises.[11] Saumur, however, had not developed

[8]Paul F. Grendler, *Schooling in Renaissance Italy* (Baltimore: Johns Hopkins University Press, 1989), 379.

[9]As cited in Pierre Mensard, "La piétas litterata de Jean Sturm et le dévelopement à Strasbourg d'une pédagogue oecuménique (1538–1581)," *Bulletin de la société d'histoire du protestantisme français* 111 (1965): 298; hereafter cited as BSHPF. Roger Chartier, Dominique Julia, and Marie-Madeleine Compère, in *L'Éducation en France*, have pointed out that the differences were minimal between the enterprises of the Protestants and Jesuit colleges and the French Protestant Academies in their initial development. The attitude of both Sturm and Calvin was that the humanities were necessary for human society and should be used in conjunction with the Scriptures to prepare young people for both the ministry and civil government.

[10]Pierre Daniel Bourchenin, *Étude sur les académies protestantes en France au xvi<sup>e</sup> et au xvii<sup>e</sup>siècle* (Paris: Grassart, 1882), 233.

[11]Three major documents pertaining to the Academy of Saumur may be found at the Bibliothèque

chairs in all of these areas, including law, exercises, and perhaps medicine, even though some chairs were intermittently filled. Each academy was under the authority of two councils: the *conseil ordinaire*, presided over by the rector and composed of the pastors of the city, the public professors, and the instructor of the first class of the college, to take care of everyday business; and the *conseil extraordinaire*, composed of pastors, public professors and some of the principal members of the Reformed church or the consistory for special selections of faculty, discipline, synod recommendations, grants, and financial matters.[12]

Article 22 of the Edict of Nantes (1598) states, "We order that there will not be made any difference or distinction in regard to the said religion to receive scholars to be instructed of the universities, collèges, and schools...."[13] The Protestant academy was considered a university by the standards of the day, even though not all of the academies had all of the chairs of the traditional French university, which would have included theology, law, medicine, mathematics, languages, and the arts. Protestant academies hoped to have the requisite chairs, but circumstances (mostly financial) dictated what they could provide. Some academies specialized in law and medicine.

Models for the Academy at Saumur were the Academy of Strasbourg, the Academy of Geneva, and the University of Leiden.[14] These three institutions were very influential in the sixteenth century. All stressed the centrality of the Bible, the recognition of a highly educated *docteur* in religion to teach theological matters, the need for advanced learning for pastors to be able to teach their flocks, and the necessity for students to become proper gentlemen with Christian values. Furthermore, the overall structure, class

---

Municipale at Saumur: (1) *Papier et Registre des affaires de l'Académie à Saumur, depuis le mois d'octobre 1613 jusqu'au 20 mars 1675*, folio ms., parchment, 229 sheets; (2) *Registre du Conseil Académique de ceux de la R. P. R. de Saumur, mis à l'Hôtel-Dieu en 1686, du 20 juin 1683 au 6 décembre 1684*, folio ms., parchment, 18 sheets; and (3) *Papier de Recette des deniers Académiques, du 1er novembre 1651 au 20 janvier 1685*, folio ms., parchment, 113 sheets.

[12]Michel Nicolas, "Les anciennes académies protestantes," BSHPF 2 (1854):156–57.

[13]Léonce Anquez, *Histoire des assemblées politiques des réformés de France, 1573–1622* (Paris: Auguste Durand, 1859), 494.

[14]For the organization of the Strasbourg Gymnasium according to Johann Sturm's basic curricular plan of 1538, see Charles Schmidt, trans.; "Mémoire de Jean Sturm sur le projet d'organisation du gymnase de Strasbourg (Fév. 1538)," BSHPF 25 (1856): 505; for Geneva's Laws of the Classes from "the Order of the College of Geneva," see Reid, "Founding of the Academy of Geneva," 26–29; for a brief discussion of Leiden's offerings, see J. J. Woltjer, "Introduction," Th. H. Lunsingh Scheurleer and G. H. M. Posthumus Meyjes, eds., *Leiden University in the Seventeenth Century: An Exchange of Learning* (Leiden: Universitaire Pers; Leiden/E. J. Brill, 1975), 5.

organization, methods of promotion, disputation requirements, and authors studied were very similar.[15]

In 1593 Philippe du Plessis-Mornay, a layman serving as special advisor to the king and governor of the city of Saumur, obtained letters patent from Henry IV to found an academy at Saumur. Duplessis-Mornay chose Leiden as a model because of its academic strengths in science and mathematics and its excellent faculty.[16] Academies had been authorized by the 1559 Discipline of the Reformed Faith; the Reformed General Assembly at Saumur in 1596 endorsed the selection of Saumur as a suitable location for an academy.[17] I hope to offer a raison d'être for almost all of the texts listed in the official programs of study at the Academy of Saumur to understand better what a late, but fairly standard Renaissance education was and to evaluate the quality of the education at Saumur. There are three basic plans—all of them coming toward the end of the Academy's existence but which continue to reflect earlier practices.[18] The earliest reference I have to an entire curricular plan is a 1680 *advertissement* for the Academy; the other two, one for 1683 and the other for 1684, are from extant records of the governing body of the institution at Saumur, the *Conseils Académiques, ordinaire & extraordinaire*. An indication of an earlier program may be detected from the period of 1618–1626 when John

[15]Janet Glenn Gray, "Lay Leadership among the Calvinists: Duplessis-Mornay and the Academy of Saumur" (Ph.D. diss., University of Missouri, 1993), 160–78. Strasbourg had an elementary school included in its structure, which Saumur did not, and the acting of plays is specifically mentioned in the plans of 1538, 1565, and 1578, as well as Euclid for geometry. Geneva had a very similar list of authors with the addition of Xenophon or Polybius in Greek and Livius in Latin for the Second Class. Leiden had similar authors in history, logic, and languages, but much more emphasis was on the sciences, such as botany, optics, physics, and engineering.

[16]*Mémoires et correspondance de Duplessis-Mornay*, 12 vols. (Paris: Chez Treuttel et Würtz, 1824), 9:293, and Roul Patry, *Philippe du Plessis Mornay: Un huguenot homme d'état (1549–1623)* (Paris: Librairie Fischbacher, 1933), 437 n. 254.

[17]Quick, *Gallia reformata*, xxvi–xxvii and 1:177, and Jean Aymon, *Tous les synodes nationaux des églises réformées de France*, 2 vols. (La Haye: Charles Delo, 1710), 197, and I. Huisseau, *La discipline des églises réformées de France* (Genève: Chez René Pean & Jean Lesnier, 1666), 55. As cited in chap. 3, sect. 5: "And the present Synod judgeth this City of Saumur a most convenient place for a College, & whenever God shall bless us with ability, for an Academy also; & entreateth the Lord du Plessis, Governor of this place, to continue the Tokens of his good will and kindness to this Noble & most Godly Design, which he hath so much affected, & the Deputies of this Assembly are entreated to excite their respected Provinces to promote it vigorously."

[18]*Mss Français*, No. 15829, 365–68. A 1623 payment schedule lists 700 livres for professors in theology, 400 for languages and the two professors in philosophy, 100 for the rector, and 210 to cover most of the régents.

Cameron dominated the Academy of Saumur with a curriculum developed by John Melville in Scotland.[19]

Some of the first French humanists, Guillaume Budé, Lefèvre d'Etaples, and Melchior Wolmar, had recommended the biblical languages, Hebrew, Greek, and Latin for students of theology.[20] Hebrew commentaries and grammar were considered vital to train pastors for correct understanding, continuing scholarship, and preparing sermons. At Saumur, notice of a salaried professor of Hebrew can be found in a 1612 financial report[21] and a letter of 1615 that establishes the presence of the renowned Louis Cappel as Hebraist.[22] Later, for example, in an upper-division course in 1680, the book of Zechariah and the Psalms were to be used in Hebrew language studies. New Testament studies were undertaken as well, with Greek as the basis of exegesis. Further references to studies at Saumur can be found in official documents.

In a 1664 report to the central government by Jean-Baptiste Colbert, Controller General of Finances, the following reference was made to the Academy of Saumur:

> The other University [besides the University of Angers], or rather Academy, is at Saumur, held and exercised by those of the alleged reformed religion, which unites there all of the people of spirit in their party, in order to render it famous and flourishing. There is for training five classes of grammar, humanities and rhetoric; two classes in philosophy, a professor of the Hebrew language, one

[19]Armstrong, *Amyraut Heresy*, 44–45. From Thomas McCrie, *Life of Andrew Melville*, 2 vols. (Edinburgh, 1819), 1:72–74. Cameron probably brought this curriculum with him from Scotland (1618–1626): "He began by initiating them into the principles of Greek grammar. He then introduced them to the study of Logic and Rhetoric, using, as his textbooks, the Dialectics of his Parisian master, Ramus, and the Rhetoric of Talaeus. While they were engaged in these studies he read with them the best classical authors, as Virgil and Horace among the Latins and Homer, Hesiod, Theocritus, Pindar and Isocrates, among the Greeks.... Proceeding to Mathematics and Geography, he taught the elements of Euclid, with the Arithmetic and Geometry of Ramus, and the Geography of Dionysius.... Moral Philosophy formed the next branch of study; and on this he read Cicero's Offices, Paradoxes, and Tusculan Questions, the Ethics and Politics of Aristotle and certain of Plato's Dialogues. In Natural Philosophy he made use of Fernelius, and commented on parts of the writings of Aristotle and Plato. To these he added a view of Universal History, with Chronology and the art of Writing. Entering upon the duties of his own immediate profession, he taught the Hebrew language.... He then initiated the students into Chaldee and Syriac; reading those parts of the books of the Galatians in the Syriac version. He also went through all the common heads of Divinity according to the order of Calvin's Institutions, besides giving lectures on different books of Scripture." Works in this model may be compared with the details given by the documents from the Academic Councils in the 1680s.

[20]Gray, "Lay Leadership among the Calvinists," 119.

[21]Quick, *Gallia reformata*, 1:387.

[22]"L'Académie de Saumur, Cinq lettres à Du Plessis-Mornay, 1598–1618," comp. Léon Audé, ed. Paul Marchegay, BSHPF 18 (1869): 471.

particularly for the Greek language...two professors of theology, who give every other day two public lessons; and, furthermore, a special school of eloquence, which they call a profession of eloquence, separate from rhetoric, whose professor, Douille [a Scotsman] is very skilled.[23]

Colbert gives information on the classes being taught; his report corresponds to records of faculty payments from 1623. Synodical and manuscript records point to some of the philosophical subjects at Saumur through discussion of methods used and authors followed.

In philosophy, the main subject of the faculty of arts at Saumur, Aristotle remained predominant at the academy during the seventeenth century, despite efforts from the 1620s to the 1660s by a professor of theology, John Cameron, and his disciple, Moïse Amyraut, to reduce Aristotle's influence. They sought to use more of Calvin's thought and the logical methods of Peter Ramus.[24] However, Beza and his followers at Geneva's academy continued to stress the importance of Aristotelian constructs, probably from their own training on the necessity for a rational system of final causation.[25] Aristotle was again predominant in philosophy, after Cameron and Amyraut, when in 1664 a young Cartesian, Jean-Robert Chouet of Geneva, who had been attracted to Saumur because of its reputation for quality and liberality, decided to seek the chair of philosophy. The opposing candidate was an older professor (and former graduate of Saumur) from Saintone, Pierre de Villemandy. The examination program requirements were as follows:

1. Two particular lessons were to be given on the texts of Aristotle on physics and ethics.
2. Two other public lessons were to be given on the texts of logic and metaphysics.
3. A fifth lesson was to be on the subject of ethics, without a book, after two hours of preparation.
4. Public debate on theses drawn from all of philosophy.[26]

---

[23]As cited in Paul Marchegay, "L'Académie des protestants à Saumur," *Revue de l'Anjou et de Maine et Loire*, 4 vols. (Angers: Librairie de Cosnier et Lachèse, 1852), 1:344–45.

[24]Walter J. Ong, S.J., *Ramus and the Decay of Dialogue* (Cambridge, Mass.: Harvard University Press, 1958). Cf. Paul Oskar Kristeller, *Renaissance Thought: The Classic, Scholastic, and Humanist Strains* (New York: Harper Torchbooks, 1961), 43. Renaissance humanists like Ramus and Nizolius followed Valla's lead in attempting to reform Aristotelian logic with the help of rhetoric; Ramist methods were followed by some professors in the latter part of the sixteenth century and well into the seventeenth century in Germany, Great Britain, France, and America.

[25]Armstrong, *Amyraut Heresy*, 166. Cf. Reid, "Founding of the Academy of Geneva," 26–29.

[26]*Papier et Registre des affaires de l'Académie Royale établie à Saumur, depuis le mois d'octobre 1613*

This is the last major contest recorded in the Registre of the Academy. Chouet obtained the chair and introduced some Cartesian philosophy into the academy to be taught along with the traditional Aristotelian courses. However, Villemandy returned in 1669 with his major dependence on Aristotle.[27]

In the 1680 Saumurian documents, philosophy consisted of instruction in the *Institutionibus Logicis*[28] and several of Aristotle's works, including his *Organum*.[29] Aristotle's *Physics* and the *Metaphysics* were included, along with an abridged text of the *Ethics*. The *Ethics* could be either the *Nicomachaen Ethics*[30] or the newly found *Eudemian Ethics*.[31] If it were the latter, it would substantiate the argument of Paul Oskar Kristeller that, although the scholastic reliance on Aristotle remained as a convention from the late Middle Ages, the Renaissance humanists used their own knowledge of classical Greek on original texts along with new manuscripts and new translations. Thus, the Aristotle of the Renaissance could be different from the Aristotle of the late Middle Ages.[32] The use of Aristotle does not necessarily mean scholasticism in the sense of narrow adherence to traditional teachings, doctrines, or methods. It can simply be included as part of the corpus of the *via antiqua* for educational purposes. Aristotle was considered essential for his source material strength, systems of ideas, and methods of discussing material and problems.[33] As John Randall

---

*jusqu' au 20 mars 1673*, folio ms., and Josephe Dumont, *Histoire de l'Académie de Saumur depuis sa foundation en 100 par Duplessis-Mornay jusqu'à sa suppression en 1685* (Angers: Librairie de Cosnier et Lachèse, 1862), 75.

[27]Gray, "Lay Leadership among the Calvinists," 248.

[28]This title is obscure, but could refer to Seneca's *Institutiones*, which contrasts dialectic and rhetoric. See Lewis W. Spitz and Barbara Sher Tinsley, *Johann Sturm on Education* (St. Louis: Concordia Publishing House, 1955), 120.

[29]See Spitz and Tinsley, 241, where Sturm's views on the *Organum* are discussed: "We want this book to be used forever by dialecticians in school so that young people may read, teachers may explain, and all may follow in these matters and in the things that pertain to disputations that are contained in a communion of liberal arts."

[30]In an analysis of the work of Saumurian Moïse Amyraut (from the Academy as both student and professor) on ethics, *La Morale chrestienne* (1660), strong elements of the *Nicomachean Ethics* may be found. Cf. Paul O. Kristeller, *Renaissance Thought II: Papers on Humanism and the Arts* (New York: Harper Torchbooks, 1965), 20, and Armstrong, *Amyraut Heresy*, 125.

[31]George E. Ganss, *Saint Ignatius' Idea of a Jesuit University* (Milwaukee, Wis.: Marquette University Press, 1954), 141. During the Italian renaissance, the great teacher, Vergerius, suggested that moral philosophy is a "liberal art" in that its purpose is to teach men the secret of true freedom.

[32]Paul Oskar Kristeller, *Classic, Scholastic, and Humanist Strains*, 39.

[33]Spitz and Tinsley, 391 n. 24: "The number of categories enumerated by Aristotle varies in several passages, but includes substance, quality, place, activity/passivity, relation, quantity, time, position, and state."

observes, "The coming of Aristotle introduced a body of materials too impressive to be ignored."[34] Aristotle was part of a standard Renaissance curriculum. However, both Calvin and Ignatius recommended moderation in the use of Aristotle due to his status as a pagan.[35]

New pedagogical methods and ideas were frequently welcomed and new commentaries were constantly being produced in the Reformed academies of France, but especially at Saumur (see fig. 1). At that academy, Jean Benoist, a physician and professor of Greek, had printed a Latin translation on the complete works of Lucien of Samosata in 1619 and in 1620 an exacting work on a translation of Pindar.[36] From 1665 to 1685, Tanneguy Lefèbvre wrote commentaries on many of the ancient texts listed in the programs offered in the 1680s. These texts included *Phaedra's Fables*, Aeliani's and Eutropius' histories, Horace, Virgil, and Terence.[37]

In addition to languages, the Bible, and Aristotle, the Academy of Saumur's upper division had instruction in eloquence, rhetoric, and mathematics. Ornateness of language, strategies of argumentation, reasoning, effective presentations—these were techniques needed for writing and scholarly disputations to be given in public for theological certification and for philosophy classes. Standing on one's own feet in argument was considered the mark of a scholar. Students were given compositions to write and disputations to argue on specific days. After successfully completing his examinations, a candidate for a master's degree had to sustain his thesis publicly from several points of dogma.[38] The reasons for the study of mathematics must have been similar to the one given for the University of Leiden, namely, that mathematics was a branch of practical philosophy (after Aristotle) and useful for surveyors or fortification builders as part of science.[39] Earlier—prior to 1603—Duplessis-Mornay had

[34]John Herman Randall, Jr., "The Development of Scientific Method in the School of Padua," *Journal of the History of Ideas* 1 (1940): 180.

[35]Ganss, *Saint Ignatius' Idea*, 327, and Reid, "Founding of the Academy of Geneva," 14–15. Loyola urges a Christian adaptation to the works of a pagan when the end is service to God, and Calvin wants to make certain that the arts form solid learning and are used properly to bring men to a true knowledge of the sovereign God. By that he meant recognition that the gifts of pagan authors were possible only through the Holy Spirit.

[36]Dumont, *Histoire de l'Académie*, 22.

[37]Ibid., 61–62.

[38]Bourchenin, 273–77. From Archives Nationales, TT. 239. Theses in logic, metaphysics, physics, and ethics of several students of philosophy professor Pierre de Villemandy were published by the church of Saumur (1681) and conserved in the Archives Nationales under the title of *Assertiones ex variis philosophiae partibus selectae*. An example of the first assertion should suffice as a sample: "Ex Logica. / Assertio Prima / Cum ad Rerum cognitionem facti / simus. Philosophandum certe: / sed ad distinctam rerum praestantiorum ac utiliorum cognitionem; / quae una cognitio est vera Philosophica."

[39]Scheurleer and Meyjes, *Leiden University*, 3.

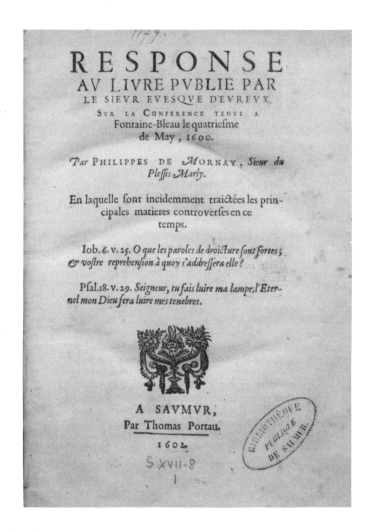

Fig. 1. Title page from a rare book by Duplessis-Mornay
From the Bibliothèque Publique de Saumur, photo by W. James Gray.

written about the importance of the Quadrivium' in a liberal education,[40] but my studies indicate no trace of music or astronomy in the curriculum.

[40]Mornay's *Mémoires* was accepted by the synod in 1603. See Mornay, *Mémoires et correspondance*, 5:65–71. Here, in a letter (ca. 1591) of advice to the Princess of Orange on the education of her

In a brief overview, one sees that students first attended elementary schools (*petites écoles*), separate from the Protestant academies, to learn the rudiments of reading, writing, and grammar. However, in rural areas in sixteenth-century France there was often little in the way of primary education. From about age ten to sixteen Protestant boys attended the six-level secondary school (*collège*, or *école classique*), then went on to the university-level *école publique*.

Beginning with the most primary, or Sixth Class, of the 1680 college at Saumur, the purpose for student exercises and required texts will be examined. Noun declinations and verbal conjugations in Latin were studied first, so that the student could become familiar with Latin speech and begin to translate sentences into Latin forms, a necessary step toward becoming fluent in the language of the Renaissance scholar. Latin had to be mastered for its structure and vocabulary, not to mention the humanist ideal of knowing and imitating ancient writers and interpreting historical documents. However, no specific Latin text is listed for the most elementary class.

The Fifth Class had a more specific application of Latin grammar and syntax along with the addition of Mathurin Cordier's *Colloquies*, which consisted of dialogues with an original Latin text, along with a facing French translation, for exercise in the two languages.[41] The text was designed to introduce the student gradually to Latin studies. An emphasis on the vernacular was unusual in Latin schools of the time, but to the Protestants it was extremely important for correct speaking on the part of pastors in the pulpit and gentlemen in governmental service. Often the dialogues included moral precepts intended to inculcate good morals and manners.[42] In the second semester Cato's *Disticha de Moribus*, a collection of aphorisms from the late Roman Empire, was used as a beginning Latin reader.[43] Its use was for the formation of language and its purity by stressing

---

son, Mornay establishes the importance that a child come to God, then mentions the necessity of mathematics, languages, histories, grammar, rhetoric, dialectic, and astronomy. The Latin authors he favors are Cicero, Caesar, Sallust, Tacitus, Pliny, Seneca, Virgil, and Horace. Among the Greeks he prefers Isocrates, Demosthenes, Xenophom, Thucydides, Hesiod, Homer, Theognis, and Phocyllides. He also recommended the Proverbs of Solomon.

[41]*Colloquiorum scholasticorum libri quatuor* (Geneva, 1563).

[42]Gabriel Compayré, *Histoire critique des doctrines de l'education en France depuis le seizième siècle*, 1, 2d ed.(Paris: Librairie Hachette et Cie, 1880), 150.

[43]Ganss, *Saint Ignatius' Idea*, 89. An example of a distich follows: "S*i deus est animus, nobis ut carmina dicunt, Hic tibe praecipue sit pura mente colendus.*" (If God is a spirit, as the poems tell us, this spirit above all should you worship with a mind undefiled.)

subject matter and vocabulary.[44] In addition, an introduction was made to Greek through the study of the Greek alphabet. Greek was essential to understanding New Testament writers as well as for comprehending the philosophical and rhetorical works of Aristotle, the poetry of Homer and Pindar, and the orations of Isocrates.[45]

In the Fourth Class more Latin syntax, coupled with grammar and the use of Latin, was exemplified in the text, *Aurelius victor*, which concerns Marcus Aurelius. This Roman emperor was a model for the importance of family life and leadership in his work, *Thoughts*.[46] *Aurelius victor* accomplished the twin goals of language studies and content of a didactic nature for character development in the context of history.

Advanced study of Greek included *Radices linguae graecae*, which focused on the roots of nouns and verbs in helping to develop facility in speaking and reading. The *Colloquies* of Erasmus replaced Cordier's dialogues. Erasmus demonstrated his Christian-humanist precepts in all of his writings, and particularly in his emphasis on rhetoric, oratory, and letters.[47]

In the second semester of the Fourth Class, the first three books of Justinian's *Institutes* were to be studied for examples in freedom and justice in order to provide a firm introduction to Roman law. The first four books constituted an introductory textbook designed to be a starting place for the whole study of law.[48] Along with law was practice in imitating the style, grace, and expression of Ovid's *Letters*.[49] In the afternoon, Ovid's *Tristia*, a text considered acceptable at the time, was to be pursued to enhance Latin verse.[50] Greek grammar from New Testament passages was used as practical application for an expanded understanding of Greek. Paul's writings were studied for grammatical structure as well as content, vocabulary, metaphor, and style.

When a student arrived at the Third Class, he encountered more New Testament Greek as well as the drama of Terence's *Phormio* and *Hecyra*.

---

[44]Sturm, "Concerning the English Nobility (1551)," in Spitz and Tinsley, 193.

[45]The recommendation of early humanist scholars plus Protestant studies in Greek pushed the Jesuits into pursuit of this language to keep up with disputations. Here the Protestants acted as a catalyst for the Jesuits.

[46]Ellwood P. Cubberley, *Readings in the History of Education* (Cambridge, Mass.: Riverside Press, 1920), 29.

[47]James D. Tracy, "Erasmus among the Postmodernists," in *Erasmus' Vision of the Church*, ed. Hilmar M. Pabel (Kirksville, Mo.: Sixteenth Century Journal Publishers, Inc., 1995), 11.

[48]Cubberly, *History of Education*, 141.

[49]Gray, "Lay Leadership among the Calvinists," 144.

[50]François de Dainville, *L'Éducation des Jésuites* (XVIë-XVIIë siècles) (Paris: Les Editions de Minuit, 1978), 169, and Grendler, *Schooling in Renaissance Italy*, 378.

These comedies were used to give conversational exercises in systematic Greek eloquence and purity of language as well as argument stated in dramatic form to correspond to the student's developmental stage of enjoying argument.[51] Johann Sturm had earlier recommended Terence's and Plautus at Strasbourg as stage plays to promote cheerfulness among the students.[52] Evidently the Protestants were not worried about Terence harming the "purity of souls," as was Ignatius of Loyola in his *Constitutions.*[53]

Poetry, which was covered on the third level, was a compilation collected by Gérard-Joseph Vossius to give practice in verse to instill style, harmony, grace, and good rhythm. Books 4, 5, and 6 of Ovid's *Metamorphoses* formed a literature section. This collection of Roman and Greek myths and legends was intended to delight and enrich the educational experience.

During the second semester, more New Testament Greek was to be studied. Virgil's *Aeneid* was also a popular choice because the level of Latin poetry mastered by the Third Class was appropriate for introducing students to this Roman epic poem praising Roman virtues. From the early days of the Renaissance it was recommended that Virgil be memorized.[54] The Latin historian, Sallust, known for his brevity and vividness, was likewise part of the curriculum. His *Bellum Iugurthinum* is a likely text since this was the text cited in the Ratio studiorum, the Jesuits' original curricular plan.[55]

The Second Class offered more advanced studies. The first semester consisted of Greek syntax. The literary text was *Cornelius Nepos*, a small text in Latin of biographical sketches (*The Lives*) on seven Greek heroes and leaders covering the late phase of the Peloponnesian War.[56] These short accounts are not exaggerated, hagiographic essays, but rather candid

[51]Selections from Dorothy L. Sayers, "The Lost Tools of Learning," in *A Matter of Eternity*, ed. Rosamond Kent Sprague (Grand Rapids, Mich.: Wm. B. Eerdmans, 1973), 127.

[52]Johann Sturm to Michael Bosch, Teacher of the Third Class, 1565, in Spitz and Tinsley, 282. See also letter 12 to Jonas Bitner, 1569: "Moreover, your comic and tragic plays will be appropriate for this academy of ours. For these exercises are for everyday usage of the Latin language, yes, more sure than was the everyday speech of Romans and Athenians. The theatre and scenes preserve the praises of eloquence longer than do the forum and lawsuits." In Spitz and Tinsley, 337.

[53]Ganss, *Saint Ignatius' Idea*, 327.

[54]Cubberly, *History of Education*, 205. Battisto Guarino, the son of Guarino da Verona (1374–1460), writes this in a letter (1459). From a letter, W. H. Woodward, trans., *Vittorino da Feltre* (Cambridge: Cambridge University Press, 1897), 161–72.

[55]Grendler, *Schooling in Renaissance Italy*, 378. Cf. Sturm, in Spitz and Tinsley, 102: Sturm recommends Sallust because of the balanced brevity of his materials, his distinctive use of words, and his specific appropriate usage.

[56]*Cornelius Nepos*, ed. E. S. Shuckburgh (Cambridge: Cambridge University Press, 1914).

political reports that emphasized virtue. Exercises in poetry rounded out the morning hours. Afternoon classes studied Virgil's *Bucolica* for rules of Latin forms.[57] These were pastoral poems dealing with life in agricultural settings. For history Ælian's *Varia histori*, a collection of curious tales of men and manners, was listed.[58]

The second semester provided for a summary of Horace. Horace was a popular author to imitate in the seventeenth and eighteenth centuries[59] after the Renaissance had rediscovered him. He was honored for his language of manners, rhythm, and variety as well as his own love of Greek literature.[60] The Protestants, with their emphasis on "things Greek" as part of the new learning, appreciated Horace's Greek content.

Along with poetry, oratory was considered essential for language skills. Cicero's *Pro Marcello* was the selection. Cicero was the preferred author of the Renaissance for his turn of phrase as well as his praise of the civic function of the orator in persuading others to lead just and reasonable lives.[61] His work included general observations, criticisms, praises, defenses, ornamentations, arguments, and a great number of figures of speech. The variety, breadth, and depth of his reasoning provided much material for imitation and memory.[62] Poetry and oration were studied together since they were considered desirable for the perfection of speaking with correct cadence and elocution.[63]

A more practical orientation in the curriculum is indicated by work with tropes and figures, an investigation of classifications, forms, and figures of speech with shades of expression for training in rhetorical skills. Students were to gain more facility in communication. In the afternoon they studied Ovid's *Epistles* (nos. 6, 7, 8, 9, 10, 12, 13, and 17), which were examined for their literary patterns. The ancient Athenian orator, Isocrates, provided the standard piece, *Oratoria ad Nicoclem*, which exhibits high standards in using correct forms to teach speech composition and

---

[57]Cf. Sturm, "For the Lauingen School (1565)," in Spitz and Tinsley, 231: "To the higher precepts of grammar are thus added in this poetical spot metrical verse or meter, which are called *feet* by most people, after the forms of poetry. In this matter see Vergil's *Bucolica*...."

[58]Claudi Aeliani, *Varia historia*, ed. Mervin R. Dilts (Leipzig: B. G. Teubner, 1974), xiii.

[59]See Dainville, *L'Éducation des Jésuites*, 176.

[60]From Horace's *Carmina*, 4.2.5–8. Cf. Spitz and Tinsley, 164, 393 n. 40.

[61]Charles T. Davis, "Education in Dante's Florence," *Speculum* 40 (1965): 420.

[62]Sturm, "On the Lost Art of Speaking (1538)," *De Amissa dicendi ratione*, in Spitz and Tinsley, 127. "There is no doubt about Cicero who reconciled eloquence with the study of wisdom. I could wish his example were followed in our own age," explains Sturm in his enthusiasm for the Roman master of letters.

[63]See Dainville, *L'Éducation des Jésuites*, 173.

in utilizing arguments to come to harmonious conclusions. Cicero acknowledged his "indebtedness and gratitude" to Isocrates for his own development.[64]

The First level called for a specific rhetoric text, *Rhetorica contracta Vossij*, for selections that would improve speaking and writing; in addition, more of the two volumes of Horace's *Epistles* were stipulated. Older students were expected to master historical study through the Greek historian, Herodotus, whose *History of the Persian Wars* gives a detailed narrative of the last years of the Archaic period. Herodotus excelled in rhetoric and making distinctions. History had been stressed from the earliest days of Renaissance-humanist education.[65]

Argument was a priority at level one, and the perfect master for teaching the subject was Cicero. His *Pro Ligario* and *De oratore* provided examples of language ornamentation and embellishment as well as lessons on the variations of style.[66] Cicero was known for insights, jest, and word patterns. His speeches fit into the new learning's attempts to break away from formalistic constraints of scholasticism. In the *Defense of Quintus Ligarius*, Cicero uses rhetorical questions, logic, and smooth persuasion for Caesar to pardon Legarius and return him from exile to his beloved brothers.[67]

In *On the Character of the Orator*, Cicero's object is to present the important rhetorical treatises of Aristotle, Isocrates, and other ancients in a pleasing form.[68] He speaks of compactness, coherence, smooth and equal flow, and harmony almost like that of poetry to eschew rude manners of language, and to add to its enjoyment. This short exposition is about an appropriate selection of materials, the content an orator should include, and how a speech ought to be completed.

Cicero's *Pro Lege Manilia* was to be examined in the second semester. In his *Defense of the Proposed Manilian Law*, Cicero addresses the Roman Assembly to support Manilius' proposition in giving Pompey power to conduct war against King Mithridates of Pontus—a fine example of the application of eloquence to the conduct of public business.[69]

---

[64]Dainville, *L'Éducation des Jésuites*, iv.

[65]Sturm, "Liberally Educated Nobility, for the Werter Brothers (1549)," in Spitz and Tinsley, 138: "Above all the knowledge of history especially helps. In history we may see the different ways states rise to power, how they have been preserved, and how changed and overthrown. Moreover, it supplies to men perplexed in life many counsels and varied examples."

[66]See Reid, "Founding of the Academy of Geneva," 28.

[67]"Speech on Behalf of Quintus Ligarius," in *Cicero the Speeches* (Cambridge, Mass.: Harvard University Press, 1961), 458–93.

[68]*Cicero on Oratory and Orators*, ed. J. S. Watson (Philadelphia: David McKay, Publisher, 1897), 12.

[69]Ibid., 150.

Herodotus was to be continued from the previous semester in the spring term. Homer's *Iliad* (books 5 and 6) was designated for this class. The style and structure of the *Iliad* demonstrate an artistic unity in vocabulary despite a long oral tradition.

Juvenal's *Satires* (nos. 1 and 10) were used at Saumur. Juvenal is known for his style of masterful attacks on the vices of Imperial Rome, along with excellent hexameters of "gaiety and stateliness" and satirical epigrams.[70] Satire represents an educational tool in showing how to use the mind sharply in changing meanings freely and drawing together material. For pedagogical purposes the Huguenots were attracted to such concise intellectual parody with moral overtones.

This concludes the analysis of the 1680 curriculum. The 1683 and 1684 programs have only minor changes in some of the books of the scriptures for the faculty of theology. The faculty of arts remained the same.

On the secondary level, the curriculum of 1684 at Saumur had the same program as that of 1680 in the Sixth and Fifth classes. Since the 1683 curriculum omits these studies, one can assume that the program was the same. I shall briefly discuss the textbook changes from the Fourth to the First classes in the 1683 and 1684 programs.

Differences appear in the Fourth Class of 1683. Emphasis is still on Latin, but Erasmus' *Colloquies* gave way to Justinian's books on law (nos. 2 and 3), and *Phaedrus' Fables* in Latin were pursued along with biblical studies on the Gospel of St. Mark. Ovid's works were omitted.

In 1684 Latin and Greek were to continue with Aesop's Greek fables added to the Latin to give anecdotes with a moral for junior students. Erasmus' text is no longer the entire *Colloquies*, but the long section, *Erasmi pietas puerilis, et convivium religiosum*, which well expresses his ideal of a union of classical and Christian learning.[71] The Academic Council of Saumur preferred that its students imitate a more focused model. The selection in history was by Eutropius, a Latin historian of the fourth century who had written a history of Rome. This is the only mention of Eutropius. Ovid's *Tristia* was retained for this level.

In the Third Class of 1683 a change was made in the comedy selected. Instead of Terence, Plautus was chosen for the sake of variety; the play was *Amphitruo*. In general, Plautus was considered more bawdy than Terence, since he had a fondness for farcical intrigue and comical songs. The more refined, sophisticated Terence is back in 1684 with *Andria* and *Eunuchus*. Ovid's *Epistolae V* was added to his *Metamorphoses* for Latin studies. The

---

[70]Juvenal, *The Satires*, trans. Niall Rudd (Oxford: Oxford University Press, 1992), xxxiv.
[71]Tracy, "Erasmus among the Postmodernists," 32, 38.

text of *Cornelius Nepos* was changed to the Third of 1684, since the material could be handled at a lower level.

For history at the Third level, Caesar's *Commentaries* (books 1 through 4) were listed instead of the 1680 history selection of Sallust. Strong, bold wording and excellent Latin made his work more of an oration than a history, and it was designed for the students' pleasure as well as example.[72] In 1683, biblical studies were Matthew and the Acts; in 1684 a general reference was made simply to New Testament Greek.

In 1683 the Second Class had Terence's *Heautontimoroumenos* and *Adelphi* for drama. Virgil's *Aeneid* replaced the *Bucolica*, and Cicero's offering was *De officiis*, a major moral treatise which relates the idea that beauty and proportion are to be found "not only in external things," but "just as much in speech and behavior."[73] It contributed to the precepts of oration and general knowledge. Religious studies included Mark and John along with Greek grammar.

In 1684 there were several changes in both semesters, reflecting a more practical orientation to the program, but continuing with a strong humanistic curriculum. History instruction included the *Aeliani variarum historiarum* (books 1 and 2) and *Quintus Curtius*, written by a legendary Roman patrician. Biblical studies covered Acts and the Gospel of Luke. For more language studies, the *Dialogi selecti Luciani*, a series of selected dialogues of Lucian, a Greek writer of dialogues of the second century, completed direct language work. There were also all four selections from Cicero's *Catilinaria*, speeches against Catiline's conspiracy to overthrow the lawful government.[74]

The First Class in 1683 also was to study Cicero for imitation in expression. In addition to *Pro Marcello*, a defense of Cicero's former teacher and Greek poet, the *Pro Archia* was specified. This oration is not only a model of praise literature, but also a defense of the liberal studies, especially of literature and its practical application in the public forum.[75] Horace's poetic selections included books 3, 4, and 5 of the *Carminum* and, in Greek, the class was to read Homer's *Odysseus* (books 1, 2, and 3) in teaching principles of relating to others.

In the second semester, Latin texts were predominant. Florus, a contemporary of Trajan, was offered for Roman history. The *Second Philippic*

---

[72]See also Sturm, "The Correct Opening of Elementary Schools of Letters (1538)," in Spitz and Tinsley, 94.

[73]Tracy, "Erasmus among the Postmodernists," 34 n.127.

[74]*Cicero on Oratory and Orators*, 24.

[75]Ibid., 114.

was listed. It could be the title of Demosthenes after the program at Geneva,[76] or Cicero's speech of the same name replying to Mark Anthony, but patterned after Demosthenes' work. It was meant to shape the students' speaking and writing. Another unusual text in 1683 was Ancreon's selections of poetry, *Anacreontis carmina selecta*. The author was a Greek poet of the fourth to third centuries B.C., known for his brilliance and grace.

In 1684, Cicero's orations were the difficult legal defense speeches, *Pro Roscio Amerino* and *Pro Publio Quinctio*. The second semester of the First Class had a new title, which consisted of the first two books of *Pharsalia*, or *Bellum civile*, written in the first century by Lucan, a nephew of the philosopher, Seneca. This account of the Roman civil wars placed Julius Caesar against the senatorial class; it was useful for Roman history as well as letters and was a fitting complement to many of Cicero's speeches. It demonstrates intellect and wisdom for a citizen.[77] The year 1684 was the last for the Academy of Saumur.

Now to some conclusions based on the examination of texts of a standard Renaissance education at the Academy of Saumur. The program of the faculty of arts was almost exclusively Aristotelian for logic, physics, metaphysics, and ethics. Humanist critics of scholasticism regularly exempted Aristotle from their attacks;[78] thus, the use of Aristotle does not necessarily mean scholasticism. And professors at Saumur were busy with their own knowledge of Greek to provide new editions or commentaries. The instructional methods seem to have been left to individual professors, since Ramus and Descartes were used in the early and mid-seventeenth century by specific professors. For theology, Hebrew and Greek were applied to Old and New Testament texts with explications emphasized. Theology and contemporary controversies were addressed, such as those relating to Socinianism and Arminianism. Plato and St. Augustine were studied in connection with Calvin's thought for reasoning, purity of speech, and clarity of meaning.[79]

On the secondary level (école classique) the classics were emphasized. But religious studies in the New Testament were also prescribed. Cicero, Homer, Herodotus, Ovid, and Virgil were the medallion authors; standard manuals, such as Cato's *Disthica* or Cordier's 1539 exercises, were used for

---

[76]See Reid, "Founding of the Academy of Geneva.".

[77]Cf. Sturm, "Liberally Educated Nobility, for the Werter Brothers (1549)," in Spitz and Tinsley, 141.

[78]Kristeller, *Classic, Scholastic, and Humanist Strains*, 43.

[79]Ibid., 55, 57, 63 n. 33.

language studies.[80] Classes were steeped in poetry and moral literature, with exercises from the *Colloquies* of Cordier and Erasmus and fables in Latin and Greek with moral lessons to be learned. Moral instruction and heroic adventures constituted an important part of the educational curriculum. Satires and plays were added in the upper grades for intellectual stimulation, developing insights, providing an element of pleasure, and practice in critical thinking, argumentation, and oral presentation. Attention was given to broadening students' horizons. A comparative approach demonstrates that texts in the classics were almost exactly the same at the Academy of Saumur as those of municipal and Jesuit schools of the time.

Greater emphasis was placed on classical authors instead of Christian authors because they were considered to be excellent in inculcating values, character, language, literature, and subject matter. Nevertheless, Christian values were addressed and a Christian lifestyle, derived from the Scriptures, was to be followed in everyday matters to make the world in the here-and-now a better place. Teachers at Saumur stressed creative human power and the *ars antiqua* for training future leaders. The overall program was that of Renaissance humanists. The Renaissance is best defined by its educational program, and it seems that its educational borders extended in France way beyond 1600, even to the end of the seventeenth century.[81]

To answer Léonard, educational depth is apparent at the Academy of Saumur, but the length of study time is somewhat less than the Jesuit program by one to three years; however, in practice the gap is not so broad, since students in theological studies at Jesuit schools took time out to teach and undergo a year of spiritual training.[82] At Saumur and the other Reformed academies, there was little emphasis on the church fathers and their philosophies, which would account for a few months' time. Nevertheless, since the goal of the French Protestant academies was to train pastors and statesmen, one can conclude that the program at Saumur offered an opportunity for a good classically based Renaissance education. It fulfilled the needs of the Reformed community for pastoral and civic leaders. Moreover, its influence reached beyond the closing of the Academy of

---

[80]Compayré, *Histoire critique*, 150 n. 2.

[81]See, for instance, a thesis from Berlin's Collège Français of 1696 directed by Étienne Chauvin, a French Protestant refugee from Nimes. *Disputatio Prima Philosophica, in qua Quid ipsa sit Philosophia, genuinaque Philosophandi ratio expenditur,* publio eam examini pröponunt JOH. CHRISTOPHORUS THEODORUS, Octobris Anno 1696, Coloniae Brandenburgicae, Imprimebat Ulricus Liebpertus (1696). Sub Praesidio…DN STEPHANI CHAUVIN, Pastoris dignissimi Philosophiae Professoris praestantissimi. Berlin: Staatsbibliothek Preussische Kultürbesits, Sign. 7 in Nh 260.

[82]George E. Ganss, S.J., interview by author, 30 September 1992, St. Louis University, St. Louis, Mo. Cf. Gray, "Lay Leadership among the Calvinists," 197–98, and Karl Hengst, *Jesuiten an Universitäten und Jesuituniversitäten* (Paderborn: F. Schoningh, 1981).

Saumur in early 1685 through those who had trained along the banks of the Loire and participated in the Huguenot diaspora.[83]

[83]See Janet Glenn Gray, "Reformed Protestant Academies Impact Life in Berlin," paper presented in Charleston, S.C., 15–17 May 1997; forthcoming from the University of South Carolina Press. Several pastors and teachers at Berlin's Collège Français were graduates of the Academy of Saumur, e.g., Pastor Jacques Abbadie and pre-Enlightenment figures Jacques Lenfant and Issac de Beausorbe.

# "NOT FOR MATTERS OF TREASON, BUT FOR LOVE MATTERS"

## Margaret Douglas, Countess of Lennox and Tudor Marriage Law

*Kim Schutte*

IN TUDOR ENGLAND MARRIAGE FOR THE WELL-BORN was not merely a matter of private housekeeping; it was very much bound up in the politics of the day.[1] Both Henry VIII and Elizabeth I showed an unusual reticence in arranging marriages for members of the extended royal family, as is well demonstrated by Henry's failure to complete marriage negotiations for any of his own children. If a member of the royal family (other than the reigning monarch) took matters into his or her own hands, the results could be disastrous. The person who most personified the possibilities and the dangers of marriage law in early modern England was Henry VIII's niece, Margaret Douglas, later the countess of Lennox. She was imprisoned no less than five times for marriage-related crimes.

Margaret herself was the product of troubled marriage alliances. She was born in 1515, the daughter of Henry VIII's eldest sister Margaret (widow of James IV of Scotland) and her second husband Archibald Douglas, the earl of Angus. The marriage was not a happy one, and it soon broke down. Margaret's mother would eventually obtain a divorce and marry for a third time. This action would cast some doubt on Margaret's legitimacy.

Margaret spent much of her youth with her father in wildly varying circumstances. The high point was when he served as regent for Margaret's half-brother, James V of Scotland, from 1525 to 1528. Soon, however,

---

[1] David Starkey, "Rivals in Power: The Tudors and the Nobility," in *Rivals in Power: Lives and Letters of the Great Tudor Dynasties*, ed. David Starkey (New York: Grove Weidenfeld, 1990), 8.

circumstances were to take a turn for the worse. When James seized control of the government in 1528, Angus became an outlaw and took his daughter with him. For several months they were refugees in the turbulent English-Scottish border region. Angus then sent Margaret to live at her uncle's court in England. He believed that England was a much more stable and safe environment for his teenaged daughter.

Margaret seems to have fit in well at the court of Henry VIII and everyone apparently was pleased with the arrangement. Undoubtedly it was expected that Margaret would quickly be married off to an appropriate husband. She was by many accounts a beautiful girl who looked very much like her Tudor relations.[2] She does not seem to have been well educated—certainly not by humanist standards—but she could write the kind of poetry that was fashionable among the young people of the court and was well-mannered enough to serve as an ornamental figure at court functions. She served all but the first (Catherine of Aragon) and the third (Jane Seymour) of Henry's wives as a senior lady-in-waiting,[3] and she was a prominent participant in the court revels. Undoubtedly Margaret and her parents assumed that Henry would arrange a brilliant marriage for her.

Until that marriage came about, Margaret was content to move in the most exalted and fashionable circles at court. She came to England just as Henry was sloughing off his first marriage to Catherine of Aragon, and Anne Boleyn was very much the ascendant figure. Anne took an interest in the king's niece, and Margaret became a lady-in-waiting to Anne when she became queen. Here she would meet the people who would inadvertently lead her to her first serious clash with Tudor marriage policy.

One of the well-connected young men that Margaret met in the Boleyn circle was Thomas Howard. Thomas was the half-brother of the third duke of Norfolk and the uncle of Margaret's great friend, Mary Howard, the duchess of Richmond (married to Henry VIII's natural son Henry Fitzroy). Thomas Howard was a wealthy young man, who spent liberally on those around him. He was considered quite good-looking and

<hr />

[2]Muriel St. Clare Byrne, ed., *The Lisle Letters* (Chicago: University of Chicago Press, 1981), 1:15; Antonia Fraser, *The Wives of Henry VIII* (New York: Knopf, 1992), 204; E. T. Bradley, *The Life of the Lady Arabella Stuart* (London: Richard Bentley, 1889), 1:16.

[3]Retha Warnicke, *Women of the English Renaissance and Reformation* (Westport, Conn.: Greenwood, 1983), 37.

very personable.[4] He had come to court just after Margaret, in 1533, was twenty-one years old, and very much a marriageable young man.[5]

With the encouragement and connivance of Anne Boleyn and Mary Howard, the twenty-year-old Margaret began a liaison with Thomas in 1535.[6] With such well-connected supporters, the couple must not have feared any ill effects from the great romance. As was typical of young couples, there was an exchange of small gifts. He gave her a cramp ring and she presented him with a miniature of herself. This seems to have been the extent of the intimacy between them. They agreed to marry at Easter in 1536.[7]

In this hope they were both naive and unlucky. Considering Margaret's importance as the niece of the king of England, the half-sister of the king of Scotland, and the daughter of the dowager queen of Scotland, she was a valuable commodity on the marriage market. Henry would want to exploit that commodity to his own advantage, rather than throw her away on a younger son of a native noble house. In agreeing to this marriage Margaret was acting outside the accepted norms for women of her social class: She had contracted what has been termed a "defiant match."[8] Still, Margaret and Thomas might have succeeded in carrying through on their desire to marry if other events had not intervened. In spring of 1536, Anne Boleyn and five men were arrested on charges of adultery. The queen was executed on May 16. This incident would prove to be a disaster for the couple. They had been very much a part of the former queen's circle, and she had been one of the great supporters of their match.

On June 8, Margaret and Thomas were arrested and sent to the Tower. At this point the precise nature of their crime was a bit cloudy. It was not yet illegal to enter into a precontract of marriage without the approval of the king. Margaret was taken by barge to her prison from the court at Greenwich.[9] The imprisonment of these two well-connected young people

---

[4]Gerald Brenan and Edward Philips Statham, *The House of Howard* (London: Hutchinson and Co., 1907), 1:90.

[5]David M. Head, "'Being Ledde and Seduced by the Devyll': The Attainder of Lord Thomas Howard and the Tudor Law of Treason," *Sixteenth Century Journal* 13 (1982): 5–6.

[6]Byrne, *Lisle Letters*, 4:179; Warnicke, *Women of the English Renaissance and Reformation*, 39.

[7]J. S. Brewer, ed., *Letters and Papers, Foreign and Domestic, of the Reign of Henry VIII: Preserved in the Public Record Office, the British Museum, and Elsewhere in England* (London: Her Majesty's Stationery Office, 1867; reprint ed., Vaduz: Kraus Reprint Ltd., 1965), 11:48. Henceforth cited as *LP*; Maria Perry, *The Word of a Prince: A Life of Elizabeth I from Contemporary Documents* (Woodbridge: Boydell, 1990), 23; Head, "Being Ledde and Seduced by the Devyll," 6 and n. 16.

[8]Barbara Harris, "Power, Profit, and Passion: Mary Tudor, Charles Brandon, and the Arranged Marriage in Early Tudor England," *Feminist Studies* 15 (1989), 62.

[9]Brenan, *The House of Howard*, 1:93.

on such a strange charge must have served as a warning to all those who might try to better themselves through marriage without the express approval of the king.[10]

Not only was Margaret's and Thomas's crime a bit unclear, but so was the exact nature of their relationship. Were they merely betrothed, or had they entered into a binding marriage? In the sixteenth century it was easy to enter into marriage. The exchange of vows between a couple of legal age (twelve for girls, fourteen for boys) was a valid marriage according to the church. This did not require either a ceremony or witnesses.[11] The attainder that was eventually passed against Thomas Howard assumed that a valid marriage contract existed between the couple. It was assumed that they had entered into a marriage *de praesenti*, which was binding according to canon law.[12]

It was Thomas who would bear the brunt of the punishment that was meted out to the couple. He would remain in the Tower until his death in October 1537, while Margaret would be removed to Syon Abbey very soon after her arrest.[13] Henry did not prosecute the couple in the law courts. Instead he chose the more direct method of Parliamentary attainder against Thomas Howard. Only Howard was to be attainted, presumably because Margaret's eventual marriage was still a valuable commodity for Henry.[14]

The Bill of Attainder went before the Parliament on 18 July 1536.[15] The attainder included a new legal restriction,

> that if any man, of what estate, degree, or condition so ever he be, at any time hereafter take upon him to espouse, marry, or take to his wife any of the King's children [being lawfully born or otherwise commonly reputed or taken for his children] or any the King's sisters or aunts of the part of the father, [or any of the lawful children] of the King's brothers or sisters [not being married] or contract marriage with any of them, without the special license, assent, and agreement first thereunto had and obtained of the King's Highness in writing under his great seal, [or defile or

[10]R. B. Merriman. *Life and Letters of Thomas Cromwell* (Oxford: Clarendon, 1902), 1:145.

[11]Steven Gunn, "Running into the Sand: The Last of the Suffolk Line," in *Rivals in Power: Lives and Letters of the Great Tudor Dynasties*, ed. David Starkey (New York: Grove Weidenfeld, 1990), 46.

[12]Head, "Being Ledde and Seduced by the Devyll," 8.

[13]Jasper Ridley, *Henry VIII* (New York: Viking, 1984), 272.

[14]C. Wriothesley, *A Chronicle of England during the Reigns of the Tudors*, ed. W. D. Hamilton (London: Camden Society, 1875–77), 1:54; Head, "Being Ledde and Seduced by the Devyll," 10.

[15]Byrne, *Lisle Letters*, 3:748.

deflower any of them not being married,] shall be deemed and adjudged a traitor to the King and his realm....[16]

This bill was intended to be very far-reaching. The definition of the children of the king is quite broad, and gives the king a great deal of authority over his family. The penalty for breaking this law was death for both the woman and the man. However, there was a special provision made to exempt Margaret from this part of the bill.[17] The law was to be applied to Margaret and Thomas retroactively, and Thomas Howard was sentenced to death. In fact, this law and the means by which it was passed were to have a profound impact on those in the extended royal family for years. Elizabeth I would make extensive use of her right to control the marriage alliances of her cousins (two of the Grey sisters), and Margaret would again fall victim to its provisions. Ironically, even Margaret's grandson, the future James I of England, would use it against her granddaughter Arbella Stuart. This bill had created a new form of treason and a new basis for attainder in the Tudor legal system. The use of the attainder rather than trial to accomplish the king's ends marks a turning point in the legal history of the reign of Henry VIII.[18] Prior to this Henry had used trial and condemnation to get his way (e.g., Thomas More, Anne Boleyn), but from 1536 on he is much more likely to use attainder (e.g., Catherine Howard).[19]

The Imperial Ambassador Eustace Chapuys lost little time writing home about events. He reported to Emperor Charles V that Parliament had attainted Thomas Howard "for having tried, in the presence of witnesses to contract a marriage with [Margaret Douglas]." He noted that the death penalty is the legislated punishment, but "[i]t appears however, that in the present case the sentence will not be carried out on [Margaret Douglas], owing to the marriage not having been consummated, and to her having been pardoned since...."[20] Chapuys seemed to have been sympathetic to Margaret and wrote that "certainly if she had done much worse she deserved pardon, seeing the number of domestic examples she has

---

[16]*Statutes of the Realm*, ed. A. Luders, et al. (London: Record Commission, 1810–28), 28 Hen. VIII. c. 24.

[17]Stanford E. Lehmberg, "Parliamentary Attainder in the Reign of Henry VIII," *Historical Journal* 18 (1975), 692; Brenan, *The House of Howard*, 1:93.

[18]Lehmberg, "Parliamentary Attainder in the Reign of Henry VIII," 692.

[19]Head, "Being Ledde and Seduced by the Devyll," 5.

[20]Pascual de Gayngos, *Calendar of Letters, Despatches, and State papers, Relating to the Negotiations Between England and Spain, Preserved in the Archives at Simancas and Elsewhere: Henry VIII* (London: Published by the authority of the Lords Commissioners of Her Majesty's Treasury, under the direction of the Master of the Rolls, 1877; repr. Vaduz: Kraus, 1969), 5, 2:214.

seen and sees daily, and that she had been for eight years of age and capacity to marry."[21] Neither Margaret nor Thomas would face execution. However, the poor conditions in the Tower undermined Thomas' health and he died in October 1537.[22] Margaret fared somewhat better because she was being held in more comfortable lodgings at Syon Abbey. She was released two days before the death of her lover, and she seems to have taken the news of his death very hard.[23] This was likely due to a feeling of guilt. In order to procure her release and reinstatement into the good graces of the king, she had had to disavow Thomas. She had worked through Thomas Cromwell, and as early as August 1536 she wrote, "I beseech you not to think that any fancy doth remain in me touching [Lord Thomas]; but that all my study and care is how to please the King's grace and to continue in his favour."[24]

It was not enough for Margaret to humble herself; her family had to do so as well. Henry was very angry about what he saw as a betrayal of his good graces. He had a tendency to see any deviation from his wishes as a threat to his power and authority.[25] He thus needed to be assured that the guilty party was sufficiently contrite and would never repeat such a mistake. As a result, the campaign to gain Margaret's release was undertaken primarily by her mother Margaret, the dowager queen of Scotland. On 12 August 1536 she wrote to Henry begging him to forgive her daughter.[26] But Henry was not to be easily swayed. He responded to his sister's entreaties in December: "And whereas you recommend unto us your daughter, although she has so lightly used herself, as was both to our dishonor and her own great hindrance, yet doubt you not, we shall for your sake, extend such goodness toward her, as you and she both shall have cause to be therewith satisfied, and for the same to give us condign thanks accordingly."[27] Satisfaction, however, was not to come quickly. Margaret was not released from Syon until 29 October 1537.[28]

---

[21]*LP* 11:147.

[22]Wriothesley, *Chronicle*, 1:70.

[23]Ibid., Ridley, *Henry VIII*, 272.

[24]Starkey, "Rivals in Power," 92; *LP* 11:294; Ridley, *Henry VIII*, 272.

[25]Leah Marcus, "Erasing the Stigma of Daughterhood: Mary I, Elizabeth, and Henry VIII," *Daughters and Fathers*, ed. Lynda E. Boose and Betty S. Flowers (Baltimore: Johns Hopkins University Press, 1989), 402.

[26]Markham John Thorpe, ed., *Calendar of State Papers, Relating to Scotland Preserved in the State Paper Department of Her Majesty's Public Record Office, the Scottish Series of the Reigns of Henry VIII, Edward VI, Mary, Elizabeth, 1509–1589* (London: Longman, Brow, Green, Longmans, and Roberts, 1858), 2:36; *LP* 11:293.

[27]*The Hamilton Papers: Letters and Papers Illustrating the Political Relations of England and Scotland in the Sixteenth Century, Formerly in the Possession of the Dukes of Hamilton Now in the British Museum*, ed. Joseph Bain (Edinburgh: Her Majesty's General Register Housed, 1890), 1:36.

[28]Patricia H. Burchanan, *Margaret Tudor, Queen of Scots* (Edinburgh: Scottish Academic, 1985), 258.

The arrest of Margaret Douglas amply demonstrates the danger of being too closely related to the king. She was not free to arrange her own marriage, even though in her eyes, she was more than ready for marriage. Henry's reluctance to arrange a suitable marriage for her was to remain a source of some frustration for several years. She was now bound by a new law that stated that she would forfeit her life if she undertook another such romantic adventure. Nevertheless, Margaret would once again attempt to deal with the matter of her marriage in her own way.

In fact, her next foray into the dangerous waters of romance would come in 1541 during Catherine Howard's short tenure as Henry VIII's queen. Margaret continued in her usual role as a senior lady-in-waiting to the queen. In this capacity she met and began a serious flirtation with Catherine's brother, Charles Howard.[29] Margaret had undoubtedly decided that if she did not handle things herself she would never marry. At twenty-six, she was already old by contemporary standards. This romance followed much the same pattern as had the relationship with Thomas Howard five years earlier. A secret marriage was arranged with the conniv-ance of the queen.[30]

In the fall of 1541, however, word of the planned marriage was leaked to Henry, and he did not react positively to the idea. Charles was banished from court, despite Catherine's best efforts, and eventually fled the coun-try. He remained in Holland and France until 1543. Margaret found her-self in her old place of confinement at Syon Abbey.[31]

Margaret would remain at Syon until November when she was moved to Kenninghall, the country residence of the duke of Norfolk. There she was in the company of her good friend Mary Howard, the duchess of Rich-mond. This was necessary because Catherine Howard's own indiscretions had come to the attention of the king, and she was lodged at Syon before being moved into the Tower. The young women were joined in the coun-try by the duke of Norfolk, who came immediately following the trial of the men accused with the queen.[32]

Before she left for Kenninghall, Margaret was visited by the arch-bishop of Canterbury, Thomas Cranmer. The archbishop had been briefed on his mission in a letter from Ralph Sadler:

> His Majesty's pleasure is, also, that tomorrow…you shall call apart to you my Lady Margaret Douglas, and first declare unto her how indiscreetly she hath demeaned herself toward the King's

[29]Neville Williams, *Henry VIII and His Court* (New York: Macmillan, 1971), 209.
[30]Brenan, *The House of Howard*, 1:306–7.
[31]Ibid.
[32]*LP* 16:1331; Williams, *Henry VIII and His Court*, 210.

Majesty, first with Lord Thomas and secondly with Charles Howard; in which parts, you shall, by discretion, charge her with overmuch lightness, and finally give her advice to beware the third time, and wholly apply herself to please the King's Majesty.[33]

Perhaps this repeat performance convinced the royal uncle that he needed to arrange an acceptable marriage for his niece. She showed every indication that she would continue to take matters into her own hands if something were not done. The man selected by Henry as a bridegroom was Matthew Stewart, the fourth earl of Lennox. He was an important Scottish nobleman, who indicated a willingness to further Henry's policies in Scotland in return for a suitable reward. The best part of that reward was to be the hand of Margaret Douglas. The couple was married on 29 June 1544 in the presence of the king and his new wife Catherine Parr.[34]

This marriage was an unqualified success. Even before they met, there were reports that they were in love.[35] Despite her relatively advanced age, Margaret had eight children. Unfortunately only two would survive, sons Henry and Charles.[36] These boys would be the cause of their mother's next problems with the marriage law. Margaret was an ambitious woman whose sons were well placed in the line of succession for both the English and the Scottish thrones. She would dedicate much of her adult life to trying to see them married as befitted their station;[37] typically noble-women worked hard to arrange advantageous marriages on behalf of their families.[38]

Unfortunately for Margaret, her sons would come of age during the reign of Elizabeth I, who seems to have had a positive phobia about marriages of the royal family. In fact she seems to have had little regard for the institution at all. Her anger at finding that any of her ladies had married is legendary. It has been argued that her experiences in childhood and adolescence soured Elizabeth on marriage.[39] In controlling the marriage

---

[33]Brenan, *The House of Howard*, 1:306; *LP* 16:1333.

[34]*LP* 19:799.

[35]*The Hamilton Papers*, 2:295.

[36]David N. Durant, *Bess of Hardwick: Portrait of an Elizabethan Dynast* (New York: Atheneum, 1978), 82.

[37]Alison Plowden, *Marriage with My Kingdom: The Courtships of Elizabeth I* (London: Macmillan, 1977), 136.

[38]Barbara Harris, "Women and Politics in Early Tudor England," *Historical Journal* 33 (1990), 260.

[39]Larissa Taylor-Smither, "Elizabeth I: A Psychological Profile," *Sixteenth Century Journal* 15 (1984), 66ff.; Simon Adams, "Eliza Enthroned? The Court and Its Politics," in *The Reign of Elizabeth I*, ed. Christopher Haigh (Athens: University of Georgia Press, 1985), 72.

patterns of the royal family, Elizabeth had the perfect weapon: the provisions set out in the 1536 Bill of Attainder against Thomas Howard.

Relations between Margaret and Elizabeth were deeply troubled. During the reign of Mary I (1553–58), Margaret was a great favorite and was often given precedence over Princess Elizabeth. There were also reports that Margaret behaved in an arrogant manner toward the princess and attempted to exploit her status as favorite.[40] When Mary died in 1558 and the princess became queen, Margaret's days as a favorite were definitively over. She and Matthew retired from court, and most of Margaret's energies were focused on the betterment of her family.

Margaret saw an opportunity in late 1560 when Francis II of France died, and left Mary, queen of Scots, a widow. Margaret was the Scottish queen's half-aunt, and she believed that a match between her eldest son Henry, Lord Darnley, and Mary would be a wonderful idea. To further this plan, she immediately sent the young man to France in order to carry condolences to the widow.[41] His trip was of some interest to the ambassadors of both England and Scotland, who watched Mary's responses carefully.[42] They concluded that they had nothing to fear. The young queen removed herself to Scotland, and Darnley returned home, an unmarried man. At this point, Mary, queen of Scots, was aiming for a bigger matrimonial prize, Don Carlos of Spain.

The apparent disinterest of the queen of Scots did not dissuade Margaret. She, and to a lesser extent, Matthew, continued to work for the match. However, Elizabeth's response to the idea was decidedly ambivalent. In 1561 and the first part of 1562, there were indications that she was seriously displeased with the countess of Lennox for sending Darnley to France. So displeased in fact, that the part of the family that was in England found itself imprisoned in June 1562. Matthew was held in the Tower and Margaret and her youngest son, Charles, were in the care of Sir Richard Sackville at Sheen. The charges against them were twofold: first, "with secret intimation that she [Margaret] has a right to the Crown of

[40]James Anthony Froude, *History of England from the Fall of Wolsey to the Defeat of the Spanish Armada* (New York: AMS, 1862–70), 2:72; Anne Somerset, *Elizabeth I* (New York: Knopf, 1991), 36; Christopher Hibbert, *The Virgin Queen: Elizabeth I, Genius of the Golden Age* (Reading, Mass.: Addison-Wesley, 1991), 44; Maria Perry, *The Word of a Prince: A Life of Elizabeth I from Contemporary Documents* (Woodbridge: Boydell, 1990), 85.

[41]Antonia Fraser, *Mary Queen of Scots* (New York: Dell, 1969), 218; Martin A. S. Hume, *The Great Lord Burghley: A Study in Elizabethan Statecraft* (London: James Nisbet, 1898), 114.

[42]*Calendar of the State Papers, Relating to Scotland, Preserved in the State Paper Department of Her Majesty's Public Record Office*, vol. 1: *The Scottish Series, of the Reigns of Henry VIII, Edward VI, Mary, Elizabeth, 1509–1589*, ed. John Markham Thorpe (London: Longman, Brown, Green, Longman's and Roberts, 1858), 169–70.

England next to the Queen," and, second, that she was involved in a "secret compassing of marriage betwixt the Scottish Queen and her son." Margaret had implausibly denied all charges. As a condition for the family's release, Margaret had to promise to give up the idea of the Scottish match for Darnley.[43] The imprisonment was quite short; they were all at liberty by mid-November. The Lennoxes were soon back at court and in favor with the queen.[44]

But the English queen's attitude changed somewhat in late 1562 and 1563 when Mary's intentions toward Don Carlos became clear. In Elizabeth's eyes, the choice of husband for the queen of Scots was a very important thing. It was vital that the man not pose a threat to English interests. Don Carlos, the son of Philip II of Spain, did pose such a threat. Henry, Lord Darnley, was an infinitely preferable match from the English point of view.[45]

It was in the period following the death of Francis II that Elizabeth wrote to Mary on behalf of the earl of Lennox, saying that his Scottish estates should be restored to him.[46] He had forfeited his lands in Scotland in 1545 when he married Margaret and transferred his allegiance to England. This forfeiture was, of course, of great concern to the Lennoxes and they hoped that with Mary in Scotland their fortunes would improve. In 1564 Elizabeth granted Matthew permission to travel to Scotland to see about the restoration of his lands.[47] There was a great deal of opposition among the Scottish nobles to the return of the earl of Lennox. The English government did what it could to allay their fears.[48]

When the earl wrote asking permission for his eldest son, Henry, Lord Darnley, to join him in Scotland, Elizabeth granted the request. The young man was granted a three-month passport in February 1565.[49] She must have known the true purpose of Darnley's trip north, but she was playing a game of fence-sitting that was familiar to those around her.

---

[43] *Calendar of State Papers, Foreign Series of the Reign of Elizabeth, Preserved in the Public Record Office,* ed. Joseph Stevenson (London: Her Majesty's Stationery Office, 1863), 4:980, 5:91 and 170; Perry, *The Word of a Prince,* 184.

[44] *Calendar of State Papers, Foreign Series,* 6:1027, 5:1123.

[45] Alison Plowdon, *Elizabeth Tudor and Mary Stewart: Two Queens in One Isle* (Totowa, N.J.: Barnes and Noble, 1984), 86; William Ferguson, *Scotland's Relations with England: A Survey to 1707* (Edinburgh: John Donald, 1977), 85; John Knox, *The Works of John Knox,* ed. David Laing (New York: AMS, 1966), 2:481.

[46] *Calendar of State Papers, Foreign Series,* 3:806; *Calendar of State Papers, relating to Scotland,* 191.

[47] Knox, *Works,* 2:469–70; *Calendar of State Papers, relating to Scotland,* 191.

[48] *Calendar of State Papers, relating to Scotland,* 199.

[49] Gordon Donaldson, *The First Trial of Mary Queen of Scots* (New York: Stein and Day, 1969), 24.

The marriage between Darnley and Mary, queen of Scots, was vigorously opposed by William Cecil. He believed that it would give undue encouragement to those who supported the claims of Mary to the English throne. He was especially concerned about the reaction of the English Catholics who might be tempted to support the claims of the couple.[50]

Despite the opposition of the English government, the marriage between Darnley and the queen of Scots took place in March 1565. Mary seems to have been very impressed with her cousin. She is reported as thinking that he was "the lustiest and best proportioned long man" she had seen.[51]

The earl of Lennox and Darnley were well beyond the grasp of Elizabeth; however, the same cannot be said for Margaret. When word reached England of the marriage, Elizabeth was determined that the countess would pay for her ambition. On 26 April, de Silva, the Spanish ambassador, wrote to Philip II:

> Lady Margaret sent word to me that she had gone to the Queen's Chamber and that her Majesty had refused to speak to her and afterwards sent an order that she was not to leave her apartments, giving her to understand she was to consider herself a prisoner, as she had received letters from a foreign prince without her permission and without conveying the contents to her. Lady Margaret answered that it was true she had received a letter from the Queen of Scotland by her Secretary, and had gone to the Queen's chamber for the purpose of showing it to her Majesty who had refused to speak to her, and consequently it was not her fault. An answer came from the Queen to the effect that although she was detained in her apartments, there was no intention of preventing her friends from visiting her, as is usually done her in cases where persons are placed under arrest.[52]

The confinement in Margaret's apartments at court did not last long. Margaret was soon transferred to the Tower and kept in the same lodgings as she had occupied in 1536.[53] The countess, however, was not held in

[50]B. W. Beckingsale, *Burghley: Tudor Statesman, 1520–1598* (London: Macmillan, 1967), 106; Plowdon, *Elizabeth Tudor and Mary Stewart*, 138; Conyers Read, *Mr. Secretary Cecil and Queen Elizabeth* (London: Jonathan Cape, 1955), 318.

[51]Plowdon, *Elizabeth Tudor and Mary Stewart*, 137.

[52]*Calendar of Letters and State Papers relating to English Affairs, Preserved Principally in the Archives of Simancas*, vol. 1, *Elizabeth, 1558–1567*, ed. Martin A. S. Hume (London: Her Majesty's Stationery Office, 1892), 296.

[53]David Hume, *The History of England from the Invasion of Julius Caesar to the Abdication of James the Second, 1688* (Boston: Phillips, Sampson, and Co., 1850), 4:66.

particularly close confinement. The Spanish ambassador reported to Philip II that she was able to send and receive word from the outside.[54] Margaret was to remain imprisoned for the duration of the marriage between Mary and Darnley. Her young son Charles was placed in the care of the archbishop of York.[55]

The queen of Scots wrote a letter to Elizabeth on 12 February 1566, protesting the confinement of the countess of Lennox. She inquired if Margaret deserved to be punished merely for wanting the best for her son.[56] This was typical of Mary. She tended to see most things in personal rather than political terms. Thus here she was making a fundamental mistake about the nature of marriage under the Tudors—and especially under the last of the Tudors. This was not a personal matter, but rather a matter of great concern to the queen. Those members of the royal family who forgot that, and who forgot the power of the law poised against them, did so at their own peril. Katherine and Mary Grey (the sisters of the unfortunate Jane Grey) attempted to marry men of their own choosing, and both were imprisoned for their pains. The closer a person was in blood to the throne, the more dangerous it was. Elizabeth had determined not to marry; thus the matter of her heir was of great concern. She saw all potential heirs as potential usurpers and took steps to minimize that danger. She frequently used the 1536 law to do that. In 1562 a foreign observer wrote, "The prison will soon be full of the nearest relations of the Crown."[57]

Since Mary, queen of Scots, saw her own marriage in primarily personal rather than political terms, it was very important to her that the union be fulfilling on a romantic level. Unfortunately, the marriage between Mary Stuart and Henry, Lord Darnley, was not a happy one. Margaret's son seems to have been an immature, unpleasant young man. His determination to be king of Scotland in his own right (as opposed to just the crown matrimonial) would lead to a serious breach between the couple. He soon was spending a great deal of time in the brothels of Edinburgh. Despite this unhappiness, Mary did manage to conceive a child, who was born on 19 June 1566. With the birth of the future James VI (I of England), Darnley became disposable. He had made himself odious to

---

[54]John Hungerford Pollen, *Papal Negotiations with Mary Queen of Scots, during Her Reign in Scotland, 1561–1567* (Edinburgh: Scottish History Society, 1901), 470; *Calendar of Letters and State Papers relating to English Affairs*, 305; Reginald Henry Mahon, *The Tragedy of Kirk O'Field* (Cambridge: Cambridge University Press, 1930), 247–48.

[55]*Calendar of Letters and State Papers relating to English Affairs*, 307.

[56]*Calendar of State Papers, relating to Scotland*, 228.

[57]Lacey Baldwin Smith, "English Treason Trials and Confessions in the Sixteenth Century," *Journal of the History of Ideas* 15 (1954), 472; *Calendar of State Papers, Foreign Series*, 4:980.

everyone of consequence in Scotland. In 1567 he was murdered, with Mary's complicity, at the palace of Kirk O'Field.

When the word of the death of Margaret's son reached England, the attitude of the English government changed toward the countess. Both Cecil and Elizabeth seem to have felt genuine sympathy for her. Cecil's wife, Mildred, was one of the two women who were sent to the Tower to tell Margaret about Henry's death. She was quickly released and restored to favor with the queen.[58] Matthew returned from Scotland, and they embarked on a largely unsuccessful campaign to hold Mary, queen of Scots, and her accomplices accountable for the murder.

When Mary was driven out of Scotland and forced to abdicate in favor of her son James, a series of regents governed on behalf of the boy. In June 1570 the earl of Lennox was appointed by Elizabeth as regent.[59] He was killed on 4 September 1571, leaving Margaret truly on her own with serious financial difficulties and equally troublesome parental responsibilities in the form of her son Charles. In 1574, when Charles was eighteen, Margaret referred to him as her "greatest dolour."[60]

Margaret would attempt to solve both problems in a very dangerous manner—through a marriage alliance for Charles. This time, however, she set her sights somewhat lower. Charles was not destined for a great alliance; instead Margaret would satisfy herself with a solid marriage into a good English noble family.

In the first half of the 1570s, however, Margaret was not the only formidable noble lady with children to marry. Her equal in scheming and ambition was Elizabeth, countess of Shrewsbury, better known as Bess of Hardwick. This lady also understood the importance of marriage and had married repeatedly herself, each time climbing higher on the social ladder. She had children from her second marriage to William Cavendish for whom she was determined to do well. In 1574 she had one daughter, Elizabeth, left to marry. Bess had been advertising the girl heavily but had not yet found a suitable match.[61]

The ambitious mothers seem to have hatched a scheme to bring their two very marriageable children together. There is no indication that either

[58]Pearl Hogrefe, *Women of Action in Tudor England* (Ames, Iowa: Iowa State University Press, 1977), 21; Perry, *The Word of a Prince*, 192.

[59]Hume, *The History of England*, 4:129–30; E. T. Bradley, *The Life of the Lady Arabella Stuart* (London: Richard Bentley, 1889), 1:20.

[60]Caroline Bingham, *The Making of a King: The Early Years of James VI and I* (Garden City: Doubleday, 1969), 60–61; Susan Doran, *Monarchy and Matrimony: The Courtships of Elizabeth I* (London: Routledge, 1996), 120; Hume, *The History of England*, 4:155; Durant, *Bess of Hardwick*, 82.

[61]Durant, *Bess of Hardwick*, 81.

one considered approaching the situation through appropriate channels: that is, asking permission from the queen. Instead they contrived an elaborate plot that was designed to preserve deniability for the older women. In October 1574, Margaret sought, and received, permission to travel north to some of her estates in Yorkshire. She took her son Charles with her. On the way they were met, as was only hospitable, by Elizabeth Shrewsbury and invited to rest for a time at her house of Rufford. Once there, Margaret's health gave way, and she was forced to take to her bed for four or five days and was tenderly nursed by her hostess. During the period of Margaret's illness, Charles and Elizabeth Cavendish fell in love and took it upon themselves to make unbreakable vows to one another. There was nothing for the mothers to do but to regularize the union and then inform the authorities of the situation.[62]

Not surprisingly, the ruse did not fool anyone, least of all the queen. She was very familiar with both of the mothers in the situation and was immediately convinced that the match had been arranged to satisfy their ambitions. Blame, however, was not equally apportioned. Undoubtedly because of Margaret's past problems in conforming to the marriage law, Elizabeth saw Margaret as the most guilty party. She, more than anyone else, knew the risks that were being taken in this marriage. By the terms of the 1536 bill, both the mothers and their children were guilty of treason and faced a possible death penalty.[63]

Somewhat ironically, the marriage did nothing to improve Margaret's financial situation. She seems to have hoped that Elizabeth Shrewsbury's third husband, the earl of Shrewsbury, would provide a healthy dowry for his stepdaughter. This did not happen, so Margaret not only ran afoul of the law but also gained dependents.[64]

When Queen Elizabeth I found out about the marriage between Charles Stewart and Elizabeth Cavendish, she reacted in two ways. First, she ordered Margaret and Charles to present themselves in London, while the bride and her mother were to keep to their house for the time being. Second, the queen ordered a thorough investigation of the circumstances surrounding the marriage to be conducted by the earl of Huntingdon. During the course of the investigation the countess of Lennox and the young couple (Elizabeth Cavendish having been granted permission to join her husband) were confined to Margaret's house at Hackney.[65]

---

[62]Durant, *Bess of Hardwick*, 83–81; Hogrefe, *Women of Action*, 65.
[63]Durant, *Bess of Hardwick*, 87; Hogrefe, *Women of Action*, 65.
[64]Durant, *Bess of Hardwick*, 95.
[65]Ibid., 84–85.

It is somewhat unclear why the queen took such a hard line in this case. The marriage could pose no real dynastic threat to her.[66] It is possible that her long-standing antipathy toward the countess of Lennox played a part. Margaret had been a matrimonial schemer for so long that perhaps the queen could not believe that there was not more to this marriage than was readily apparent. It is also possible that Elizabeth suspected a conspiracy centered on Mary, queen of Scots. Mary Stuart was a prisoner in England, and her primary custodian was the earl of Shrewsbury, the bride's stepfather. Despite Margaret's repeated claims to have nothing but loathing for the murderess of her son, Elizabeth might have thought otherwise.[67] Finally, it is conceivable that Elizabeth's anger had nothing more behind it than a typically Tudor suspicion of anything that happened behind her back. The 1536 law gave the queen the right to control the marriages of the members of the royal family, and any abrogation of that right could be construed as a threat to royal authority in a more generalized way.

Margaret wasted little time in presenting her side of the story to important men around the queen. She wrote to William Cecil with her version of events on 3 December 1574. In this letter she totally denies that there was any plan between the mothers to arrange the match. She writes, "Now my Lord, for that hasty marriage of my son Charles, after that he had entangled himself so that he could have done none other, I refer the same to your Lordship's good consideration, whether it was not most fitly for me to marry them, he being my only son and comfort, that is left to me. And your Lordship can bear me witness, how desirous I have been to have a match for him other than this...." A week later, she wrote to Robert Dudley, the earl of Leicester, asking him to influence the queen in favor of the marriage.[68]

Margaret was placed in the Tower for a short period for her part in this marriage. The exact date of her release is not clear, but she was back at her house in Hackney by the end of the year. There she was joined by Charles and his wife.[69] This marriage was not to be long-lasting either. Charles

---

[66]This did not always make any difference; one of the Grey sisters was imprisoned for marrying a guardsman.

[67]Durant, *Bess of Hardwick*, 86.

[68]Cecile Goff, *A Woman of the Tudor Age* (London: John Murray, 1930), 305–6; *Calendar of State Papers, Domestic Series, of the Reigns of Edward VI, Mary, Elizabeth, 1547–1580, Preserved in the State Paper Department of Her Majesty's Public Record Office*, ed. Robert Lemon (London: Her Majesty's Stationery Office, 1856), 48a, vol. 99:12, 12i, and 13.

[69]Bradley, *The Life of the Lady Arabella Stuart*, 1:34–35.

died eighteen months after his wedding.[70] He was married long enough to have a child with his wife. This child was the Lady Arbella Stuart who was to have her own matrimonial problems during the reign of her cousin, James I.

During her last encounter with the marriage law that had been passed in response to her first indiscretion in 1536, Margaret wrote the following: "Thrice have I been sent into prison not for matters of treason, but for love matters. First, when Thomas Howard, son of the Duke of Norfolk, was in love with me; then for the love of Henry Darnley, my son, to Queen Mary, lastly for the love of Charles, my younger son, to Elizabeth Cavendish."[71] In this Margaret draws a line between "love matters" and politics. She knew that this was a false line. Her meddling in marriage alliances had little to do with romance and a great deal to do with ambition and politics. In her own case, her relationships with both Thomas and Charles Howard would have married her into the most powerful noble family in England. Both men had close relations with Henry VIII's Howard queens (Anne Boleyn and Catherine Howard). Thus these marriages could be counted on to keep her at court and in the center of power. The ambitious motives that lay behind the marriage of Henry Darnley and Mary, queen of Scots, are obvious. Presumably, by 1574 she had begun to look to the future. Her son, Charles, stood in close relation to the line of succession in Scotland as well as England; any child he had would be a very important person indeed.

In her own lifetime, Margaret's ambitions came to little; both of her sons died young, but in the next generation her plotting bore fruit. Not even in her wildest speculations could she have imagined that her grandson would sit on the thrones of both England and Scotland. There was fruit of a less healthful type as well. During the reign of James I (James VI of Scotland), her other grandchild Arbella Stuart repeatedly came into conflict with the government over the issue of her marriage and the strength of her claim to the throne. Eventually, like her grandmother before her, Arbella would take marriage matters into her own hands. She married William Seymour, duke of Somerset, without governmental permission. In many ways this union was reminiscent of the previous generation. The erstwhile groom was himself the product of a marriage contracted in defiance of the 1536 marriage law; his paternal grandparents were the Lady Catherine Grey and Edward Seymour, earl of Hertford. This couple had married without permission in the reign of Elizabeth I and had

---

[70]Durant, _Bess of Hardwick_, 93.
[71]Goff, _A Woman of the Tudor Age_, 306–7.

been imprisoned in the Tower for the offense. Arbella and William were immediately imprisoned. Following a dramatic escape, Arbella was recaptured and spent the rest of her life in the Tower of London.

Margaret Douglas, countess of Lennox, was important for the very texture of Tudor political culture. Her career bears a striking witness to the artificiality of the line between love and politics. One could easily become the other, and Margaret understood this truth. Her pursuit of political advantage through marriage caused the passage of the Bill of Attainder of 1536, which gave the Crown maximum scope in regulating all royal marriages. Margaret herself ran afoul of this law more than any other royal personage. Her whole life demonstrates the vital role that marriage played in the politics of Tudor England and the dangers inherent in marital politics.

# "FOR I AM WELSH, YOU KNOW"

## Henry V, Fluellen, and the Place of Wales in the Sixteenth-Century English Nation

*Robert S. Babcock*

FLUELLEN: Your majesty says very true; if your Majestie is remembered of it, the Welshmen did good service in a garden where leeks did grow, wearing leeks in their Monmouth caps; which your majesty knows to this hour is an honourable badge of service, and I do believe your Majesty takes no scorn to wear the leek upon Saint Tavy's day.

KING HENRY: I wear it for memorable honor; for I am Welsh, you know, good countryman.

FLUELLEN: All the Water in the Wye can not wash your Majesty's Welsh plood out of your pody, I can tell you that. Got pless it and preserve it as long as it pleases his Grace and his Majesty too.[1]

IN THIS EXCHANGE FROM *HENRY V*, THE SPEAKERS are a Welsh officer in the king's army at Agincourt and Henry V himself. It is an exchange that is jarring equally to the medievalist and the modernist, to our understanding of nationality and identity in the sixteenth and twentieth centuries. For as Prince of Wales, heir to the English throne, Henry had presided over the pacification of the native Welsh and the destruction of Owain Glyn Dwr's rebellion against his father, Henry IV.[2] Yet the exchange illustrates well the complexities of being Welsh—and being in Wales—in the sixteenth

---

[1] *Henry V* 4.7.87–98.

[2] For an account of Henry's activities in Wales with a stridently contemporary view of nationality, see Desmond Seward, *Henry V: The Scourge of God* (New York: Viking, 1987), 13–26. For more judicious assessments, see Christopher Allmand, *Henry V* (Berkeley: University of California Press, 1992),

century of Tudor kings and queens of a self-consciously English nation. It has long been recognized that the century saw the achievement of both Tudor absolutism and English national consciousness. For the Welsh, the former meant the rise of the gentry, inclusion into the shire administration, and the application of English law to Welsh affairs. But what of the latter development in early modern Britain, the growth of English national consciousness? What role were the Welsh to play in this expansive, assertive English nation? As with so many other issues of sixteenth-century Britain, William Shakespeare's plays may provide the beginnings of an answer to that question. Fluellen and Henry speak to the ways—service, administration, and a shared, if mythical, sense of history—that the Welsh were to fit into the strident English identity the Tudor realm had become. Shakespeare's treatment of Fluellen, however, also shows how differences in language and culture made that fit a difficult one.

Shakespeare's works are particularly useful tools to address such political and cultural issues. Critics who are generally lumped together as "new historicists" have argued that royal figures in Elizabethan plays are statements of royal authority and identity, quite often statements in synch with the prevailing aspirations of the monarch on the throne.[3] Shakespeare was the object of both royal and aristocratic patronage at court; his plays and his players received their backing from figures intimately involved in the royal politics of the age and figures who were also part of the audience. His works cannot help but be part of the political discourse of the realm and commentary on that discourse.

Similarly, they are both shapers of the emerging national sentiment and reflectors of the new English identity. As Philip Edwards noted, "the English drama never shows its closeness to the nation more strikingly than in the large body of plays written in the last fifteen years of Elizabeth's reign with English and British history as their subject."[4] In *Forms of Nationhood: The Elizabethan Writing of England*, Richard Helgerson examines a number of literary genres of the sixteenth century and concludes:

---

16–38, and R. R. Davies, *The Revolt of Owain Glyn Dwr* (Oxford: Oxford University Press, 1995), 242–43.

[3]See, among others, Jonathan Goldberg, *James I and the Politics of Literature* (Baltimore: Johns Hopkins University Press, 1983); Stephen Greenblatt, *Renaissance Self-Fashioning* (Chicago: University of Chicago Press, 1980); Peter C. Herman, "O, 'tis a gallant king: Shakespeare's *Henry V* and the Crisis of the 1590's," in Dale Hoak, ed., *Tudor Political Culture* (Cambridge: Cambridge University Press, 1995); and Stephen Orgel, *Illusion of Power: Political Theater in the English Renaissance* (Berkeley: University of California Press, 1975).

[4]Philip Edwards, *Threshold of a Nation* (Cambridge: Cambridge University Press, 1979), 1.

"Though the forms of nationhood imagined by these various texts are many, the political issues that engage them can...be reduced to just two. One of these concerns the monarch and monarchic power. The other involves the inclusion or exclusion of social groups from privileged participation in the national community and its representation."[5] Shakespeare and his contemporaries were especially concerned with who ruled the nation and who had the right to claim membership in it.

Such concerns make instances in which an English king proclaims "For I am Welsh," as Shakespeare has Henry V say twice,[6] especially important. The exchange with Fluellen becomes an assertion of the legitimacy of an English monarch to rule Wales as well as a statement of the acceptance of the Welsh into the English nation. Indeed, all of *Henry V* would seem to be about the British peoples, represented by Fluellen, Mac-Morris [Irish], and Jamy [Scots], united behind an English king against a common, foreign foe. Certainly this is the theme emphasized in Laurence Olivier's 1945 film of the play, made when the peoples of Britain were united against Nazi Germany. Such a theme was important in the sixteenth century as well, for Shakespeare wrote *Henry V* in the summer of 1599 at a moment when his countrymen were facing the prospect of a bloody foreign war perhaps not unlike the Hundred Years' War of the play, and Welsh soldiers would have to play a disproportionately large role in it.

In 1593 Hugh O'Neill, earl of Tyrone, had united with Hugh O'Donnel and other Irish leaders to begin a drive against the English. In 1598 the English were soundly defeated at Yellow Ford and the Pale itself became open to Irish incursions. During the entire campaign, the Irish rebels actively solicited money, supplies, and troops from Philip II of Spain, and the spectre was raised of a Catholic and perhaps Spanish stronghold menacing Protestant England's western flank. To raise the massive invasion force necessary to prevent this, Elizabeth's government desperately raised money through loans, forced and otherwise, and the sale of Crown lands, and began to levy troops from English and Welsh counties. The main parts of departure for service in Ireland were Bristol, Chester, and Milford, making the Welsh shires and their human and economic resources especially valuable, and making Welsh service and loyalty to the Crown essential.

---

[5]Richard Helgerson, *Forms of Nationhood: Elizabethan Writing of England* (Chicago: University of Chicago Press, 1992), 9.

[6]The first is to Pistol, while in disguise 4.1.50.

Between 1594 and 1602, some 2.9 percent of the population of Wales was called for service in Ireland.[7]

It would not be the first instance in which Welsh troops had fought in support of the king of England, nor even the first time they had fought in Ireland. The English conquest of Wales had been a long and complex process that saw generations of Welshmen reach accommodation with their conquerors as vassals, allies, and mercenaries. Welsh troops accompanied Strongbow to Ireland; the Lord Rhys ap Gruffudd brought troops from South Wales to aid Henry II in both England and France.[8] Welsh captains distinguished themselves at Agincourt.[9] In this sense, Shakespeare has history on his side; Fluellen may be a fictional character, but he represents hundreds, perhaps thousands, of Welshmen who served Henry V loyally on the fields of France. In Tudor times, Henry VII could not have won the throne without Welsh support, and Henry VIII raised troops in Wales for campaigns in France, Scotland, and Ireland. Indeed, Welsh casualties at Yellow Ford were particularly heavy.[10]

When Elizabeth dispatched Robert Devereux, the earl of Essex and holder of significant lands in South Wales, to deal with the revolt of the earls, Welshmen accompanied him as they had accompanied the Devereux earl of Essex to Ireland twenty years earlier.[11] The chorus refers to Devereux in act 5 of *Henry V*—a reference Gary Ward has called "the only explicit, extradramatic, incontestable reference to a contemporary event anywhere in the canon."[12] It is a reference that connects precisely the common cause of medieval war in France with the common cause of contemporary war in Ireland.

> But now behold
> In the quick forge and working-house of thought,
> How London doth poure out her citizens,
> The mayor and all his brethren in best sort,
> Like the senators of th'antique Rome,

---

[7]Glanmor Williams, *Recovery, Reorientation and Reformation: Wales c. 1415–1642* (Oxford: Clarendon Press, 1987), 367–68. See as well J. J. N. McGurk, "A Survey of the Demands Made on Welsh Shires...," *Transactions of the Honorable Society of Cymmrodorian* (1983): 56–68.

[8]Rhys brought troops to participate in the siege of Tutbury castle in 1174; Ralph of Diceto, *Radulfi de Decan: Londoniens 3 Opera Historian* (Rolls Series, 1876), 1:384. And he sent a thousand soldiers with Henry to France in the same year; Roger of Howten, *Gesta Regis Henri Second;* (Rolls Series, 1867), 1:74.

[9]David Walker, *Medieval Wales* (Cambridge: Cambridge University Press, 1990), 178.

[10]Williams, *Recovery, Reorientation and Reformation,* 367.

[11]Ibid., For the Devereux holdings in South Wales, see H. A. Lloyd, "The Essex Inheritance," *Welsh History Review* 7 (1974): 13–39.

[12]*Henry V,* ed. Gary Taylor, *The Oxford Shakespeare* (Oxford: Clarendon Press, 1982), 7.

With the plebeians swarming at their heels,
Go forth and fetch their conquering Caesar in—
As, by a lower but loving likelihood
Were now the general of our gracious empress,
(As in good time he may) from Ireland coming,
Bringing rebellion broached on his sword,
How many would the peaceful city quit
To welcome him? Much more, and much more cause,
Did they this Harry.[13]

The message is clear and it illustrates convincingly how connected to royal ideology Shakespeare's historical plays can be. Just as rich and poor, senators "with plebeians swarming at their heels," had united behind Caesar as all London had united behind Henry, so all Elizabeth's subjects should unite behind her for war in Ireland. By including Fluellen, the foremost spokesperson for royal authority in the play,[14] among Henry's subjects, Shakespeare suggests the Welsh should consider themselves among these legitimate, true, and steadfast subjects of Elizabeth.

Many did. Fluellen, whom some critics see as an alternative to Falstaff among the lesser gentry,[15] represents the Welshmen who actively fought in support of the English king in France and Ireland, and he also represents the emergent Welsh gentry which found its power and prosperity under Elizabeth I. What historians call the "Tudor Settlement" of the mid-sixteenth century involved essentially an alliance between Crown and local gentry.[16] Part of the assimilation of Wales into the Tudor state meant that English law had to be enforced fully in the Principality and the Marches; to do that, Thomas Cromwell, the architect of the revolution in government under the Tudors, oversaw the introduction of the office of Justice of the Peace into Wales and Cheshire in 1536. It was an office that had never existed in Wales before. It went hand in hand with the division of Wales into shires and it required local administrators to enforce the laws and carry out the wishes of the central government. Those local administrators proved to be members of the Welsh gentry.[17] Not surprisingly, this level of society which enjoyed the power, prestige, and wealth of service in the

---

[13]5.0.22–35.

[14]Jonathan Dollimore and Allan Sinfield, "History and Ideology: The Instance of *Henry V*," in *Alternative Shakespeares*, ed. John Drakakis (London: Methuen, 1983), 223: "he is totally committed to the king and his purposes."

[15]Ibid.

[16]D. M. Loades, *Politics and the Nation 1450–1660*, 4th ed. (London: Fontana, 1992), 270.

[17]W. R. B. Robinson, "The Tudor Revolution in Welsh Government 1536–1543: Its Effects on Gentry Participation," *English Historical Review* 406 (1988): 1–20, and M. Gray, "Power, Patronage and

name of the English monarch endorsed the sovereign who had so enabled them. Rhys ap Meurig of Glamorgan, for instance, wrote in 1578, "Now, since Wales was thus…enabled with the laws of England, and thereby united to the same…they are exempted from the dangers before remembered; for now life and death, lands and goods rest *in this monarchy* [emphasis mine], and not in the pleasure of the subject."[18] This interdependency between the Welsh gentry and the Tudor monarchs helped produce a political philosophy among the gentry that J. Gwynfor Evans wrote, "identified government essentially with the institution and role of the monarchy."[19] By the writing of *Henry V,* "the majority of the Welsh gentry were no longer prepared to endanger a structure that they had helped create and from which they benefited so much…. However unscrupulous and aggressive the gentry might be in their relations with others, high and low, fundamentally they were well aware where their interests lay and how dependent they were on a monarchy that eagerly promoted them."[20] The Welshmen who had public roles, those with whom Shakespeare and his audience would have been familiar, would have been like Fluellen—staunch supporters of the English monarch.

These supporters could couch their support in the Tudor myth that connected the monarch to the fabled British—that is, pre-Saxon, and thus Welsh—past. Sixteenth-century authors wrote in support of the Tudors "acknowledging their lineal descent from the Welsh *uchelwyr* and accomplishing their obligations to restore the Welsh nation its inalienable birthright."[21] Henry Tudor successfully used such traditions of Welsh revivalism to drum up support in Wales against Richard III, and like Henry VII, the first Tudor monarch, continued to give public attention to his Welsh heritage. Perhaps not unlike Shakespeare's Henry V, who took "no scorn to wear the leek on Saint Tavy's day," Henry VII joined the Welshmen at his court to celebrate St. David's Day and gave gifts to his Welsh yeomen on David's feast day. He named his first son, Arthur, hearkening back to a pre-Saxon, Celtic Britain, and he sent for his Welsh

---

Politics: Office-Holding and Administration on the Crown's Estates in Wales," *The Estates of the English Crown 1558–1640,* ed. R. W. Hoyle (Cambridge: Cambridge University Press, 1992), 137–62.

[18]Rice Merrick, *Morganiae Archaiographia,* ed. B. L. James (Barry: South Wales Record Society, 1983), 68; J. Gwynfor Evans, *Early Modern Wales c. 1525–1640* (New York: St. Martin's Press, 1994), 87.

[19]Evans, *Early Modern Wales,* 89.

[20]Ibid., 121–22.

[21]Ibid., 88.

nurse to care for his second son, the future Henry VIII.[22] Welsh poets trumpeted the myth to Henry's Welsh subjects, for as Lewis Glyn Cothi could write: "British isles were now entrusted to men of British blood."[23] To their Welsh subjects, Tudor monarchs could and did proclaim, as Shakespeare has Henry V proclaim, "For I am Welsh, you know."

Henry V would have had a particular Welsh connection in the understanding of Shakespeare's audience anyway. In writing about Henry, the Bard had chosen the monarch whose memory was perhaps the most venerated of any in the sixteenth century. Tudor monarchs made special use of the memory, "a valuable asset to the enthusiastic nationalist."[24] Elizabeth's father had courted that memory at least twice, first during the French war of 1513–14 when an updated life of Henry V was made for Henry VIII as the latter, like his namesake, went to war on the continent. Then in the 1530s as the British struggled against a foreign foe once more, this time the pope, the memories of Henry and Agincourt were evoked again.[25] Among the intertwining of truth and myth about Henry V, extant in Tudor times, must have been the story of his birth in the gatehouse of Monmouth castle. This alone might have given Shakespeare the stimulus to make Henry proclaim his Welshness, and references to it figure prominently in Fluellen's dialogue.[26]

However much the prevailing ideology of Elizabethan England may have been that the Welsh were to be included in the nation, however necessary Welsh service in war and administration may have been to the Tudor monarch, and however beneficial the relationship with the monarch may have been for the gentry of Wales, Shakespeare's treatment of Fluellen suggests that the Welsh may not have fit so neatly into the new national consciousness. Fluellen is, after all, presented as a comic figure, and what makes him funny is his language.

---

[22]Ralph A. Griffiths and Roger S. Thomas, *The Making of the Tudor Dynasty* (Gloucester: Allan Sutton, 1985), 195. See also David Rees, *The Son of Prophecy: Henry Tudor's Road to Bosworth* (London: Black Raven Press, 1985).

[23]Quoted by Griffiths and Thomas, 198.

[24]May McKisack, *Medieval History in the Tudor Age* (Oxford: Clarendon Press, 1971), 121.

[25]Christopher Allmand, *Henry V* (Berkeley: University of California Press, 1992), 432–33.

[26]4.7.9: "Ay, he was porn at Monmouth." Just how "Welsh" Monmouth was in the fifteenth and sixteenth centuries is a matter of some debate, however. For its separateness from Wales, which is emphasized on a number of maps of the period, see Gwyn Williams, *When Was Wales* (Hammondsworth: Penguin, 1991), 119–21. Today Monmouth has been incorporated into the Welsh county of Gwent, but Desmond Seward, 1, surely risks superimposing any number of modern assumptions about nationhood and national identity when he writes "It is ironical that someone who was to inflict so much misery on the Welsh should have been born in Gwent."

FLUELLEN: Ay, he was porn at Monmouth. Captain Gower, what call you the town's name where Alexander the Pig was born?

GOWER: Alexander the Great.

FLUELLEN: Why, I pray you, is not "pig" great? The pig, or the great, or the might, or the huge, or the magnanimous, are all one reckonings, save the phrase is a little variations.[27]

By butchering spoken English through the use of Welsh mutations, Fluellen, noble as his character may be, thus becomes an object of derision not dissimilar to Evans in *Merry Wives of Windsor.*

Fluellen and Evans are not Shakespeare's first Welsh characters, nor are *Henry V* and *Merry Wives* the only plays in which the Welsh language and Welsh accents have had roles. Language and nationality are key in *Henry IV,* part 1, in which Owen Glendower figures prominently. Indeed, the play suggests Shakespeare had more than a passing acquaintance with Welsh speakers, for Mortimer's bride sings to him in Welsh.[28]

In *Henry IV,* part 1, Glendower and the Welsh are the enemy, yet perhaps because he must be taken seriously as a threat and perhaps out of some kind of respect, the leader of the Welsh revolt does not speak English in the comical accent of Fluellen or Evans. Indeed, Shakespeare underscores the point: "I can speak English, lord, as well as you," he has Glendower tell Hotspur.[29] Nevertheless, language is a key means by which otherness—non-Englishness—is defined. In a play in which English turncoats figure prominently, their flirtation with the enemy is portrayed in starkly linguistic terms. In succumbing to his bride, Mortimer "surrenders both his Englishness and his marital masculinity," an act Michael Neill calls "linguistic submission."[30] Mortimer proclaims to his Welsh love:

But I will never be a truant, love
Till I have learn'd thy language, for thy tongue
Makes Welsh as sweet as ditties highly penn'd.[31]

By *Henry V,* perhaps to underscore the message that the Welsh, however badly they may mangle the English language, are part of the nation, Shakespeare reaches an accommodation. The language difference need

---

[27]4.7.9–14.

[28]*1 Henry IV.*

[29]3.1.119–20. Michael Neill, "Broken English and Broken Irish: Nation, Language, and the Optic of Power in Shakespeare's Histories," *Shakespeare Quarterly* 45 (Spring, 1994): 1–32, suggests that the changing nature of Glendower, who elsewhere is "irregular and wild" (1.1.40–46), adds to his threat.

[30]Neill, "Broken English and Broken Irish: Nation," 17.

[31]11.204–8.

not define the other in a situation in which Welsh and English were united against a common foe. Language and culture need not separate Fluellen from participation in the nation. Gower speaks the words in defense of both Fluellen and the "leek" that the Welsh captain has made such a symbol of his—and Henry's—identity.

> Will you
> mock at an ancient tradition began upon an honourable
> respect, and worn as a memorable trophy of predeceased
> valour, and dare not avouch in your words? I have seen
> you gleeking and galling at this gentleman twice or thrice.
> You thought because he could not speak English in the
> native garb he could not therefore handle an English
> cudgel. You find it otherwise, and henceforth let a Welsh
> correction teach you a good English condition.[32]

Despite Gower's admonition that handling an English cudgel was more important than speaking "English in the native garb," and despite the metaphorical message that Welsh military service was more important than cultural conformity, the Welsh language and culture did—or could—exclude Welshmen from participation in the nation. The legislation collectively known as the Acts of Union, legislation designed to assimilate Wales into an English administration, cemented the alliance between the English monarch and the Welsh gentry and deemed that English was to be the official language of the new Tudor state. One of the acts in 1536 included the statute that no persons "that use the Welsh speech shall have or enjoy any manner of office or fees within the realm."[33] Welsh gentry began to teach their sons English, enabling them to participate fully in the new English administration and by the end of the sixteenth century, in the expanding English economy.

There was a time when modern national historians, writing in a period of heightened cultural awareness and close association of the Welsh language with Welsh identity, were especially harsh on the Acts of Union in this regard, presenting them almost as if they were designed to destroy the Welsh language and Welsh cultural tradition.[34] In fact, the uniformity the supporters of the acts desired was legal and administrative rather than cultural, and the Welsh gentry that was empowered by its participation in the English-speaking Tudor state was the same Welsh gentry who patronized

[32]5.1.62–70.
[33]Glanmor Williams, *Recovery, Reorientation and Reformation*, 269.
[34]See, for instance, Gwyn Williams, *When Was Wales*, 121 ff.

bards and patronized or practiced antiquarianism. Men like Sir John Wynn of Gwydir produced family chronicles and others like George Owen of Henllys wrote county histories that preserved Welsh history and cultural traditions.[35] While the quality of Welsh poetry did decline, gentry interest in the language certainly did not. William Herbert, the first earl of Pembroke, "spoke Welsh more readily than English," for instance.[36] Moreover, the humanist tradition encountered by Welsh who sought their education in the English or the European style drove some to try to fit their native language into its deserving place alongside other European tongues, a drive which would produce the first Welsh dictionaries.[37] And the Tudor Reformation, with its need for Protestant Bibles and prayer books, produced a whole new venue for the Welsh language to perform.[38]

This potential conflict within those who became full members of the Tudor—and thus English—state but who maintained participation and interest in their Welsh culture is prophesied in Shakespeare's Fluellen, if only inadvertently on the part of the author. No character in *Henry V* is more aware of history than Fluellen; no one refers to it more often nor more precisely. In the exchange with Henry V that began this essay, Fluellen makes clear and pointed reference to his cultural heritage in the leek metaphor for Welsh culture that Shakespeare uses throughout the play. "Welshmen," he says, "did good service in a garden where leeks did grow, wearing leeks in their Monmouth caps." He goes on to express his loyalty to the English monarch in terms that recall the Tudor myth that the rulers of England were of British blood. However problematic it may read to the reader in the late twentieth century, for Fluellen, as it would be for so many of the Welsh gentry of the sixteenth century, there seemed to be no difficulty in professing loyalty to the Crown of England, even participating in the English nation, while at the same time professing and rejoicing in his Welsh identity.

In the sixteenth century, humanism, with its conscious mining of the past for the edification of the present, played a role in the creation of early modern national identities. Mimicking Virgil, humanist poets strained to write national epics worthy of the new states that were emerging. As Philip Edwards has noted, the Tudor state generated no national epic during this

---

[35]Trevor Herbert and Gareth Elwyn Jones, eds., *Tudor Wales. Welsh History and Its Sources* (Cardiff: University of Wales Press, 1988), 18.

[36]Glanmor Williams, *Recovery, Reorientation and Reformation,* 466.

[37]Ibid., 449–50.

[38]For a brief and judicious assessment of the effects of the Acts of Union on Welsh cultural life, see Evans, *Early Modern Wales,* 210–14.

period.[39] Instead, the British past was mined and reshaped, the English identity shaped and recorded in the series of history plays; the foremost are those of William Shakespeare. Creating a national identity and memory, however, when there had been scant before—especially when there are competing identities and memories such as those of the Welsh—led to numerous rough edges in the myth of Tudor Britain. It is to Shakespeare's credit and to our benefit that the national epic he was crafting in his history plays captured these rough edges for us to examine.

[39]Philip Edwards, *Threshold of a Nation*, 1.

ACKNOWLEDGMENT

A significantly different version of this paper, titled "The Problem of Fluellen for Shakespeare and for Historians," was given at the 29th International Congress on Medieval Studies, Kalamazoo, Michigan, in May 1994. I would like to thank Frederick Suppe, Martin Davis, and Huw Pryce for their very helpful comments at that presentation.

Cardiff Castle

# HUMANIST TREATMENTS OF BATTLE ACCOUNTS DURING THE RENAISSANCE

## Guy Wilson

BETWEEN THE LATE FOURTEENTH AND LATE SIXTEENTH CENTURIES, major changes occurred in the art of narrative. These changes were especially marked in the written descriptions of battles, which were more integrated, detailed, and analytical in the sixteenth century than in earlier times.[1]

In medieval works, the structure of the narrative was weak, rambling, and episodic. In Renaissance histories, time, space, and logical connections usually organize battle accounts. Medieval writers, like Jean Froissart, sometimes forgot these organizing principles. Froissart sometimes interrupts what happens on one part of the battlefield to recount an incident completely unrelated by time, space, or logic. By the sixteenth century, narratives were more tightly organized and interruptions of this type had disappeared.

Medieval chroniclers used dialogues to describe events and to keep a narrative moving. One individual would comment on what he was seeing, or on what he had just seen, to another individual. This was the main descriptive device employed in Froissart. In the sixteenth century such descriptive dialogues were relegated to plays—Shakespeare still used the technique in *Henry V.* Renaissance historians learned to describe events directly to the reader. Authors still indulged in dialogues and speeches, but more to highlight points than to describe events. By the 1570s, they were introducing long asides to expound tactical theories or comment on personalities.

---

[1]For a fuller analysis of many of the issues discussed here, see Guy Wilson, "The Effects of Technology on Sixteenth-Century Military Thought" (Ph.D. diss., University of Missouri–Columbia, 1991).

The sense of time in medieval chronicles is vague when compared to the time sense of sixteenth-century histories. Time becomes a stronger organizing principle in Renaissance military narratives. The same is true of battlefield topography, which becomes more sharply defined. Whereas the development of a sense of time is slow and evolutionary, the development of a sense of terrain is abrupt. Until the beginning of the sixteenth century, terrain could be completely ignored in writing about a battle—as when Leonardo Bruni (in the middle of the fifteenth century) wrote about a battle for a bridge without mentioning the bridge.

Renaissance writers were interested not only in noblemen, but also in the actions of units. Sixteenth-century writers describe the organization of men and their placement on the battlefield in terms of units, not of their leaders. They placed individuals into the context of units and placed these in their proper spots on the battlefield. This is probably linked to the ability to identify details of battlefield terrain. Writers who ignore terrain tend to write about leaders; authors who detail the topography of battlefields are more prone to write about units. Terrain provides units with physical context; units provide terrain details with meaning.

The Renaissance's greater attention to detail is seen in more abstract ways as well. As the Renaissance progressed, historians attributed actions on the battlefield to an expanding range of motivations. Honor and desperation, along with religious fervor in crusades, were the common coin of thirteenth- and fourteenth-century chroniclers. The fifteenth-century authors added patriotism to the repertoire, while the early-sixteenth-century historians included greed, cowardice, treachery, and a desire for glory in their accounts. Later in the sixteenth century, the whole gamut of human emotions came into play. Whether this reflected a heightened psychological sophistication or the intensity of emotion associated with the Wars of Religion is unclear. Also, in the Middle Ages, motives were ascribed to leaders, but later authors ascribed them to masses of soldiers as well.

All of these factors fueled the Renaissance ability to analyze battles. Renaissance historians could look at why battles were won or lost in terms of what motivated men, physical characteristics of the battlefield, differences in tactics, the role of the weather, and other factors. By Machiavelli's time, military writers and historians were no longer just describing; they were looking for reasons and finding them.

These seven characteristics—smoothly flowing narrative, use of narrative (rather than dialogic) description, increased attention to space and time, understanding of psychological motivation, attention to military units (not just to nobles), analysis of the decisive elements in the combat, and the extraction of useful lessons from them—can be traced through a selection of chroniclers, historians, and military authors. Jean Froissart, chronicler of the Hundred Years' War, writing at the beginning of the fifteenth century, is a useful starting point. He will be contrasted with two major humanist historians of the fifteenth century, Leonardo Bruni and Flavio Biondo, whose works deal with the Italian city-states. Moving forward, significant changes will be traced in the work of Alessandro Benedetti and Niccolò Machiavelli. Benedetti wrote in the wake of the French invasion of Italy in 1494, while Machiavelli, writing some two decades later, was still influenced by that war and its aftermath. The last three authors wrote during the French Wars of Religion. Estienne Pasquier was a humanist lawyer and historian. His contemporaries, the Huguenot general François de La Noue and the Catholic marshal, Blaise de Monluc, were not properly humanists, but were heavily influenced by humanism, and their work shows how far the humanist-influenced battle narrative had spread. La Noue and Monluc also are indicative of the way humanist forms became married to mundane military practice to produce the military narratives of the next four centuries.

Jean Froissart is very representative of the medieval style. Philippe Contamine has noted that Froissart's topographical descriptions are so vague that his placement of the English army on the battlefield of Poitiers hardly makes sense when walking the battlefield or looking at a map. In another instance, Contamine is unable, based on Froissart's account, to determine on which bank of a river to locate the battlefield of Cocherel. Froissart's *Chronicles,* his account of the early years of the Hundred Years' War, contain a strong formulaic element, and it is easy to extend the few instances Contamine notes. These take the form of models that are imposed on the preparations for battle, stereotyped incidents during the battle, and phrases reminiscent of the oral formulas used by bards.[2]

The two most important battles recounted by Froissart are Poitiers (1356) and Crecy (1346). The model of the preparatory actions before these two battles has six parts. It begins with the king and nobles engaging in pious activities (such as hearing mass or praying) before holding a council of war. The king issues orders and Froissart then describes the dispositions (distribution of bodies of troops on the battlefield). A reconnaissance of the enemy's positions is described. This leads to the king receiving and accepting advice. Not only does he follow this model in both cases,

---

[2]Philippe Contamine, "Froissart: Art militaire, pratique et conception de la guerre," in *Froissart: Historian,* ed. J. J. N. Palmer (Totowa: Rowman and Littlefield, 1981), 134, 136.

but the wording is almost identical in places. Furthermore, it is notable that the fighting in these two instances follows similar patterns. Excluding the deeds of Sir Eustace d'Aubrecicourt (which intrude in the middle of the Poitiers narrative), there are four separate movements to the fighting, as there are in the Crecy account. In reality, there seem to have been more than four phases to both battles. Likewise, both narratives insert a chapter on the heroism of a small number of men in the midst of describing the French king's actions. In the Crecy narrative, this insertion is the death of the king of Bohemia; while in the case of Poitiers, the actions of the king of France and his capture are split by the chapter, "Of two Frenchmen that fled from the battle of Poitiers, and two Englishmen who followed them." Finally, in Crecy and Poitiers, Contamine's points about the ending and aftermath of the battle are crystal clear. The fighting begins with the advance of armies and banners marked by passages with almost identical, formulaic wording.[3] Both accounts end in the manner Contamine notes, with the accrual of honor, the enrichment of the victors, and the sadness of the vanquished.[4]

The humanist battle narratives of the early fifteenth century have some of the same characteristics, but also display new developments. Leonardo Bruni generally ignores the details of terrain and time even more than Froissart. In writing about the battle of Anghiari (1440), a battle for a bridge, Bruni fails to mention the bridge.[5] It is impossible to tell how long a given battle lasted in Bruni's contemporary histories. The details in his accounts focus on individuals, as in Froissart, but also, to some extent, on the units of the armies. Instead of focusing only on honor or desperation as motives, he adds civic patriotism and treachery as reasons for behavior. Dialogue is displaced by speeches and monologues to carry the descriptions and explanations. This is particularly true of his recounting of the battle of Montaperti (1260), where speeches occupy two-fifths of the narrative.[6] The real advance over the narrative methods of Froissart occurs in Bruni's ability to organize narratives. These are compact and informative. The reader does not have to wade through masses of minor details and rambling accounts, as was previously the case.

---

[3]Jean Froissart, *Chroniques de Jean Froissart* (Paris: Société de L'histoire de France, 1872–74), 3:173, lines 16–18; 5:19, lines 19–20.

[4]Contamine, "Froissart," 136.

[5]Leonardo Aretini (Leonardo Bruni), *Rerum suo tempore gestarum commentarius*, in L. A. Muratori, *Rerum Italicarum Scriptores*, vol. 19, pt. 3, 458.

[6]Ibid., 34–39.

Some fifteenth-century humanists present a clearer picture. Flavio Biondo's account of Anghiari is a model of clarity, at least insofar as the preparations for the battle are concerned. The topography of the battle-field is delineated in a manner superior to any other narrative so far considered, although some of the information given is not particularly useful at the tactical level. Likewise, the Florentine deployments are described clearly. There is even a tactical appreciation of the terrain and disposi-tions.[7]

Early-fifteenth-century humanist historians anticipate the character-istics of the sixteenth-century military writers. The logical structures of their narratives are at least as good, if not superior to those of the sixteenth century. However, Bruni and Biondo lack the psychological understanding of their successors when explaining the motivation of combatants. Nor does the action flow so well as in the sixteenth-century writers. Bruni and Biondo rely heavily on speeches and monologues to describe and move the action forward, whereas the late-fifteenth- and the sixteenth-century authors directly describe the course of action to the reader, without using historical figures to narrate the battle.

Writers at the fifteenth century's close, and throughout the sixteenth century, had a better command of battle narratives than earlier humanists. The Venetian physician and humanist, Alessandro Benedetti, gives a clear, eyewitness account of the battle of Fornovo (1495).[8] As in Biondo, battle-field topography and troop deployments are well defined. Curiously, in defining the placement and movement of the armies, Benedetti is as dependent as Froissart on the names of leaders and notables; however, unlike the earlier author, Benedetti is precise regarding numbers and placement. His reliance on names probably had more to do with the struc-ture of Venetian forces, in which units were generally named for the indi-vidual who first raised or led them.[9] This naming convention was general among the other forces at Fornovo. Benedetti does not fail to see units as units.

Benedetti keeps speeches to a minimum and conventionally classical. They do not carry the action of the battle, but rather give some basis for

[7]Flavio Biondo, *Le Decadi (Historiarum ab inclinatione romanorum decades)*, 32 vols., trans. Achille Crespi (Forli: n.p., 1963), 906–9.

[8]Alessandro Benedetti, *Diaria de bello Carolino (Diary of the Caroline War)* (New York: The Renaissance Society of America, 1967), 85–111.

[9]For the naming of Venetian units, see M. E. Mallett and J. R. Hale, *The Military Organization of a Renaissance State: Venice c. 1400 to 1617* (Cambridge: Cambridge University Press, 1984), 20–65 passim.

assessing the motivations of the combatants in fighting. Benedetti delin-
eates the motives of several of the participants in the battle of Fornovo,
but, like Bruni, expresses them chiefly in terms of patriotism, desperation,
greed, or glory. The latter comes through in the case of Francesco
Gonzaga, the Italian leader, both through his actions and his speech at the
beginning of the battle. That Benedetti did not apply motives mechani-
cally to the combatants is shown by his attribution of patriotism to the
Italian condottieri, notorious for their greed.[10]

In comparison with later writers, Benedetti fails only in two respects:
He has no clear grasp of time or duration and his analysis of events lacks
depth. Military events happen simply one after another, or meanwhile
*(interea),* and the whole battle takes only an hour.[11] The more modern
clock-based sense of time to appear in the second half of the sixteenth century is weak. Likewise, in his account of Fornovo he tends only to report
and editorialize, but does not explain in depth why things happened as
they did.

With the generation of Machiavelli, new developments appear in battle narratives. Their greater narrative specificity and control is sometimes
spoiled by fixed ideas and preconceived notions, particularly in Machiavelli. In Machiavelli's recounting of the battle of Anghiari, for example, a
four-part narrative structure appears.[12] This narrative structure consists
of an introductory phase, the movement of the opposing armies, the
actual combat, and the decisive moment and resulting collapse of the los-
ing side. This is a reasonable structure for a battle narrative, but it is not
common for this period and tends to gloss over the actual course of action.
The four-part form runs through much of Machiavelli's work and does
violence to the battles throughout his writings. Machiavelli also discounts
aspects of Anghiari which violate his overriding theses that citizen-soldiers
are superior to mercenaries and that infantry armed after the Roman fashion are superior to cavalry or artillery. He highlights only those aspects of
the battle that support these notions. In short, he treats his account of
Anghiari as an argument in favor of his military ideals. The results are dramatically different from other accounts of this 1440 battle. To show that
condottieri were cowards who shunned hard fighting and bloodshed, two
hours of hard fighting are compressed into three sentences, reporting the
casualties as "none dead," save for a couple of men who fell from their

[10]Benedetti, *Diaria de bello Carolino,* 92–93.

[11]Ibid., 91, 97, and 105.

[12]Niccolò Machiavelli, *History of Florence,* 5:33, in Allan Gilbert, trans. and ed., *Machiavelli: The Chief Works and Others* (Durham: Duke University Press, 1965), 1279–80.

horses and drowned. By comparison, Flavio Biondo gives the Milanese casualties as sixty dead and four hundred wounded, while the Florentines, he reports, lost ten dead and two hundred wounded. In addition, six hundred horses were killed by artillery fire.[13]

Machiavelli moves directly from the crisis of the battle to the rout of the Milanese. Throughout, he avoids discussion of fighting and emphasizes events supporting his antimercenary arguments: the mercenaries' overreliance on stratagems, the bloodlessness of their warfare, and their cowardice. All authors tend to suppress some details and highlight others. In many cases, this is an editorial choice, but when done consistently or egregiously, it reveals biases and peculiarities of thought. In the three Anghiari narratives reviewed, those of Bruni, Biondo, and Machiavelli, we have seen that Bruni so ignored topography that he failed to mention the bridge, for which the battle was fought, that Biondo described only the Florentine troop deployments, and that Machiavelli failed to give details of the fighting and casualties.[14] Bruni elsewhere ignored terrain, and this fits with Donald Wilcox's assertion that fifteenth-century Florentine historians ignored the environment, focusing instead on the actions of men.[15] Thinking about terrain was not what a historian did, for history was chiefly about morality. That Biondo failed to describe the Milanese deployments at Anghiari may be a result of his own patriotism or of lack of information.

Machiavelli did something entirely different. Guided by a belief in the pragmatic, as opposed to moral, value of history, he consciously suppressed those aspects of battles which did not fit his ideas of proper military practice. In essence, Machiavelli used battle descriptions as devices to prove the points he made in his theoretical writings on war and politics. In this he was firmly in the humanist tradition, even though his methods and theories ran counter to mainstream humanist thought.

What is new with Machiavelli's battle narratives, as with so much of his historical writing, is his analysis. Obsessed as he was with the factors that made or broke states, and convinced that the constitution of a state could be good only if its armies were built on correct principles, Machiavelli was naturally interested in why battles were won or lost. To some extent this must have preoccupied him in his active political career. He had

[13]Pasquale Villari, *Niccolò Machiavelli and His Times,* trans. Linda Villari (London: Kegan Paul, 1878–1883), 4:311–12.

[14]Machiavelli, *History of Florence,* 634–35.

[15]Donald J. Wilcox, *The Development of Florentine Humanist Historiography in the Fifteenth Century* (Cambridge: Harvard University Press, 1969), 182–86.

drafted the ordinances, decided the organization, raised, and administered the Florentine Republic's militia army from its inception to its defeat by the Spanish in 1512. In several chapters of the *Discourses,* he drew lessons from historical battles to back his conclusions. When he embarked on actual historical writing, in the *Life of Castruccio Castracani* and *History of Florence,* Machiavelli chose combats that supported his conclusions about the proper ways to wage war, as formulated in the *Discourses* and *Art of War.* When he analyzed battles to find the reasons for success and failure, his analyses were heavily biased. Nevertheless, he demonstrates that early-sixteenth-century humanists were moving beyond narrative and superficial explanations into the military-historical analysis of battles.

The analysis of battles, campaigns, and armies to determine better means of organizing and administering armies and of fighting battles is the necessary precursor to the evolution of both modern military history and military theory. The beginnings of both are found in Machiavelli. The depth of his interest in these subjects is indicated in a thought experiment he included in *The Art of War.*[16] The culmination of this dialogue is an exposition of an idealized battle. Machiavelli uses this to illustrate the analysis of military organization, equipment, and tactics made in the earlier parts of the work. It is also an analysis of how to win a battle. It is a theoretical, rather than a historical exercise, but it is of a piece with his historical battle accounts.

If Machiavelli marks the growth of military-historical analysis, its full flowing occurs in the *Discours politiques et militares* of François de la Noue. La Noue, a Huguenot general, was not a humanist, but rather an autodidact who was well read in classical and humanist authors, including Machiavelli. His *Discours,* like the main body of Machiavelli's work, was an attempt to understand how a nation might become great or how it might recover from disaster, and this included its military constitution and tactical doctrines. La Noue relates several battles in a narrative form with concomitant analysis, but in one case, he departs entirely from narrative and simply analyzes the battle of Dreux (1562), observing six unusual points about it.[17] Dreux was the first battle of the Wars of Religion and La Noue begins by lamenting that the political situation in France had deteriorated to the point of war. The first of his six notable points is that the Catholic army under Montmorency and Guise and the Huguenot army under

---

[16]Machiavelli, *History of Florence,* 2:634–36.

[17]François de La Noue, *Discours politiques et militaires,* ed. F. E. Suttcliffe (Geneva: Droz, 1967), 660–67. For a narrative account of this battle, see Charles Oman, *A History of the Art of War in the Sixteenth Century* (1937; reprint, Novato, Calif.: Presidio Press, 1989), 412–14.

Condé and Coligny remained within the range of each other's artillery for two hours without skirmishing (or firing). Then, as later, this was unheard of. La Noue goes on to note the steadfastness of the Swiss infantry in the face of heavy casualties or when cut off. This is an obvious rebuke to the French infantry, which was frequently unreliable. It was this firmness, combined with Guise's patience, according to La Noue's third point, which won the day for the Catholics. He is here, as elsewhere, criticizing impetuous generals (and indirectly criticizing Machiavelli, who praises impetuous behavior in war). La Noue's fourth point is simply an observation, that the battle of Dreux lasted for four hours, when most contemporary battles took scarcely an hour. His fifth point is that two leading generals were captured, the real criticism being that battles at this time were rarely pressed so far that commanders risked capture. Again, this is a rebuke of contemporary practice. Finally, he notes that the battle ended without pursuit. This was hardly an unusual occurrence and explains the reasons for this curious chapter—La Noue was analyzing the battle of Dreux to highlight the most common failings of contemporary French armies. Specifically, he was critical of their lack of steadiness, their impetuosity, inability to press home an attack or exploit an advantage, and their failure to destroy their defeated enemies.

In contrast to La Noue's attempts to analyze and draw lessons from battles, his contemporary, the humanist and lawyer Estienne Pasquier, wrote compact, factual accounts of the same combats. In his *Lettres historiques pour les années 1556–1594*, Pasquier narrates a number of battles, including Dreux.[18] Like Leonardo Bruni, more than a century before, he omits discussion of terrain and other environmental factors. Unlike Bruni, whose accounts were colored by his political opinions, Pasquier's are straight reporting—he does not filter out politically inconvenient events or facts. In this way, Pasquier was closer to a modern war correspondent than to his humanist predecessors.

An older contemporary of both La Noue and Pasquier was Blaise de Monluc. Less well educated than La Noue, he was personally close to the humanists. Monluc counted among his friends Montaigne and the humanist soldier Pietro Strozzi (himself the son of a friend of Machiavelli). Although the original draft of his *Memoires* was a personal defense in which he sought to demonstrate his loyalty to the Crown in the face of trumped-up charges, the later, printed version sought to expound sound tactical principals, as well as tell a good story. In recounting the various

[18]Estienne Pasquier, *Lettres historiques pour les années 1556–1594* (Geneva: Droz, 1966), 1:117–23, 452–57.

skirmishes and battles of his fifty years as a soldier (his first battle was in 1522 and his last in 1568), Monluc demonstrates the characteristics of the fully developed, sixteenth-century battle narrative. The best example of this is his narration of the battle of Ceresole (1544).[19]

Ceresole, one of the few pitched battles between France and the Empire in this period, had a central place in Monluc's defense, and also allowed him to show off his ability to innovate tactically (he had worked out a new way to use arquebusiers and pikemen together). Ceresole is therefore the most fully developed of his battle accounts. The narrative moves smoothly from episodes directly involving, or within sight of Monluc, who was leading the French skirmishers, to a more general view of the combat from the perspective of François d'Enghien, who commanded the French army. Monluc recounts several brief conversations and one long speech, which he claims to have given to his infantry, but these are primarily included to make points about tactics. The speech, in particular, is an analysis of infantry tactics comparing the Swiss and German methods of fighting with pikes.[20] He fixes the reader's attention on the important terrain features of the battlefield—particularly a house around which much of the infantry fighting flowed—and clearly lays out the deployments of the opposing armies. There is a clear sense of duration and of time in this account. Elsewhere, in describing the assault on Rabastens in 1568, Monluc gives very precise time references based on the church clock.[21]

Although personalities figure prominently in his description of the battlefield, Monluc is equally concerned with the character and tactics of the units they command, sometimes minutely so, as when he expounds on tactics or comments on morale. Monluc also understood the motivations of men in battle as no historian could, so that his account of the battle is more psychological than any discussed previously. Indeed, Monluc is not ashamed to admit his own fear and to question those who claim not to be afraid in battle. He also shows in his speech to the French infantry how to reassure and motivate men to fight. In short, it is a very modern account of a battle.

Taken together, these authors illustrate the development of narrative and analytical ability over the course of two centuries. The evolution of the battle narrative is directly related to the general development of humanist historiography. Machiavelli is a pivotal figure in redirecting the historical

---

[19]Blaise de Monluc, *Commentaires: 1521–1576* (Paris: Gallimard, 1964), 150–67.
[20]Ibid., 158.
[21]Ibid., 779–82.

traditions created by Bruni, Biondo, and others into broader and more analytical channels. Because he placed such emphasis on the roles of the military and war in society, Machiavelli's battle narratives are important parts of the new direction he forged.

La Noue and Monluc, who cannot be described as humanists—no matter how strongly they associated with humanists—developed the traditions of military history and thought begun by Machiavelli. They demonstrate how, by the 1570s, humanist and Machiavellian history and ideas had penetrated the ranks of military officers. They are both an indication of how far humanistic ideas had diffused in society and also foreshadow things to come. Military intellectuals, combining humanistic and scientific ideas with the practical understanding of war, weapons, and soldiers, would dominate both military history and military theory for centuries to come.

Turning to specifics, the ability to construct logical and compelling narratives progressively evolved from the quasi-oral tradition of Froissart's rambling accounts to the time-sensitive, detailed, edge-of-the-seat recollections of Monluc. Benedetti was able, by the 1490s, to abandon completely the use of dialogues to narrate action.

The same evolution is seen in describing the motivation of combatants. To Froissart's honor and desperation, the humanists gradually added patriotism (in Bruni, Biondo, and Benedetti), greed, cowardice, treachery, and glory (from Machiavelli onwards) to flesh out the psychological details of the battlefield. The human dimensions of battle also deepened as attention shifted from a few men to the behavior of masses. More slowly, details of time and space grew, until Monluc finally gave precise time references in the midst of combat.

The most notable change is the ability to analyze battles. Even if Froissart sought to derive lessons from the French defeats of the 1340s and 1350s, his mental equipment was inadequate—like Bruni and Biondo, he is essentially a reporter of battles, not an interpreter. Benedetti is more perceptive, but is concerned only with the perceived Italian victory at Fornovo. Machiavelli, with his blend of imagination, dissatisfaction with earlier historians, and prejudices, is the first to look beyond the particulars of battles to general reasons for success or failure. La Noue's analytical abilities were less constrained by prejudices than Machiavelli's had been. A practical soldier, he drew pragmatic and universal lessons from his analysis of Dreux.

In the end, it was the soldiers who reaped the fruits of humanistic military historiography. By the late sixteenth century this approach had given rise to the tools which soldiers and theorists needed to understand battles and sieges. The blossom of humanist military history yielded the heavy fruit of military theory.

# TWO SPIRITUAL DIRECTORS OF WOMEN IN THE SIXTEENTH CENTURY

St. Ignatius Loyola and St. Teresa of Avila

*Jill Raitt*

IN SIXTEENTH-CENTURY SPAIN THERE LIVED TWO GREAT SAINTS both of whom met the challenges of reform within the Roman Catholic Church by founding or reforming religious societies. St. Ignatius of Loyola founded the Society of Jesus, which although it has inspired many women's religious societies, is unique in not allowing a female branch. In order to bring about reform of the Carmelite house which she joined in her youth, St. Teresa of Avila had to found new houses which became a separate Carmelite order. Both Ignatius and Teresa provided written spiritual direction for women, Ignatius through letters and Teresa in nearly all of her works, including her letters.

In this essay I compare the principles of spiritual direction of Ignatius and Teresa in their writings for women. I shall therefore consider Ignatius' direction of three women who represent three classes of women: Juana, daughter of Emperor Charles V and sister of Philip II of Spain; the noblewoman Joanna of Aragon caught in an abusive marriage; and Teresa Rejadella, a Benedictine nun. Of Teresa of Avila's writings, I have chosen brief passages from five letters and three passages about spiritual direction from her autobiography. The results of this study are in one sense predictable and in another sense, surprising and gratifying.

## Ignatius of Loyola

Ignatius of Loyola (1491–1556) lived to see the successful foundation of his own order, the Society of Jesus whose members came to be called Jesuits, and the beginnings of the Catholic Reformation as embodied in the first two sessions of the Council of Trent. Ignatius is credited with establishing not only one of the most successful and controversial religious orders, but also with working out an effective method of spiritual renewal and direction called the *Spiritual Exercises.* He was canonized in 1622 with his close friend, Francis Xavier, S.J., and two other sixteenth-century saints, Teresa of Avila and Philip Neri, founder of the Oratory of Divine Love.

Ignatius' correspondence is voluminous, but his letters to women account for a relatively small number. They have been edited by Hugo Rahner, who had to overcome a prejudice long held by previous anthologists of Ignatius' letters.[1] Rahner tells us that "Nobody has so far dared to attempt to include these letters (to women) with the rest of Ignatius' *Correspondence.*"[2] The inclusion of letters *from* women to Ignatius might be considered even more daring and Rahner did include them, which makes our task easier since we have the voices of the women as well.

Why did it take so long to collect Ignatius' letters to women? In selecting letters for anthologies, those addressed to women were seen, perhaps, in the light of their recipients, as written to persons of little interest or historical importance compared to those written to men:

> In comparison with these (6,813 letters and instructions of Ignatius and 956 letters addressed to Ignatius) the correspondence with women can indeed be called scanty. What is still preserved of it, in letters and answers of which the full text exists, amounts to only 139 documents. There are besides twenty lists of contents of letters to women in the *regesta.* A critical examination of the surviving letters further shows that a comparatively large number of such letters have been lost, as they were kept for only a short time in Ignatius' files and then destroyed as being of no historical importance; or else they disappeared in course of time without a trace from among the papers of the recipients or their heirs. So we have to-day only a compact group of 139 letters, of which Ignatius wrote eighty-nine to women and received fifty.[3]

We should perhaps be grateful that so many survived the culling of historians who found letters to women uninteresting. We should also give

---

[1]Hugo Rahner, ed., *Saint Ignatius Loyola: Letters to Women,* trans. Kathleen Pond and S. A. H. Weetman (Freiburg: Herder, 1960).

[2]Ibid., 1.

[3]Ibid., 3.

Hugo Rahner credit for his interest in them as early as 1956, in a decade when the women's movement had reached a particularly low point.[4]

Rahner organized his book hierarchically. First are letters to and from royal women followed by those to noblewomen. These are followed by letters to benefactresses. Rahner tells us that

> it was from the women of his time that he got the most abundant help, from the early years of his own spiritual development to the period of the Society's magnificent expansion. The letters to his benefactresses bear grateful witness to this.[5]

The fourth chapter contains letters of spiritual direction. What did women seek from Ignatius to help them lead lives of greater spiritual value? It is from these letters that we learn of the desire of some of these women to found societies of female Jesuits and Ignatius' refusal to consider such a thing. As a result and as a matter of historical record, many women's religious societies were founded on the base of the Rule of the Society of Jesus modified appropriately for women.[6] The fifth chapter presents the letters to and from mothers of Jesuits in which is revealed, Rahner tells us, Ignatius' motherly heart. In the last chapter are letters springing from friendship.

Rahner gives us more helpful information as he tells us that Ignatius' letters, all of them that he wrote himself, were the result of reading and rereading his correspondence and then writing and rewriting drafts of his responses. In spite of all this care, or perhaps because of it, his letters are deliberate rather than spontaneous. Rahner compares them, in this regard unfavorably, with the lively outpourings of Teresa of Avila who almost never reread, let alone rewrote, her letters.[7]

Rahner adds that "he [Ignatius] wished to help those souls in whom he found the capacity for the love of God, for the inner life, for works of

---

[4]Rahner tells us why he did so:"We have had two aims in view. Firstly, these letters constitute a veritable biography of the saint and give us a more concrete understanding of his innermost thoughts than any number of psychological reflections. Secondly, their contents, taken as a whole, give us access to a hitherto almost unknown territory in the history of the spiritual care of women at the beginning of the ecclesiastical reform in the sixteenth century." Ibid. Hugo Rahner deserves full credit for his concern for this aspect of the history of the spiritual direction of women which stemmed probably from Rahner's own interest in the direction of women.

[5]Ibid., 4–5.

[6]Some examples are: The Sisters of Mercy, the Religious of the Sacred Heart, the Religious of Our Lady of the Cenacle.

[7]Ibid., 6. But see Charmarie Blaisdell's essay comparing the letters of Ignatius and Calvin to women. Her assessment is that Ignatius is less formal than Calvin. "Calvin's and Loyola's Letters to Women: Politics and Spiritual Counsel in the Sixteenth Century," in *Calviniana: Ideas and Influence of*

charity. This capacity he found more in women than in men."[8] Nevertheless, Ignatius withdrew from the direction of women more and more.
After reflection upon his experiences, Ignatius came to a decision recorded
in these words by Rahner:

> from now on he would not only study more thoroughly and not
> let himself be distracted by any pious undertakings; he would do
> more. He would go to the University of Paris, where he did not
> know the language of the country, *and so could not act as spiritual
> director to women*; he would win recruits for the great work he
> planned for the kingdom of Christ. In Paris we first recognize the
> future saint, the man who sought to win *men* for God.[9]

Ignatius turned to the formation of the Society of Jesus and to the recruit-
ment of men. However much women had responded to his direction and
were willing to support him, Ignatius found their company and conversation too complicating, even, it seems, too dangerous. And yet, the direction of women could not simply be set aside; later in his career, Ignatius
gave rules for his own guidance and to help his "sons" to avoid the pitfalls
into which he had stumbled.

Among these rules, even first among them, was to avoid common
women and lower-class women. This was not because they were more
dangerous in themselves but because conversation with them was more
likely to be misinterpreted. Conversations with noblewomen, on the contrary, were less likely to be misconstrued. Ignatius' direction stems from
his own experience, Rahner tells us, but we must look more deeply. Common and lower-class women were judged less noble with regard to virtue.
Nobility was thought to include virtue. Perhaps it did in the sense that
noblewomen were usually attended by servants, companions, guardians of
their virtue. Common women were less guarded. They were therefore
more dangerous. Ignatius gave two examples of instances when Jesuits visited women to hear their confessions and to give them spiritual direction.
Later the women were found to be with child and were it not for the discovery of the women's lovers, the Jesuits would have been suspect. In spite
of their care, however, the Jesuits' ministry to aristocratic women caused
the people of Rome to raise their eyebrows. Jesuits therefore were told

---

*Jean Calvin*, ed. Robert V. Schnucker, Sixteenth Century Essays and Studies, 10 (Kirksville, Mo.: Sixteenth Century Journal Publishers, Inc., 1988), 235–53.

[8]Rahner, *Saint Ignatius Loyola*, 6.
[9]Ibid., 13. Emphasis added.

never to converse with women except in the company of another Jesuit. Hearing confessions had to be exempted from that rule, however, since confessions fall under the seal of absolute secrecy.

And so we turn to Ignatius' letters to women. In his introduction to this chapter, Rahner tells us that only two persons wrote spiritual homilies to Philip II of Spain: Ignatius and "the great St. Teresa."[10] While Teresa wrote to Philip because she needed to do so (and indeed she succeeded in winning Philip over by her wisdom), Ignatius gained access to the Hapsburg men through their women: "We are not then wrong in stating that Ignatius gained access, as it were, to the inner counsels of imperial policy through his friendship with the women of the House of Hapsburg."[11] In fact, Rahner writes with amazement, Juana, regent of the Spanish kingdoms and daughter of the Holy Roman Emperor, Charles V, was made the only female member of the Society of Jesus![12] Because of her sovereign position, she could not be refused and so, under the pseudonym of Mateo Sanchez, was allowed to make the vows of a Jesuit scholastic. These vows of poverty, chastity, and obedience bound the one making them, but the Society of Jesus could dissolve the vows at any time. They were intended for Jesuits still in training, but they provided a solution to the problem of Juana who was beautiful and marriageable and as the daughter of Charles V and sister of Philip II, might become a pawn in the royal marriage game. Rahner says of her that she was exceedingly beautiful, "but more than that, she displayed a truly masculine intelligence and strength of will."[13] Ignatius learned that while he could count on Juana for support, both political and financial, he would also have to obey her as regent of Spain, a peculiar twist since she had vowed obedience, under God, to Ignatius. It was as Ignatius' sovereign that Juana acquired the right to command two Jesuits, Francis Borgia and Antonio Araoz. The plans of Philip II to marry Juana to

[10]Rahner, *Saint Ignatius Loyola*, 32.

[11]Ibid.

[12]In none of the volumes about Philip II have I found more than a few lines about Juana (1535–73) and in none of them is there mention of her membership in the Society of Jesus. She was the widow of John of Portugal (d. 1553) and mother of Sebastian of Portugal (b. 1553) whom she left in Portugal when she returned to Spain in 1554 to become regent of Spain while Philip II left for England (1554–59). Indeed, the longest references to Juana concern the effort of her brother Philip II to marry her to her nephew, Don Carlos. Some authors say that she wished the marriage, but all agree that Don Carlos was vehemently opposed to marrying the aunt who was twice his age. It is surprising also that Juana's years of regency elicit no comment beyond the fact. Juana founded a discalced Carmelite convent and ended her days there. Perhaps this was the best retreat for the austere, lonely female Jesuit. Cf. Geoffrey Parker, *Philip II*, 3d ed. (Chicago: Open Court, 1988).

[13]This attribution of masculine traits to a woman who displays an independent mind and firm resolve is an ancient and abiding characteristic of men writing about women from antiquity to the present.

various European princes failed and she maintained her life as a princess and a Jesuit until her death in 1573.

The correspondence of Ignatius with the noblewoman Joanna of Aragon, who was married in 1521 to Ascanio Colonna, provides us with insight into marriage relations when the husband, as Rahner describes him, was a "rough and avaricious warrior."[14] Ascanio delighted in warfare and joined his kinsman Vespasiano Colonna in attacking Rome itself in 1526 and then sacking it in 1527. He was known for his extravagance and his anger which led to violence inside and outside his home. Joanna bore him six children, but their marriage was marked by her withdrawals from the Colonna palace to the cultured life at a castle at Ischia owned by her friend, Constanza de Avalos. After the birth of her sixth child, Joanna and Ascanio separated. Their marriage difficulties were becoming public knowledge and therefore a scandal. The pope was concerned not only about Joanna's marriage, but about her religion. In Naples, Joanna was also attending the sermons of Juan Valdes, a humanist and a reformer who was beginning to be suspected of heresy, that is, of turning Protestant. In 1539, at the pope's request, and it seems also at the request of Ascanio Colonna, Ignatius sent the Jesuit priest Nicolas Bobadilla to Naples and to Ischia. He found that Joanna's faith was not in danger, but her marriage was. Bobadilla was followed by Antonio Araoz. Both Jesuits failed to reconcile Joanna to her husband. That reconciliation was their object is quite clear. In their minds, a wife belonged with her husband; it was her duty to live with him. Joanna, on the other hand, found it impossible to do so. In response, Ascanio cut Joanna's budget for both herself and their six children. By 1550, pope and emperor were equally upset with the bitter recriminations now publicly aired and politically explosive. Joanna, together with her son Marcantonio, was for Spain and the Emperor. Ascanio accused Joanna of being a whore. Joanna accused Ascanio of "unnatural acts" and of siding with France against the emperor. In 1552 Duke Ascanio called on Ignatius and persuaded him to visit Joanna.[15]

When he failed to persuade Joanna to return to Ascanio, Ignatius wrote to her, presenting her with no less than twenty-six numbered reasons for her capitulation. Ignatius opened his letter by reminding Joanna of their conversations and of the "means of agreement with Senor Ascanio,

---

[14]Rahner, *Saint Ignatius Loyola,* 134.
[15]Ibid., 139.

which I feel would be more in conformity with his divine will and which becomes Your Grace more than anything else...."[16]

There is no question in Ignatius' mind that marriage means that spouses live together; divorce is out of the question and separation is hardly better. Since this was the mind of the church and therefore of Ignatius, it was also the will of God and to this will Joanna must try to conform. Ignatius then told Joanna that

> Your Grace should arrange, with a generous mind and trusting in the Lord, to go to Senor Ascanio's house, putting yourself entirely in his power, without seeking for other security or making any other conditions, but freely, as a wife is normally, and ought to be, in the power of her husband....

Ignatius does not question that a woman should obey her husband and trust him to do her no harm. Joanna had no grounds for putting such trust in Ascanio, nor had God protected her from him in the past. Indeed, she accused Ascanio of trying to murder her. When, in response to the visit of Ignatius, she asked Ascanio for guarantees regarding her financial and social position, Ignatius asked her to forgo all such contractual arrangements. Second, she should submit to her husband out of Christian humility. Since no agreement would be possible without one side or the other submitting, it is fitting that the wife should do so: "it is much more reasonable that the wife should be distinguished in humility than the husband." In fact both men and God would blame her otherwise. Ignatius was correct; men, and the God whom they thought of as a sovereign like the King of Spain, as Lord and Supreme Majesty, would certainly disapprove of a proud woman while tolerating a proud and violent man. Third, wrote Ignatius, even though Joanna might risk bodily harm, should she not exercise courage and magnanimity and be willing to face death? In this way she would win a heroic battle over herself both with regard to fear and to her aversion to her husband. Ignatius argued that Joanna would do better to follow Christ who loves peace and wants reconciliation and she would be more in conformity with God's laws for holy matrimony in which the woman is to be subject to her husband. By such heroic virtue and by her great charity, Joanna would bring Ascanio to "a state more secure for his

---

[16]Rahner, *Saint Ignatius Loyola*, 141. The letter goes to 145; subsequent quotations will be to these pages until otherwise indicated.

salvation." She would also relieve him of domestic cares and give him peace and contentment.

We are already at point ten in Ignatius' list of reasons for Joanna to return to Ascanio, and there is not a word about Joanna's peace and contentment or her burden of domestic care; rather she is exhorted to heroic virtue and constant concern for her husband. In the next arguments, Joanna is advised to think about her three daughters and Marcantonio, the only son remaining of the three boys she had borne. She should also consider the scandal involved in continued separation and the public edification given were she to return to Ascanio's house. The honor of Ascanio was that of herself and her children so she should do all she could to sustain and even increase that honor. If she did all these things, Ascanio would certainly capitulate and submit himself to her, paying her debts, dowering their daughters, and providing for their futures. Her fears for her personal safety should also be quieted by the fact that any attack on her would have serious political repercussions because the pope, the emperor, and the whole Spanish nation would rise up against Ascanio. Ignatius concluded by saying that it is all up to her; she can end the separation whenever she wishes.

Ignatius is here consistently following sixteenth-century notions about wives' duties to their husbands. Given these notions, he is also consistent in applying the principles of the Spiritual Exercises. The will of God is clear to Ignatius: Joanna must return to her husband. He appeals to her to set aside her own desires and magnanimously, even heroically, embrace God's will. Ignatius adds to this paramount consideration, all the practical and even political reasons for submitting to Ascanio. He is following rules for making a decision given in the *Spiritual Exercises*, especially in Annotations 16 and the methods for making a good election and for reforming one's life found at the end of the Second Week.[17]

Rahner assumes that Joanna returned to Ascanio, but he has no evidence that she did so. There is, rather, evidence that she did not, for Ascanio drew up a will on 17 December 1552, in which he disinherited his son and accused Marcantonio of an immoral relationship with Joanna who, "contrary to all conjugal duty, was disobedient, hostile and rebellious towards her husband."[18] In August 1553 Ignatius wrote to Father Araoz that Joanna was willing to return to Ascanio, but would prefer that he join

---

[17] *Ignatius of Loyola, Spiritual Exercises and Selected Works*, ed. George E. Ganss, S.J. (New York: Paulist Press, 1991), par. 16, 184–89.

[18] Rahner, *Saint Ignatius Loyola*, 145.

her in Naples or in Spain, that is to say, in places where her family was politically dominant. Whether such a reunion took place is not known.

At the end of this account, Rahner paints a picture of the conversation between the two old soldiers, Ascanio and Ignatius, whose battle wound led to his conversion. This gratuitous presentation of male bonding may indeed have occurred, but if so, it means that Ignatius was drawn into Ascanio's net and that Rahner's touting of Ignatius' understanding of the psychology of women means rather that Ignatius knew how to present to a woman compelling arguments based on gender expectations in the sixteenth century. And indeed he did, for he appealed not only to her honor, but to her concern for her children and her household. The end of the affair is that Ascanio was arrested for collusion with the French and died a few years later in a Naples prison. With Ascanio out of the house, Joanna returned to Rome and the Colonna palace where she was watched by the new anti-Spanish pope, Paul IV, who had excommunicated both Ascanio and Marcantonio on political grounds. Taking her safety into her own hands, Joanna, her daughter, and her daughter-in-law fled in male peasant disguises, and then mounted horses to reach the safety of her duchy of Tagliacozzo. She returned to Rome only after the death of Paul IV. Joanna and her children remained devoted and generous supporters of the Jesuits, whose founder had been so solicitous for her conjugal fidelity.

The third set of letters I would like to consider is the correspondence between Ignatius and Teresa Rejadella.[19] Teresa was a Benedictine nun in the convent of Santa Clara in Barcelona. Ignatius met her there sometime between 1524 and 1526 and tried to help her and ten other nuns reform the lax convent. In 1536, Ignatius wrote a long letter of spiritual direction to Teresa. He had recognized in her a courageous and ardent person to whom he responded just as he would to any of his Jesuit sons. The letter explains to Teresa how to distinguish the action of the devil from the action of God, a matter on which Ignatius had written succinctly in his *Spiritual Exercises* in a special directive on distinguishing spirits. In this instance, he applied his principles to a particular case.

> When, however, we make ourselves humble, he (the devil) tries to draw us into false humility, that is, into humility which is exaggerated and corrupt. Of this your words are clear evidence, for after you relate certain weaknesses and fears which are true of you, you say, "I am a poor nun, desirous, it seems to me, of serving Christ our Lord"—but you still do not dare to say: "I am desirous of

[19]Cf. *Ignatius of Loyola*, 332–38.

serving Christ our Lord" or: "The Lord gives me desires to serve him," but you say: "I seem to be desirous." If you look closely, you will easily see that those desires of serving Christ our Lord do not come from you, but are given you by our Lord. Thus when you say: "The Lord has given me increased desires to serve him," you praise him, because you make his gift known and you glory in him, not in yourself, since you do not attribute that grace to yourself.[20]

Ignatius writes to Teresa as to one who can understand the nuances of his direction and profit thereby. Thus Ignatius tells her that when the devil tempts her to despair because of God's justice, she should consider her sins and God's mercy. He concludes this section by quoting Eccl. 13:11: "Beware that thou be not so humble that in excessive humility thou be led into folly."

Unfortunately, many of Teresa's letters to Ignatius were not kept, so one must guess at them from the responses Ignatius sends her. In a second letter, Ignatius counsels Teresa to get enough food, recreation, and rest since

Much can be achieved with a healthy body; with a sickly one it is difficult to accomplish anything. A healthy body can be a powerful factor either in the doing of much evil or of much good—evil if the will is depraved and one's habits sinful; good if the will is wholly devoted to God's service and formed to the habit of the virtues.[21]

Ignatius does not speak of Teresa's body as a weak or sinful body because it is a woman's body. He tells her what he would tell a man—the body is essentially good and can be turned to either good or evil by a good or bad will and the impulse of good or evil habits. Ignatius describes what he considers to be the human condition, not a problem particular to women. He tells her to dwell on God's love for her which is certain so that her thoughts should be of gratitude and of repaying love for love. In another straightforward passage he tells her:

Do not worry about bad, obscene or sensual thoughts, nor about your wretchedness or lukewarmness, when it is against your will that you experience such things.... Just as I shall not be saved through the good works of the good angels, so I shall not be

---

[20]Cf. *Ignatius of Loyola*, 332.
[21]Ibid., 336–37.

damned through the bad thoughts and weaknesses suggested to
me by the bad angels, the world and the flesh.[22]

How sensible this direction is and how free of any indication that a woman
has special kinds of problems with imagination and with the flesh. Teresa
is simply an ardent person to whom Ignatius responds with his best
insights.

Besides spiritual direction, Teresa also desired that her convent be
reformed. Since she got nowhere on this point, she and eleven like-minded
nuns sought for years to be taken under the Jesuit wing and to form a
female branch of the order. There was good precedent for the request since
the Benedictines, the Carmelites, the Dominicans, and the Franciscans all
had convents of women under their Rules. Ignatius, however, was ada-
mant. There was to be no female branch of the Society of Jesus. Neither
the frequently repeated requests of the nuns nor the advocacy of the Spanish Jesuits, nor the intercession of the nobility could move Ignatius. One of
Ignatius' reasons was that Jesuits had to be a mobile unit. They could not
be tied down to the sacramental and spiritual service of nuns bound, by
canon law, to remain in one place. One senses, however, that while Ignatius was willing to direct individual women of noble lineage and independent means, he was not willing to take on communities of nuns and the
problems of providing guidance for their government, their shelter, and
their income. But matters at Santa Clara took a turn for the worse as the
simoniacally elected abbess was supported by the local Benedictine abbot
and the rebellious reformers told to conform. They refused to do so and
appealed to Rome. Requests to Ignatius to "accept us as your daughters"[23]
were renewed with increasing passion and despair. Father Araoz, provincial of Spain, who had first asked Ignatius to allow Teresa and her group of
reform-minded nuns to come under the obedience of the Society of Jesus,
now asked Ignatius again to grant their request. But even the intercession
of this loved kinsman and Jesuit did not move Ignatius from the position
he had taken. The campaign continued for three years, from 1546 to 1549,
when the nuns accepted the fact that they could not become female Jesuits.
Their problems remained severe as they were persecuted by the abbess and
the lax nuns.

In all the pages of correspondence to and from Ignatius and written by
the nuns and by their advocates, there is never an appeal to their female
weakness. Their requests are always made on the basis of the divided

---

[22]Cf. *Ignatius of Loyola*, 337.
[23]Ibid., 349.

convent and the impossibility of living under such conditions. Even when they had to give up all hope of joining the Jesuits, the nuns spoke frankly of their difficulties but also of their having to bear the cross in whatever form it presented itself. For Teresa, the solution came in her death in 1553. Her last hours were reported by Juan Qeralt, S.J. She exhorted the nuns to fidelity and perseverance. Obviously moved by her fervor and strength, Qeralt wrote to Ignatius: "Truly, dear Father, to assist at such a deathbed was enough to convert a Turk!"[24]

If we look at these three instances of direction of women, we see that when faced by an unalterable political situation, namely the desire of a woman who, as Spain's regent, could demand Ignatius' obedience, he found a unique and gracious way to obey her by providing her with the means to fulfill her deep desire; she became his only spiritual daughter in the Society of Jesus. Thus Juana escaped the limitation of her gender through her position as Ignatius' political superior while Teresa of Rejadella could neither command nor move Ignatius to admit her and her suffering sisters into the Society of Jesus. Nor did it occur to Ignatius to go beyond the conventional attitude toward married women in the case of Joanna of Aragon. His advice to her was governed by gender stereotypes of husband and wife supported by laws and customs. Ignatius did not see beyond these limited and limiting views of women. Women seeking spiritual advice were treated differently.

While class stereotypes and fear of women and scandal governed Ignatius' directions to Jesuits regarding whom to assist spiritually, once a woman had passed the safe test, Ignatius' letters regarding spiritual matters are gender indifferent. Spiritual direction follows the same rules for women as for men. This is not an uncommon phenomenon; it is true of Augustine and Francis of Assisi as well as other masters of the spiritual life from Ignatius' time to the present. The circumstances of the woman and the man receiving spiritual direction usually resulted in different kinds of practical realizations of their spirituality, but the manner of direction did not differ.

## Teresa of Avila

Teresa of Avila (1515–82) could have been a sister of Iñigo Loyola. Except that she was born in Castile and Iñigo in Basque country, these two fiery Spaniards spoke of God similarly, addressing God as "Your Majesty" and yet utterly convinced of God's most tender love for them, experiencing

---

[24]Cf. *Ignatius of Loyola*, 368. It should be remembered that the Turks were a constant threat to the Holy Roman Empire throughout the sixteenth century.

that love in ways that drove them to found or reform orders and to write works that are the foundations of major spiritualities.[25]

Ignatius prepared his sons to move quickly and sometimes alone to the farthest parts of the globe, as did St. Francis Xavier within the first decade of the foundation of the Society of Jesus. The Carmelites, however, were mendicants, a movement begun in the thirteenth century. There remains a close connection, nevertheless, between Teresa's reform and the Jesuits. As a Carmelite nun, Teresa turned by preference to Jesuits for direction and advised her daughters to seek someone learned (*letrado*), a reputation the Jesuits already had by the time Teresa began her foundations.

Not long after Teresa had made her profession as a Carmelite, she became ill and lay in a coma for three days. She recovered, but it was three years or more before she could walk again. Like Ignatius, whose conversion began with his recovery from war wounds, Teresa read books during her convalescence that would guide her all her life. But unlike Ignatius, it was another twenty years before Teresa resolved the tension she felt between God's call and the worldly life of the inmates of the convent of the Incarnation. For a time, she gave up prayer altogether, something she later deeply regretted. Teresa then experienced a conversion which marked the end of her old life and the beginning of a new life of prayer based on a deep trust of Christ which allowed her to rest, to listen, to learn through a prayer of quiet, a kind of passive openness to God that often resulted in union with God that was deeply transforming. In fact, she experienced a habitual resting in God that, paradoxically, drew her out into an increasingly active life as she attempted to reform the lax Carmelite convent where she lived. She then began an extremely active life, founding convents based on a reformed Carmel, the sign of which, among other things, was sandals rather than shoes, hence the Order of Discalced Carmelites by which Teresa's reform is distinguished from the Carmelite order that she had originally joined.

Teresa, that giant among human beings, that doctor of the church, spoke of herself as a simple woman who would not presume to write except under obedience. She declared that she was no theologian, had no literary talent, and yet she towers over other mystics, male and female, and proved to be one of the greatest guides of the spiritual life who ever lived. Teresa's first book was written in an effort to make her experiences in prayer known to her confessors. *The Way of Perfection* was written for her

---

[25]For a brief introduction to Teresa's life and spirituality, see *Teresa of Avila: The Interior Castle*, trans. Kieran Kavanaugh, OCD and Otilio Rodriguez, OCD (New York: Paulist Press, 1979), xi–29.

nuns. Although Teresa called herself a simple woman, reflecting the conventions of her times, she knew very well that she was the equal of most men, and eventually she felt that nuns direct nuns better even than her favored Jesuits or her spiritual son, John of the Cross. Priests were needed for confession, but direction, except of herself, she could handle as could the superiors she appointed for her convents.

Teresa's direction was marked by great sensitivity to the working of the Holy Spirit and by great common sense in discerning what was from God and what from the human spirit. Teresa also enjoyed a robust sense of humor and gaiety and encouraged her nuns to dance and sing on occasion.[26] Her great simile for the journey to God still helps many people: it is that of an interior castle or mansion, *morada*. Conversion and penance are the way in. Once there, one progresses through various rooms until one comes into the bridal chamber and is united with the bridegroom. The delightful part of this simile is that one has the freedom of the castle, at least of those rooms one has already occupied. So Teresa tells her readers that they must not be alarmed if they find themselves in a room near the front door from time to time. Progress for her was not linear and there was nothing wrong with going back to spend time in a room that would seem to be less advanced, even to the ramparts of the castle. Teresa's own prayer was spiced with humor as she reproached her Lord for the time she spent traveling in rickety carts over rutted roads to found convents. It was during another journey that Teresa died reciting verses from the Song of Songs and professing her joy in being a daughter of the church. Toward the end of her life, and again like Ignatius, Teresa experienced profound intellectual visions of the Trinity in which she conversed with the three divine persons.

We turn now to Teresa's correspondence.[27] Teresa's letters outnumber those of Ignatius, but far fewer, only 435, have come down to us. She wrote to Philip II, king of Spain,[28] to some of the same noble ladies to whom Ignatius wrote, to John of the Cross, her spiritual son and father, and to her nuns. She wrote to Jesuits, Franciscans, lords, and inquisitors. Her

---

[26]Victoria Lincoln, *Teresa, A Woman: A Biography of Teresa of Avila*, ed. Elias Rivers, and Antonio T. de Nicolás (New York: Paragon House, 1984), 269: "When Mother Foundress joins / Our recreation joys / We start to dance and sing / And make a noise." This bit of verse was written by Isabelita, a nun in the Carmel of Seville.

[27]There is some disagreement about the number of letters Teresa wrote. Some say 1,200, some 5,000, and still others 15,000! (See Introduction, p. xi of *Santa Teresa de Jesus (1515–1582): Obras Completas*, ed. Isidoro de San Jose OCD (Madrid: Editorial de Espiritualiad [sic], 1963). However that may be, less than 450 have come down to us.

[28]For example see *Obras Completas*, letters 50 (xlv), 83 (lxxvii), 201 (cxcx), 206 (cciv).

form of address to each of these is appropriate as one would suppose, but what is overwhelmingly evident is that Teresa's style did not vary. No matter whom she addressed, she was spontaneous, courageous, and as free of condescension toward inferiors as she was direct with superiors, including the powerful king of Spain. The gender of her correspondent had little to do with the tone of her letters. She scolded monk, friar, priest, nun, lady, or courtier with equal vigor if they deserved it. She encouraged them or set forth her plain business as the occasion required. Teresa complied with the gender requirements of the time in that she traveled veiled, but she traveled! She was largely self-educated, and it did not occur to her to try to attend a university. She had enormous respect for learning and insisted that she and her nuns have the benefit of learned confessors since ignorant priests could cause much harm.

In a letter to Mother Ana de San Alberto in Caravaca,[29] whom Teresa addresses as *mi hija* (my daughter), Teresa writes of her joy in writing to help her daughters, no matter how much work she has or how late she must stay up to take care of business and correspondence. She writes of the painful struggles to maintain the Discalced in spite of opposition in high places. She praises Father Jeronimo Gracian, on whose behalf she had written to Philip II and to whom many of her letters are addressed. On another occasion, she writes from Medina del Campo to comfort the widow of Juan de Mejía. Teresa asks God to give strength to the widow and urges her to seek "more and more light in order to understand the mercy of Our Lord." Teresa promises to pray for her as well, assuring the widow that His Majesty will act powerfully to help her go on with her life.[30] She writes in quite a different vein to her niece, who took the same name as her aunt, Teresa de Jesús.[31] This letter of direction deals with a young nun, "Teresica," who suffers from scruples. Teresa writes: "it seems to me that Our Lord is already treating her like a strong person and so wishes to prove the love she has, whether it is as strong during aridity as in times of delight. Take it as a very great mercy of God."[32] The young nun should forget herself. Whenever an evil notion comes to her, even if it is very bad, she should regard it as nothing. Teresa writes that she too has struggled with

---

[29] *Obras Completas*, 194 (clxxxiv).

[30] Ibid. "más y más luz para que entienda la merced que hace Nuestro Senor a quien saca de ella…; Su Majestad lo haga como poderoso, y sea companía de vuestra merced de aquí adelante, de manera que no eche menos la muy buena que ha perdido."

[31] Ibid., 324 (cccxxix).

[32] "paréceme que la trata ya Nuestro Senor como a quien tiene por fuerte; pues la quiere probar para entender el amor que le tiene, si es también en la sequedad, como en los gustos. Téngalo por merced de Dios muy grande."

aridity and that when temptations arise, it is best to say a *Paternoster* or strike one's breast and try to think of something else. Teresa is never condescending toward those struggling along a path she too has trod, but rather gives them hope and sound advice. To a superior, Mother María Bautista in Valladolid, Teresa writes a brief line about governing with love. "Todo va con amor" (everything goes with love).[33]

With regard to spiritual direction, Teresa had come to have great confidence in the superiors of her order, and it is clear in a letter to Mother Maria de San Jose that she thought they were capable of the spiritual direction of their daughters. In difficult cases, they should write to Teresa herself:

> The prioress of Veas writes telling me that her nuns make their confessions to one priest to whom they speak of nothing but their sins, so that he hears the whole community in half an hour; she adds that this plan ought to be observed everywhere. The sisters are perfectly contented and greatly attached to their prioress as they treat of their souls with her. Your Reverence may tell your daughters to write to me for direction, as I have had some experience, for why should they search for others who perhaps had less than I?[34]

I have selected only a few passages from Teresa's letters; indeed, most of her letters have to do with the business of foundations, with protecting the Discalced from their enemies and the like. It is in her other works that her deep spiritual understanding is best revealed.

Teresa had too much sense to ignore her observations of the women with whom she lived or with whom she corresponded. The evidence she acquired was clearly contrary to the stereotypes of women then current. In her autobiography, she commented on these instances just enough to make us wish that she had written much more on the subject. We will look at three examples. The first has to do with spiritual correction. Teresa is writing about the highest mystical state, that of union, and what the soul sees with regard to other souls.

> Oh, what power that soul possesses which our Lord raises to this state! how it looks down upon everything, entangled by nothing!

---

[33] *Obras Completas*, 344 (cclxxvi): This is the entire letter: "Sepa que no soy la que solía en gobernar; todo va con amor; no sé si lo hace que no me hacen por qué, o haber entendido que se remedia así mejor."

[34] *The Letters of Saint Teresa*, trans. the Benedictines of Stanbrook (London: Thomas Baker, 1921), 2:263. The original Spanish is found in *Obras Completas*, 183 (clxxiii).

how ashamed it is of the time when it was entangled! how it is amazed at its own blindness! how it pities those who are still in darkness, especially if they are men of prayer, and have received consolations from God! it would like to cry out to them, that they might be made to see the delusions they are in: and, indeed, it does so now and then; and then a thousand persecutions fall upon it as a shower. People consider it wanting in humility, and think it means to teach those from whom it should learn, particularly if it be a woman....The soul at times cannot help itself; nor can it refrain from undeceiving those it loves....[35]

Women were not supposed to correct men; nuns were not supposed to correct priests. Teresa did both. Her insight was such that she could not refrain from speaking out when she saw a gifted soul fail to make progress through its own ignorance when she possessed the knowledge to help. She attributed these impulses to God's action in her. In her experience, God's action was not only not limited to men, but was more frequently effective in women:

There are many more women than men to whom our Lord gives these graces; I have heard the holy friar Peter of Alcantara say so, and, indeed, I know it myself. He used to say that women made greater progress in this way than men did: and he gave excellent reasons for his opinion, all in favor of women; but there is no necessity of repeating them here.[36]

Oh yes, Teresa, there was need for you to give those reasons; we need to hear them!

The next passage I will quote is a more complex one. Teresa is talking about the great difficulty she experienced in finding a good spiritual director. Without learned directors, she suffered much as she tried to explain to confessors what was happening to her in prayer, her experiences of both graces and temptations. She tells us:

And certainly the affliction to be borne is great, and caution is necessary, particularly in the case of women,—for our weakness is great,—and much evil may be the result of telling them [women] very distinctly that the devil is busy with them; yes, rather the matter should be very carefully considered, and they should be

[35] *The Life of St. Teresa of Jesus of the Order of Our Lady of Carmel, Written by Herself,* ed. Benedict Zimmerman, OCD, trans. David Lewis (Westminster, Maryland: The Newman Bookshop, 1943), 174.

[36] Ibid., 411. Cf. *Santa Madre Teresa de Jesus, Libro de su vida* (Leipzig: Insel-Verlag, 1921), 300–1, for the Spanish text.

removed out of reach of the dangers that may arise. They should be advised to keep things secret; and it is necessary also that their secret should be kept. I am speaking of this as one to whom it has been a sore trouble; for some of those with whom I spoke of my prayer did not keep my secret, but, making inquiries, one of another for a good purpose, did me much harm; for they made things known which might well have remained secret, because not intended for every one: and it seemed as if I had made them public myself.[37]

Teresa refers to her confessors and those to whom her confessors told her to confide the state of her soul. She goes on to say that they did not reveal any confessional secrets, but nevertheless, they revealed what she told them, at their request, in extrasacramental conversations. Teresa adds, "My meaning, then, is that women should be directed with much discretion; their directors should encourage them, and bide the time when our Lord will help them, as He has helped me."[38]

In these passages, we hear two voices. One is the voice of Teresa who rightly resents the publication of the state of her soul (it led to her examination by the Inquisition for fear that she was an *alumbrada*, one who claimed to be enlightened by God, but who sought neither sacramental nor other help in interpreting their prayer). The second voice is Teresa's ascription to herself and to other women of weakness that puts women in a particularly vulnerable position. A careful reading of these passages indicates that the priests were at fault, if not maliciously then at least out of ignorance [weakness?], and that Teresa, in this instance, uncritically accepted a misperception about women, namely that they are weaker than men. From our perspective, we can see that the supposed weakness was a result of the denial to women of a good education and the freedom that men enjoyed to gain both the learning and the experience that made men appear strong. Over the course of her lifetime, Teresa more than made up for these deprivations and understood her own ability when she undertook the direction of her nuns and approved of other superiors' doing the same, leaving to confessors only the strictly sacramental absolution of sins as in the letter to Mother Maria de San Jose quoted above.

In her actions, correspondence, and comments, Teresa rose above the misconceptions about men and women in her age. In other instances, she witnessed to them. In each of the passages cited in this essay Teresa

---

[37] *The Life of St. Teresa of Jesus,* 204–5. See also 254.
[38] Ibid.

expresses her strong sense of her own good judgment and spiritual experience. The Roman Catholic Church agreed with her and declared her not only a saint, but a doctor of the Church. Generations of Christian women and men agree and find in Teresa's works the spiritual wisdom they seek.

It is predictable that expressions about the weakness of women should occur in the writings of sixteenth-century people. It is also predictable that women should be counseled to fulfill the roles that sixteenth-century culture imposed upon them. But it is surprising and gratifying to find that, when dealing directly with women in matters of spiritual direction, both Ignatius of Loyola and Teresa of Avila treated men and women with equal respect.

Ignatius of Loyola and Teresa of Avila were great spiritual directors. Their legacies have been and remain the inspiration of tens of thousands of men and women both religious and lay. That their writings appeal to so many is due primarily to their spiritual insight and clear expression of it. But surely it is also, in some degree at least, due to their evenhanded, non-gender-specific, spiritual direction.

Ignatius of Loyola

# Scholarly Publications of Charles G. Nauert

**Books:**

*Humanism and the Culture of Renaissance Europe.* Cambridge: Cambridge University Press, 1995.

Introduction and annotations to *Collected Works of Erasmus*, vol. 11: *Letters 1535 to 1657, January–December 1525*, texts translated by Alexander Dalzell. Toronto: University of Toronto Press, 1994.

"Caius Plinius Secundus," book-length article in F. Edward Cranz et al., eds., *Catalogus Translationum et Commentariorum*, vol. 4 Washington, D.C.: The Catholic University of America Press, 1989, 297–422.

*The Age of Renaissance and Reformation.* Hinsdale, Ill.: Dryden Press, 1977; repr., University Press of America, 1982.

*Agrippa and the Crisis of Renaissance Thought.* Illinois Studies in the Social Sciences, 55. Urbana: University of Illinois Press, 1965.

**Articles:**

"Humanism as Method: Roots of Conflict with the Scholastics," *Sixteenth Century Journal*, 29 (1998): 427-38.

"Humanists, Scholastics, and the Struggle to Reform the University of Cologne, 1523–1525," James V. Mehl, ed., *Humanismus in Köln/ Humanism in Cologne*, 39–76. Studien zur Geschichte der Universität zu Köln, Bd. 10. Cologne: Böhlau Verlag, 1991.

"Humanist Infiltration into the Academic World: Some Studies of Northern Universities," *Renaissance Quarterly* 43 (Winter 1990, pub. February 1991): 799–812, and bibliography, 818–24.

"Graf Hermann von Neuenahr and the Limits of Humanism in Cologne," *Historical Reflections/Réflexions historiques* 15 (1988): 65–79.

"The Humanist Challenge to Medieval German Culture," *Daphnis: Zeitschrift für mittlere deutsche Literatur* 15 (1986, actually published in 1987): 277–306.

"The Communications Revolution and Cultural Change," *Sixteenth Century Journal* 11 (1980): 103-7.

"Renaissance Humanism: An Emergent Consensus and Its Critics," *Indiana Social Studies Quarterly* 33 (1980): 5–20.

"The Author of a Renaissance Commentary on Pliny: Revius, Trithemius, or Aquaeus?" *Journal of the Warburg and Courtauld Institutes* 42 (1979): 282–86.

"Humanists, Scientists, and Pliny: Changing Approaches to a Classical Author," *American Historical Review* 84 (1979): 72–85.

"The Clash of Humanists and Scholastics: An Approach to Pre-Reformation Controversies," *Sixteenth Century Journal* 4, no. 1 (April 1973): 1–18.

"Peter of Ravenna and the 'Obscure Men' of Cologne: A Case of Pre-Reformation Controversy," *Renaissance Studies in Honor of Hans Baron*, ed. Anthony Molho and John A. Tedeschi. DeKalb, Ill.: Northern Illinois University Press; Firenze: G. C. Sansoni, Editore, 1971, 609–40.

"Agrippa von Nettesheim (1486–1535)," in *Rheinische Lebensbilder*, Bd. 4, Dusseldorf: 1970, 57–77 (in German).

"Agrippa in Renaissance Italy: The Esoteric Tradition," *Studies in the Renaissance* 6 (1959): 195–222.

"Magic and Skepticism in Agrippa's Thought," *Journal of the History of Ideas* 18 (1957): 161–82.

Fifteen brief articles in the *New Catholic Encyclopedia* (1967).

**Book Reviews Published in:**

> *The American Historical Review*
> *Renaissance Quarterly*
> *Archiv für Reformationsgeschichte*
> *Sixteenth Century Journal*
> *Catholic Historical Review*
> *The Historian of Phi Alpha Theta*
> *Histoire sociale/Social History*
> *International History Review*
> *Anglican and Episcopal History*
> *Albion*

# Contributors

ROBERT S. BABCOCK is associate professor of history at Hastings College in Hastings, Nebraska, where he has been teaching since 1992. He earned his M.A. in European history with Charles Nauert at the University of Missouri in 1986. He has since earned his Ph.D. in medieval history at the University of California–Santa Barbara, earned a Fullbright scholarship to the University College of Wales at Aberystwyth and published articles on aspects of medieval Welsh and Anglo-Norman history.

ECKHARD BERNSTEIN is a professor of German at the College of the Holy Cross in Worcester, Massachusetts. After studying at the universities of Marburg, Germany and Exeter, England, he received his Ph.D. in comparative literature from Case Western Reserve University in Cleveland. He is the author of several monographs and numerous articles on German Renaissance humanism and German vernacular literature of that period. He currently serves as president of the Sixteenth Century Studies Conference.

GWENDOLYN BLOTEVOGEL is a graduate student in the Department of History at the University of Missouri–Columbia. She received her B.A. from Truman State University (1988) and M.A. from the University of Missouri–Kansas City (1990). She has taught history at Truman State University and currently serves on the history faculty at Columbia College in the Extended Studies Division. Gwen is completing her dissertation under the direction of Charles Nauert.

BARBARA C. BOWEN is professor of French and comparative literature at Vanderbilt University, and a past president of the Renaissance Society of America. Her monographs include *Words and the Man in French Renaissance Literature* (1983) and *Enter Rabelais, Laughing* (1998). She worked for many years with Charles Nauert on the Organizing Committee of the Central Renaissance Conference.

PAUL F. CASEY was a professor of German at the University of Missouri–Columbia who died unexpectedly 18 July 1998. He received his Ph.D. from Johns Hopkins University. After teaching at the University in Bonn (1971–79) and University College Galway, Ireland (1979–86), he joined the Department of German and Russian Studies at the University of Missouri where he specialized in German studies of the early modern period. He was a colleague of Charles Nauert since 1986.

JANET GLENN GRAY is an adjunct humanities faculty member at Maryville University and St. Louis University. She received her B.A. from Pennsylvania State University and her M.A. in liberal studies at Valparaiso University. She completed her Ph.D. dissertation at the University of Missouri–Columbia under the direction of Charles Nauert. She has also taken graduate courses at Duke University, Notre Dame University, Sangre de Cristo Seminary, and Washington University. She is the author of *The French Hugenots: Anatomy of Courage* and several articles.

PAUL F. GRENDLER taught at the University of Toronto from 1964 until early retirement in 1998. He received his A.B. from Oberlin College (1959) and his Ph.D. from the

University of Wisconsin (1964). He is the author of five books and editor of two books. He is editor-in-chief of *The Encyclopedia of the Renaissance* and was president of the Renaissance Society of America from 1992 to 1994. As a member of the editorial board of the Collected Works of Erasmus, he recruited Charles Nauert to contribute to the project many years ago.

JAMES V. MEHL is professor of humanities at Missouri Western State College. He received his B.S. from St. Louis University (1963) and his M.A. and Ph.D. from the University of Missouri–Columbia (1965, 1975), where Charles Nauert was his dissertation advisor. After teaching in the Department of History at Benedictine College in Atchison, Kansas (1969–72), he joined the Department of Communication Studies/Theatre/Humanities at Missouri Western State College. He is also currently chairperson of that department.

BONNER MITCHELL is professor emeritus of French and Italian at the University of Missouri–Columbia and a longtime colleague of Charles Nauert. He has been studying the forms of Renaissance pageantry, particularly in Italy, for more than thirty years.

JILL RAITT is professor and chair of religious studies at the University of Missouri–Columbia. She received her M.A. from Marquette University and an M.A. and Ph.D. from the University of Chicago. She is past president of the American Academy of Religion, a senior editor of the Oxford Encyclopedia of the Reformation, on the board of editors of the Encyclopedia of World Spirituality and the editor of volume 17 of the series: *Christian Spirituality: High Middle Ages and Reformation*. Her most recent book is *The Colloquy of Montbéliard: Religion and Politics in the Sixteenth Century*.

ERIKA RUMMEL is associate professor of history at Wilfrid Laurier University in Waterloo, Canada. She is the author of several books on Erasmus including *Les Colloques d'Erasme: Renouveau Spirituel et Réform*, and a number of editions and translations and most recently, *Erasmus on Women*. She shares Charles Nauert's interest in the intellectual history of the sixteenth century and credits him with inspiring her book *The Humanist-Scholastic Debate in the Renaissance and Reformation*.

KIM SCHUTTE is an adjunct faculty member of the Department of Social Sciences at Missouri Western State College. She received two B.S. degrees from Missouri Western State College in 1986 and 1987 and her M.A. from the University of Missouri–Columbia (1988), where Charles Nauert served as her thesis advisor.

KEITH A. SHAFER is is a Ph.D. candidate in classical studies at the University of Missouri–Columbia. His dissertation on Ciceronianism in the late fifteenth century is being codirected by Charles Nauert. He has taught in the classical studies at the University of Missouri and Truman State University.

PAULA SOMMERS is a professor of French at the University of Missouri–Columbia, has published a number of articles on the Heptameron and Marguerite de Navarre's poetry, in addition to her book on the queen's religious poetry (1989). She is studying the marriage topos as it occurs in the works of women writers in the sixteenth century.

GUY WILSON is employed as a webmaster at the University of Missouri–Columbia. He received his B.A. and M.A. from Central Missouri State University. He received his Ph.D. from the University of Missouri (1991), where Charles Nauert served as his dissertation advisor. He has taught European history at Spring Hill College in Mobile, Alabama, and at the University of Missouri–Columbia. His main area of academic interest is the relationship between technology and cognition.

# INDEX